S0-BRJ-429

The
Broom Closet

Writing About Women
Feminist Literary Studies

General Editor

Esther Labovitz
Pace University

Advisory Board

Marie Collins
Rutgers–Newark University

Doris Guilloton
New York University

Lila Hanft
Case Western Reserve University

Mark Hussey
Pace University

Helane Levine-Keating
Pace University

Heather Rosario-Sievert
City University of New York

Vol. 25

PETER LANG
New York · Washington, D.C./Baltimore · Boston
Bern · Frankfurt am Main · Berlin · Vienna · Paris

Jeannette Batz Cooperman

The
Broom Closet

Secret Meanings of Domesticity
in Postfeminist Novels by
Louise Erdrich, Mary Gordon,
Toni Morrison, Marge Piercy,
Jane Smiley, and Amy Tan

PETER LANG
New York · Washington, D.C./Baltimore · Boston
Bern · Frankfurt am Main · Berlin · Vienna · Paris

M. HODGES LEARNING CENTER
WHARTON COUNTY JUNIOR COLLEGE
WHARTON, TEXAS 77488

Library of Congress Cataloging-in-Publication Data

Cooperman, Jeannette Batz.
The broom closet: secret meanings of domesticity in postfeminist novels by Louise
Erdrich, Mary Gordon, Toni Morrison, Marge Piercy, Jane Smiley,
and Amy Tan / Jeannette Batz Cooperman.
p. cm. — (Writing about women: feminist literary studies; vol. 25)
1. American fiction—Women authors—History and criticism. 2. Housewives in
literature. 3. Feminism and literature—United States—History—20th century.
4. Women and literature—United States—History—20th century. 5. American fiction—
20th century—History and criticism. 6. Domestic fiction, American—History and
criticism. 7. Married women in literature. 8. Housekeeping in literature.
9. Marriage in literature. 10. Family in literature. I. Title.
II. Series: Writing about women; vol. 25.
PS374.H69C66   813'.5409'352649—dc21   97-51352
ISBN 0-8204-3953-3
ISSN 1053-7937

Die Deutsche Bibliothek–CIP–Einheitsaufnahme

Cooperman, Jeannette Batz:
The broom closet: secret meanings of domesticity in postfeminist novels by Louise
Erdrich, Mary Gordon, Toni Morrison, Marge Piercy, Jane Smiley,
and Amy Tan / Jeannette Batz Cooperman.
–New York; Washington, D.C./Baltimore; Boston; Bern;
Frankfurt am Main; Berlin; Vienna; Paris: Lang.
(Writing about women; Vol. 25)
ISBN 0-8204-3953-3

Author photo by Jennifer Silverberg

The paper in this book meets the guidelines for permanence and durability
of the Committee on Production Guidelines for Book Longevity
of the Council of Library Resources.

© 1999 Peter Lang Publishing, Inc., New York

All rights reserved.
Reprint or reproduction, even partially, in all forms such as microfilm,
xerography, microfiche, microcard, and offset strictly prohibited.

Printed in the United States of America

PS
374
.H69
C66
1999
C.2

To my husband, Andrew.
Loving him has taught me the meaning of homemaking.

ACKNOWLEDGMENTS

Heartfelt thanks to

Tuck Loui, for her close reading
and gentle direction; Belden Lane,
for his enthusiasm and deep insight;
and Wynne Moskop, for her astute,
patient and relentless clarifications,
without which I might never have
figured out what I was saying.
More fervent thanks to Dawn
Jungermann, for her serenity,
generosity of spirit and ability
to transform chaos into design.
Eternal thanks to my husband,
who ordered us pizza so I could
write about cooking; and to my
mother, who scrubbed and ironed
all those years, while I studied ideas
that would lead me to an analysis of
what she'd been doing all along.

CONTENTS

ONE

KEEPING HOUSE

The world begins at a kitchen table.

from "Perhaps the World Ends Here," by Joy Harjo

When I began researching domesticity, I lived alone in a tiny modern apartment with pickles, beer and a jar of peanut butter in the refrigerator. A year later, I had married and moved into a brick bungalow with hardwood floors, stained glass windows and a crooked sunporch. My husband and I painted cracked plaster, cursed the plumbing, yanked away tiles, planted an herb garden. He bought a drill, I bought an apron. Our friends started calling us Ward and June.

I started writing as the dust settled from a year of awkward, compulsive domesticity—which I now took to mean devotion to house, home and family life, rather than docility. I was 33, and had just left a phase of feminism marked by fierce single-minded independence and a disgusted rage at the notion of female servitude. Now that I was safely married to someone who had no intention of whipping me into kitchenly submission, I found myself genuinely interested in women's traditional work, and in the harmonious ordering of our daily life together. But I didn't have the slightest idea how to keep house.

My mother, widowed young, had kept our surroundings immaculate; she was so good at it, she used to console herself that, if she ever lost her secretarial job, she could clean houses for a living. She'd walk in the door from work, spot a string of caramel on the kitchen linoleum and drop to her knees to swipe it clean, car keys still in hand.

I never saw the payoff.

So after a decade of sloppy, self-centered basic survival, here I was, checking out Heloise's hints from the library (research serving as excellent cover) and scribbling down 100 uses for baking soda. My husband urged me back to the computer, professed deep love for frozen entrées and did all the cleaning, but laundry and cooking still beckoned, oddly seductive. Initially, their pull was a mix of novelty, conditioned guilt and new-wife role-play. Then the daily rhythms began to feel whole, psychologically healing, even spiritual. The physical immediacy of housework completely distracted me from the intellectual analysis I had conceived to make its prospect bearable.

Only when I could whisk a roux with a practiced hand and feel a measure of control over domestic chaos did my abstract curiosity reassert itself. How did housework—which I had long considered merely a hollow drudgery misassigned to females—manage to create psychological as well as physical order? Why had I—and so many women I knew—felt so tense, torn and ambivalent about these tasks? What made household chores such heavy drudgery on some days, so satisfying and peaceful on others? The most sweeping question of all: how had domesticity shaped women's consciousness, our thoughts, emotions and spirits? And how had domesticity influenced those who preferred to create with ideas and ink?

As I wondered, I came upon two fateful sentences in a book I was reading: "In the development of women, all these motions of 'home-keeping,' the cooking, the washing, the sweeping, quantify something beyond the ordinary," wrote Clarissa Pinkola Estés. "All these metaphors offer ways to think about, to measure, feed, nourish, straighten, cleanse, order the soul-life" (97). Hmm. If our souls themselves were being influenced, no wonder I was more interested in "domesticity"—a word which carried the emotional and psychological dimension of devotion to the home—than in plain "housekeeping," the maintenance and management of a household through the practice of certain predictable chores.

Eager to understand how everyday, home-oriented behaviors could cut deep enough to shape our mental, emotional and spiritual lives, I searched history, anthropology, psychology, theology and critical theory. But as I tried to synthesize ideas from that array of disciplines, the conceptual lump called "domesticity" broke apart. I had been puzzling over a single entity, when in fact domesticity was a gestalt of hundreds of different tasks and techniques falling within diverse, social, historical and cultural traditions. Domestic practices took new shape every time technology changed or social standards shifted; meanwhile, each domestic act reflected countless values and influences, some generalizable, some idiosyncratic. (It would be a mistake to generalize too much from my Aunt Mary's habit of hiding all the pots and pans on the back porch—where they sometimes froze for days—so her dinner guests wouldn't feel obliged to help with the dishes.)

The stable goals of the domestic sphere are edible food, wearable clothes, livable rooms, daily health and well-being—but each goal is a process linked to the others, not an isolated simple task. Well-being suggests hospitality, which requires shopping and cooking, which necessitates cleaning, and clothes break into buying, sewing, washing, drying, mending, ironing, folding, hanging and storing, and chores overlap in their use of water or coal or electricity, and systems intersect and affect each other.

Child care is another set of housebound tasks that help establish the home as women's domain, but in infinitely complex ways. For simplicity's sake, I avoided a detailed analysis of child care, which weaves erratically in and out of domestic issues, and spent my time scrutinizing basic assumptions about domesticity over the past century. Those assumptions show themselves in all the tasks associated with "making a home," including washing, ironing, shopping, sewing, mending, cooking, scrubbing, sweeping, polishing, dusting, decorating, making beds, doing dishes, tending the sick and extending hospitality.

Still, a white attorney ironing a shirt before her beloved husband's job interview in 1995 differs significantly from a white housewife ironing all her husband's shirts in 1955; or an Asian-American casting aside silk shantung to learn the quirks of rayon; or an African-American attorney remembering how her mother ironed other people's clothes all day and her own family's at night. "One way to understand women's consciousness is to make visible the cultures it creates," writes Bettina Aptheker in *Tapestries of Life: Women's Work, Women's Consciousness, and the Meaning of Daily Existence.* She defines a culture as "the ordered system of meanings in terms of which people define their world, express their feelings, and make their judgments" (13). Through these systems of meanings, then, we can begin to understand how domesticity has helped women bring order out of chaos.

Looking through the lens of literature brought further insight, because its allusions, linguistic infrastructure and patterns of movement not only describe social contexts but offer clues to consciousness itself. For centuries, but especially since the antebellum upsurge of domestic fiction, women writers have used images and metaphors of sweeping, cooking, ironing, weaving and other household tasks to express emotion, describe relationships, symbolize ideas and convey values. Tillie Olsen began her first short story, "As I stand here ironing," summing up years of domestic work and literary silence. Poet Deena Metzger wrote, "Each day is a tapestry, threads of broccoli, promotion, couches, children, politics, shopping, building, planting, thinking interweave in intimate connection with insistent cycles of birth, existence, and death" (7). In *Pilgrim at Tinker Creek*, Annie Dillard called the liminal space of the text a "hemline" between eternity and time, "a fabric of spirit and sense so grand and subtle, so powerful in a new way, that we can only feel blindly of its hem" (7). Even literary critics such as Elaine Showalter have pieced their texts with domestic metaphors: "the Spinster who spins stories, Ariadne and her labrinthine thread, Penelope who weaves and unweaves her theoretical tapestry in the halls of Ithaca or New Haven" (224).

Not only is literature a cultural artifact that can reveal subjective truths about domesticity, but literary production captures the tension between domesticity and creative self-expression at its most exquisite apex. Housework happens in bits and pieces, at others' beck and call; writing begs for huge chunks of uninterrupted musing. Housework is inherently repetitive and mundane; writing strives for freshness and novelty, a seduction, a climax, then closure. Housework benefits from close empirical observation and steady, methodical upkeep; writing moves by intuitive fits and starts, analysis, introspection and synthesis.

The purpose of both domesticity and literature is to pull order from the daily chaff and rubble of human experience—yet in practice, the two modes grate against each other. Women writers have resented male critics' swift dismissal of domestic subjects as trivial—but those same women writers have articulated a profound ambivalence toward their own domestic chores. Virginia Woolf dreamed of cleaning houses with a puff of wind; Tillie Olsen blamed a sense of "discontinuity" on years of domestic distractions; Adrienne Rich reminded us that "to be a female human being trying to fulfill traditional female functions in a traditional way is in direct conflict with the subversive function of the imagination" (Spender, *The Writing or the Sex* 125).

Much has been written about the "domestic fiction" of the nineteenth century, in which Hawthorne's "scribbling women" described the everyday intimacies of family life rather than adventures in the outside world. Precious few critics, however, have noted the way domesticity sneaks into more recent, less constrained fiction by women. Ann Romines' *The Home Plot: Women, Writing & Domestic Ritual* is the only deep, subtle and comprehensive work I've found that carries us well into the twentieth century, and even Romines stops at 1970, just as self-conscious feminism began to transform the topic.

Romines used literature to explore "domestic ritual," a term she allowed to encompass all physical activities that were performed regularly in a house and derived emotional and symbolic meaning from its boundaries. Viewing housework in this way allows us to see its power, its significance, and its numinous aspects: the holiness of the everyday, and the paradoxically sacred quality of time spent quietly performing the regular, simple, earthbound tasks that sustain and order our lives.

It is painfully obvious, however, that housework does not always reach the communicative and performative level of ritual; sometimes it stays in a rut. Domesticity can be the metaphorical hearth that centers a family's daily life, bringing order from chaos and linking matter to spirit. But domesticity can also empty into meaningless rote, or shatter into profane, disconnected acts used to control and manipulate the rest of the household. The simple act of sweeping can be Cinderella drudgery, spring-cleaning catharsis or a Buddhist sand-garden meditation. Shall we call it domestic ritual, regardless?

"Ritual" first emerged as a formal term of analysis in the nineteenth century, identifying what was believed to be a universal category of human experience, notes Catherine Bell (19). Scholars have since used the word to describe religion, analyze social phenomena and anchor the dynamics of culture—which surely include domesticity. In *The Magic of Ritual,* Tom Driver names its three central purposes as making and preserving order, fostering community and effecting transformation. We can easily point to the fulfillment of all three in the processes of domesticity, which battle chaos, glue together families and transform lives (71). Even if we narrow our focus to, say, rites of passage, we can easily identify acts of purification and cleansing; acts that cross threshholds, suspending time and place and altering consciousness; and acts of incorporation, a sharing of food that allows participants to reenter society on a new basis.

As Driver reminds us, performing a ritual not only reminds us of an underlying cosmic order, it helps establish that order (133). Spring cleaning, then, would not only remind us of our ability to purify and renew, but it would help us do so, internally as well as externally. Ritual orders the world, turning potential into reality. Like housework, it is deliberately repetitive, thus denying the passage of time and the fearfulness of change. Ritual offers us a social reconstruction of reality that keeps it from "slipping into the sea of indeterminacy" (137).

Unfortunately, most definitions of ritual are either too narrow or too broad: at one extreme, they limit themselves to events that occurred at an altar; at the other, they consider every human act. If ritual is simply a set of routinely repeated everyday acts that have been endowed with magical efficacy, what will hold the boundaries between the everyday and the magical, the rut and the rite?

Driver demands that any definition acknowledge the relation between ritual and nonritual activity, taking into account the "various degrees of nearly-but-not-quite ritual behavior" (69). The performers and witnesses of such acts feel no need to draw a heavy line between ritual and non-ritual; if an act is truly ritual, it will have transformative power. If someone prepares a meal with special care, acting in prescribed ways, for a symbolic purpose, on a regular and preordained basis, then shares that meal with appreciative loved ones in a communal setting, I defy anyone to deny that meal ritual status. But if the same person carelessly microwaves frozen entrees so the family can gulp them in front of the TV set, she has entered the mundane with a thud.

To avoid automatically elevating all house-bound chores to the high end of ritual's continuum, we can separate them the way society has, by the characteristics of the domestic sphere long assigned to women. Those characteristics include a cyclical, often daily, time frame; a piecemeal nature that allows distraction and interruption; and a necessary confinement to the interior of the home. The earliest gendered division of labor was, after all, biologically based: women were assigned responsibilities that could reshape themselves to accommodate pregnancy, breast-feeding and child care. Thus "women's work" became whatever tasks were located within or very near the home, could be interrupted and resumed later, and did not require the risk of life and limb. These requirements soon became self-perpetuating characteristics: "women's work" was defined as confined and confining; fragmented and to some degree mindless; and capable of existing on a small, gentle, ordinary scale. When home and workplace separated themselves from each other geographically and culturally during the Industrial Revolution, the patriarchal patterns that held sway allowed the gendered division of labor to be reified, and "women's work" became normative, an encoding of societal obligation.

Today, dividing labor by sex is no longer a nearly-automatic act of biology, common sense and instinct; and neither is it simple obedience to societal norms. The nature of work in general has changed, the societal emphasis on procreation has eased, and normative definitions of masculinity and femininity have hardened and softened in different spots. In just the last century, technology has deskilled housework and eased its manual labors, an economy centered in buying instead of making has destroyed its creativity, and feminism has struggled to break its gendered connection. Most of us hesitate now before referring to housework as "women's work." Yet women continue to do the bulk of the work, and its essential characteristics—unpaid, isolated, accountable round-the-clock, crucial yet socially devalued—have altered very little. British sociologists R.D. Barron and G.M. Norris point out that in the labor market, job characteristics often become descriptions of the people who do these jobs (Barker 2). If the same is true of unpaid labor, the implications for women's status and scope are clear.

According to the U.S. Census Bureau's *Households, Families and Children: A 30-Year Perspective*, between 1960 and 1990, the proportion of married women in the labor force had nearly doubled, rising from 30 percent to 58 percent (53). Yet in 1994, studies indicated that "superwomen" still spend 32.3 hours a week doing domestic tasks, compared to their male partners' 8.7 hours (Hellmich 05-D). In January 1995, *USA Today* noted that 76 percent of women make their bed every morning, compared to 46 percent of men. Another article that month reported that 25.5 percent of African-American men—but only 16.6 percent of white men—do more than 40 percent of the household chores (Usdanfky 01-D).

Persistent gender inequities raise an old, awkward question: Are domestic attributes inherently feminine? Sociologists Barker and Allen note the fallacy of calling women earthier and weaker, thus better suited to mundane home tasks: "One could, after all, argue that men are closer to nature because of their 'unrestrained sexuality' and 'aggressiveness' and that they are physically more vulnerable because of their external genitalia" (10). Anthropologists, meanwhile, offer us countless examples of variation in the gendered division of labor. In just one study, Margaret Mead notes "the Toda prescription of almost all domestic work as too sacred for women" (xi); the Mundugumor, who consider fishing an essentially feminine task (xiii); the Arapesh, who find it "very convenient for a man to have two wives; when one is menstruating, he has another one to cook for him" (109); and the Tchambuli, who send men to shop, resplendent in feathers and shell ornaments, wheedling and bartering but buying only with their wives' permission.

Women's disproportionate domesticity is far more likely to be societal than inherent. In *Just a Housewife*, historian Glenna Matthews measures how far away we are from reconciling domesticity with justice for all women, pointing out "a large gap in American history between the 1870s and the 1970s, when almost no one gave the issue any thought" (143). Only in the past three decades have large numbers of feminists begun to question—"interrogate" might better capture the tone—women's automatic assignment to the domestic sphere.

In 1968, the Students for a Democratic Society passed a National Resolution on Women that pointed out how "women themselves have come to act by necessity according to the function a class society has given them, hence *believe* in that function" (Roszak 256). The following year, the Women's Liberation Collective in Palo Alto, California, insisted in its manifesto that "responsibility for the home should be assumed by all family members" (Roszak 272). A succession of diatribes and declarations followed, with feminists suggesting everything from redesigned living space to communal work-sharing. By the mid-1970s, the baton passed from consciousness-raising groups to activist writers to academics such as sociologist Ann Oakley, who demanded abolition of the housewife role, the traditional family and the gender roles. "Housework is work directly opposed to the possibility of human self-actualization," she insisted, noting that it fails to provide motivation, challenge, accomplishment, responsibility, growth, advancement, pleasure, recognition (222–223).

Such radical demands failed to win wide support, however, and by 1989, Aptheker was reassuring her readers that abolition would be a transition phase: After "unpaid family care services have been largely replaced by purchased substitutes, and after equality of opportunity has been established in the workplace, it will be time to consider reviving the occupation of full-time homemaker. Then we can see if it can become an honorable, safe, and secure occupation for both mothers and fathers" (184).

Aptheker's comment sprang from the most recent period of struggle, one sometimes called "postfeminist." The term can refer strictly to the time frame of the 1980s and 1990s, but it is often broadened to describe the philosophical shift as feminism embraced postmodern analyses of race, class and patriarchy, using them to deal summarily with society's nostalgia for old gendered certainties; with a new generation of women reluctant to be called "feminists"; and with the faint insistent drummings of the men's movement. The postfeminist period is especially interesting for this study, because women writing after feminism established itself have had more time and leeway for balanced reflection on the domestic realm's multiple, varied and variable significances.

In her acerbic critique of contemporary culture, however, Tanya Modleski threw the word "postfeminist" in quotes, calling the post-mortem on feminism premature, and noting the vultures' patriarchal features. The glossary of *Feminist Readings/Feminists Reading* took a milder tack, defining "post-feminism" as "a position of having worked one's way through feminist theory to such an extent that the basic tenets of feminism can be taken as read." But the editors immediately appended a warning: "It can also mean a position where feminism is no longer nec-essary" (Mills 247). The book concluded by saying postfeminist women "are the competent, independent equals of men and who therefore no longer need to 'compromise' their femininity or their equally important roles as wives and mothers"—then added acidly, "The fact that such women are actually a very small middle-class minority within society as a whole is, of course, never said" (227).

We will avoid the ideological land mine by defining "postfeminist" chronologically, as a period that began roughly in 1980, after the "second wave" of U.S. feminism had crested, and will continue until we can iden-tify another shift. Why bother using such a red-flagged label? Because in this "postfeminist" period, we have had access to a growing body of his-torical, technological and sociological knowledge—as well as a great deal of marital, generational and societal tension—surrounding the subject of domesticity. We have seen how thoroughly and unquestioningly women were assigned to the domestic sphere; we have raged about what it cost them; we have constructed theories about both the process and its ori-gins. From this vantage point, we can see whether the associations sur-rounding "women's work" are still meaningful enough, and powerful enough, to influence our enlightened egalitarian psyches.

In Search of a Starting Point

It would be easy to assume an inherent link between women's ways of knowing the world and the domestic patterns that shape and reflect those ways. But that may be too easy, too quickly generalized, too deterministic. Certainly, the correspondences between women's reproductive functions and certain dimensions of housework—its repetition in cyclical time, its physical intimacy, its mandate to shelter, nurture and respond—are too powerful to be reduced to chronological coincidence. On the other hand, my husband scrubs our house far cleaner than I do, and tends our February pointsettia with tremendous care. It seems unfair to give biology the final say and assume that men's consciousness cannot also be shaped by domesticity. What the collective result would be, it is far too early to say; we will need to embed a sense of domestic responsibility in the male psyche and let it germinate for a century or two before the comparison is fair. But just as we cannot understand the past if we ignore its patriarchal context, we cannot look forward if we give women proprietary, biological rights to domesticity.

Nor can we continue to assume a concrete wall between public and private spheres, as liberal feminism is wont to do. We could diagram the shaping of female consciousness by measuring women's labor inside and outside the home, then tracing the political power that attends each realm; we could study the changes in family structure, social roles, institutions and technology that are loosening the gender link, and explore the possibilities now open for equality in both spheres. But women's traditional domestic role would still cut deeper into the psyche than structural shifts could account for.

First, public and private have never been as separate as they seemed, with the private sphere influencing female consciousness and the public sphere influencing male consciousness. Instead, the spiritual, symbolic, ritual and relational dimensions of domesticity set up currents of guilt, ownership, virtue, manipulation, caretaking, connection and transcendence that criss-cross social and political spheres. In the most concrete and practical ways, women's and men's lives have always interpenetrated, if only because of the intimate mutual influences of marriage. Even in the Progressive era, when their spheres of responsibility and zones of comfort were explicitly separate, women and men alike urged a "municipal housekeeping" that would make the whole world homelike.

Furthermore, housework—traditionally conceived as private-sphere activity—is more accurately an art and science of the boundaries. Boundaries between public and private, boundaries of home and family; boundaries of the body, boundaries of the psyche. Housework sweeps threshholds, opens passages to the outside world. Shopping and cooking bring goods into the home and the body; cleaning removes the filth of the world and prepares us to reenter it.

If we cannot assume split social spheres or tap conveniently into a physical core of universal femininity, what about putting a feminist spin on classical theorists such as Freud and Marx, whose work laid the foundations for so much of postmodern social and literary criticism? In a dissertation on film images titled "Keeping House: Discourses of Domestic Economy," Kathleen Anne McHugh comments dryly that Marx theorized labor and work, Freud analyzed family life, and both ignored housework. As unpaid, private labor, it breaks through the finite bounds of both Marx's political and Freud's libidinal economy: "Its practices literalize the paradoxical condition, both inside and other, often invoked to describe women's position in patriarchy; its invisibility and unsightliness are therefore congruent with the problematic representational status of women themselves" (1). Housework keeps women intimately bound up with the deepest and most fundamental parts of life, yet excluded from the sexual and economic passageways of power, and trivialized by the profane, as opposed to sacred, nature of their work.

Freudian analysis would reduce household tasks to the reduction of tension, the gratification of need and impulse, the pursuit of pleasure or the socialization of the superego, binding all domestic experiences into a finite closed system reducible to the body. Marxist analysis would show capitalism oppressing women economically as unpaid workers at home (and less-paid workers in the labor force). Socializing housework might move women into better industrial positions, but the housework itself would remain drudgery; Marxists saw no redeeming value in the traditional "women's work."

The weight of domesticity has been emotional as well as economic, and in some ways and instances it has been assumed voluntarily. In *The Feminine Mystique*, for example, Betty Friedan tells how, "after the loneliness of war and the unspeakableness of the bomb, against the frightening uncertainty, the cold immensity of the changing world, women as well as men sought the comforting reality of home and children" (182). A Marxist reduction of that search to a sublimated drive or a housewife's surplus commodity value hardly seems adequate.

Since Marx and Freud fall short, perhaps psychoanalytic feminism could unearth the ways domesticity structures consciousness? At first glance, there is nothing particularly domestic about the French contribution of *jouissance*—an orgasmic bliss that flows from the deep female state of embodiment, touch and connection—except perhaps its assertion of a kind of knowing rooted in touch, a knowing that allows the irrational to emerge through the ordinary. A second glance, however, unearths numerous parallels between attitudes toward the female body—long ascribed the messy, chthonic aspects of the earth—and attitudes toward the mud, eggshells, hairballs, feces and scum the housewife rinses into subterranean pipes. In performing domestic rituals, women use their bodies in deliberate, disciplined ways, so that "specific, finite, identifiable actions are carried out bodily at a definite time and place," which Driver lists as a characteristic of ritual in general (83). "In the measure in which the body is alienated—either by being discounted or else by being treated as a mere object that must hop, skip, and jump on cue—in that same measure will the ritual process be inhibited," he adds (85). Thus the body—so often linked categorically to femaleness—is central to domestic ritual's performance as well as its purpose.

Finally, domestic values have traveled along the "motherlines," with explicit and veiled messages alike passing from mother to daughter. Nancy Chodorow carefully describes the values and norms daughters internalize, and the conflicted messages sons receive, by bonding with a woman as the overwhelmingly primary parent. When we add unconscious attitudes toward the female body and toward the mortality signified by life's dirt and decay, depth psychology does seem a likely framework for an analysis of domesticity. But the primal substratum of domesticity is simply that; society has piled more easily identifiable layers atop it, and psychoanalysis might overread them.

Just how far *does* childhood socialization go in determining adult behavior? McHugh describes the transmission of domestic knowledge and skill as "mute pedagogy, knowledge passed on by a miming of the mother, by a wordless exchange" (9). That wordless exchange is a powerful one: housework is the first form of human work most of us observe, and we see it every day from infancy. Yet daughters can internalize their mothers' standards and rebel against them for the rest of their lives; being influenced by societal norms does not automatically guarantee that we will conform to them.

The ideal approach would seem to be a careful equilibrium, culling insights from various theoretical frameworks without relying unduly on any one of them. When Aptheker notes that "women carry the threads of many tasks in their hands at the same time," and "have a consciousness of social reality that is distinct from that put forth by men" (39), she is not blaming the doubled X chromosome. Instead, she cites the sexual division of labor and the institutional subordination of women to men, emphasizing the shared aspects of consciousness that have resulted.

The need for balanced theory is especially strong in the field of literature, which is rich with insights into consciousness but highly vulnerable to distortions of critical fashion. In *Sister's Choice*, Showalter points out that women's writing "cannot be defined by biological essences, stereotypes of femininity, or nationalist myths. It must avoid both over-feminization, the insistence that everything in women's writing can be explained by gender; and under-feminization, or the neglect of gender inscriptions in women's texts." (17–18)

Even outside the bounds of literature, we must take care. The more we learn about the social sciences, for example, the less sense it makes to explain social patterns at a single level, from a single discipline's point of reference, or by a single cause. Ritual, especially, is far too multifaceted for that: rooted in human bodies, physical environments, cultural traditions and social processes, it has multiple points of origin and means of interpretation.

The shift to more flexible, multidisciplinary kinds of analysis is coming just in time: as we approach the second millennium, the public and private spheres are collapsing into each other. Computers, fax-modems and cordless phones bring the workplace into the home, while daycare sites, cleaning services and delivered meals commercialize what once was private. The chaos and blurred boundaries of the information age have, at least in formal discourse, vanquished our yearning for a meta-narrative. It is impossible even to speak about "women" as a single group, or about language as shared meaning. Noted literary scholar Sacvan Bercovich abandoned the traditional hunt for consensus and threw his hands up, calling this era "a time of dissensus" in which Americans' common ground now has more to do with diversity, division and discord than with any harmonious commonality.

As feminists, we have filtered our concerns through a fine-meshed grid of gender, class and race, and the change has opened our eyes. For African-American women, housekeeping's history is bound up with slavery, broken by the separation of mothers from daughters, and split between other people's housework and their own. For middle-class European Americans, housekeeping belongs to a smoothly continuous (but sometimes secretly painful) legacy of private-sphere feminine identity. American Indian housekeeping rituals bear the mark of tribal spirituality and customs. Asian immigrants bring a background even more patriarchal than the American ideology that kept June Cleaver in pearls and an apron.

In her history of *The Great American Housewife,* Annegret S. Ogden points out how the Industrial Revolution's false division of public from private blinded us to the contributions of poor and working-class women who crossed between those spheres every day. Excluded from the mainstream for reasons of class, race or ethnicity, women who were forced to work outside the home developed radical alternatives to the nineteenth-century cult of domesticity, which glorified the stay-at-home female as a paragon of virtue. Scholars are only beginning to study the various ways these women integrated home, work and identity—but we know enough to realize they differed sharply from the middle-class white norm. Judging by Ogden's analysis, the only common denominator revealing Aptheker's "female consciousness" in women of diverse backgrounds has been a common vulnerability to the stereotype of the ideal housewife, achievable or not.

Women writers have been just as vulnerable to that stereotype as their sisters, and perhaps better qualified to articulate and challenge it. Most have carefully chosen their strategies: risk self-doubt by following male models; adopt "lesser" literary genres; bury subtle meanings in a more accessible and acceptable plot; or deal with central female experiences from a female perspective and see what happens.

The final strategy is the most dangerous: "Male readers who find themselves outside of and unfamiliar with the symbolic systems that constitute female experience in women's writings, will necessarily dismiss those systems as undecipherable, meaningless, or trivial," notes Rachel Blau DuPlessis. She writes about the taboos and false namings women writers have confronted, as well as "the dilemma of the male reader who, in opening the pages of a woman's book, finds himself entering a strange and unfamiliar world of symbolic significance." Unable to decipher the significance of "kitchen things," he will judge such fiction slight and aesthetically wanting (231).

In the United States, writing about female experience has often meant professional suicide—or at least a chronic case of the vapors. In *Feminism and American Literary History*, Nina Baym notes that, to qualify as American, literature must take the nation as its ultimate subject. Themes must align with the quest for identity and democracy; characters and experiences must make sense only nationally, not universally (7). Baym describes the Adamic myth, with its emphasis on informal, unconventional exploration, taming the wilderness and rejecting society, and concludes, "There is no place for a woman author in this scheme" (16).

Nor was there a place for women characters in the *Bildungsroman* genre; identity and maturation simply weren't interesting enough when confined to the home. Throughout *The Voyage In*, authors Elizabeth Abel, Marianne Hirsch and Elizabeth Longland sharply point up the difference between the adventurous outward spiral of the male *Bildungsroman* and the circular, introspective formation of the female, which either happens through apprenticeship, as she shifts domiciles from her parents' household to her own, or through awakening, a series of brief internal epiphanies that often require a break from the authority of marriage and tradition. In *The Myth of the Heroine*, Esther Labovitz describes four female characters who underwent a serious quest for identity: All began by rebelling against domesticity, recoiling from its chores, expectations and exemplars.

For less exceptional women, housework has been the only proving ground—yet it has been perceived as too mundane to merit exploration. Fortunately, feminist scholarship in the last 20 years—in literary criticism, the social sciences, the arts and the humanities—gives us ways to probe deeper meanings from women's writings about domesticity. As Romines establishes, "some of the best fiction by American women writers is dominated and shaped by the rhythms and stresses of domestic ritual" (9). We have trivialized these references to domesticity, first in submission, later in self-deprecation or rebellion. The loss is our own.

Yet the recovery of female experience does not, we are now painfully aware, mean the same for every writer. DuPlessis advises critics to consider housekeeping discourses as psychosocial fabrications of difference, and Shelley Wong warns of "literary strip-mining" that fails to reinsert detached imagery into its specific context and history as soon as interrelationships with other texts have been established. Still, even in dissensus, there is common ground. Critics of different women's literatures note shared metaphors, similar uses of language and powerful recurring myths. Needlework alone yields the quilting metaphor Showalter uses to organize American women's literary history; the stylistic notions of stitched transitions, braided plots and embroidered text; the ancient example of Penelope weaving by day and unraveling by night; the lyrical image of the Fates, who control human destiny by spinning, measuring and cutting the thread of life. Even the gentleman critics, such as Theodore Roethke, took up the metaphor, accusing female writers of contenting themselves with "the embroidering of trivial themes" (DuPlessis 221).

Theorists have speculated about how a "pure feminine writing" might look—nonhierarchical, spiraling, interwoven, pieced together without subordination or privileging. But language carries too much patriarchal culture and history in its structure, references and nuances to ever be "pure." Until we can follow Helene Cixous' advice, explode language and reinvent it from scratch, we might do better to seek domesticity in subject matter, plot, character and metaphors, rather than risk overreading by constructing elaborate theories about the structure of language itself.

With female experience gaining literary legitimacy, you'd think housework would have been done to death, scrubbed down to symbol and significance, decontextualized and recontextualized. Indeed, there are several solid areas of relevant recent scholarship: the socioeconomic implications of "women's work"; the politics of female identity; the history of housework; feminist theory and literary criticism; anthropological and theological analyses of ritual. But when it comes to representations of domesticity in literature—whose female authors have railed against

housework's burdens as vehemently as the suffragists railed about political representation—most works of any length deal with explicitly
domestic novels and nearly all stop short of the twentieth century.

The omissions are more interesting than the scant offerings: in *The
Festival of Life,* a seemingly thorough history of women in America, "The
Meaning of Work" section scrutinizes the marketplace and ignores the
home. Douglas R. Anderson's *A House Undivided: Domesticity and
Community in American Literature* acknowledges domesticity as a privi-
leged sphere of meaning in the nineteenth century, yet fails to mention a
single housekeeping task. He proves the reach of domesticity with Emily
Dickinson's dialogue with John Milton; Henry James' *The Portrait of a
Lady;* Franklin's and Thoreau's reconstruction of male identity; and the
domestic ethic of Crèvecoeur!

Why such scant acknowledgment, for a set of activities that has sustained human life, grounded the economy, glued together society's family unit, carried its idiosyncratic histories, manipulated relationships and
shored up (or torn apart) feminine identity? Housework may be a powerful and elementary arena, but unfortunately, it does not fit neatly into
any particular discipline, and it slips rather too fluidly into a multidisciplinary approach. Second, female experience has been quarantined from
intellectual inquiry for decades, treated as trivial, personal and unworthy
of analysis. Finally, housework tends to be either too concrete or too spiritual for traditional scholarship. In *The Sacred and the Feminine: Toward a
Theology of Housework,* Kathryn Allen Rabuzzi comments that the basic
purpose of domesticity as we know it, the creation of a safe, loving home
by women, "belongs to that dimension of human existence known as
tacit." Its assumptions are so basic to the culture, so implicit, fundamental and invisible that they are taken for granted. Or, at the other end of the
continuum, domestic rituals approach mystical experience and defy language altogether (3).

Why bother translating? Because if Freud was right, that work and
love form the core of our lives, then housework—ideally, work done in
love, at home—must shape our psyche, our relationships, our sense of
self and our role in society. Thus, as Ruth Schwartz Cowan said so suc-
cinctly in *More Work for Mother:* "to fail to understand the history of
housework is to fail to understand ourselves" (9).

Parameters

The writers I've chosen for scrutiny are Louise Erdrich, Mary Gordon,
Toni Morrison, Marge Piercy, Jane Smiley and Amy Tan. All six are
acclaimed female writers in the United States who have written a novel

in the last decade that dealt with women's lives, either currently or historically, in honest and thorough fashion. All six are writers eager to express deep truths about women's lives; capable of using language thoughtfully and vividly; and unafraid to include every dimension of women's experience.

They come from different economic backgrounds and filter an assortment of cultural influences: Ojibwa, Irish Catholic, African-American, Jewish, WASP, Asian-American. Initially, my care in seeking diversity was part fad and part fear; I did not want to make mistakes of exclusion. As I pored over the novels, however, my selection taught me more than I had expected, with each tradition illuminating the emphases and omissions of the others. In Erdrich's Ojibwa story, I found none of the resentment of domesticity that burned through Gordon's contemporary Irish-American women. In Morrison's and Tan's reliance on "superstition," societal oppression and folk healing made their presence known more powerfully than they ever could in a political treatise.

The novels' time frames span roughly a century and their settings circle the globe, yet the same patterns of meaning recur in all of them. Indeed, domestic rituals weave themselves through these texts in subtle but surprisingly pervasive fashion. Because housework is so often overlooked or demeaned, however, it would be easy to read these novels without stopping to acknowledge the deep significance of the domestic realm in their plot and character development. Domestic chores have had a problematic relation to female characters and female works of art ever since women began publicly rejecting responsibility for them. As a result, writers often keep domesticity's multiple, powerful meanings below the surface, and readers often let the baby slide with the bathwater.

Before we rescue that slippery baby, however, two histories must be outlined: the evolution of housework in the United States, considering technology and economics as well as societal attitudes; and the intersection of women's literature with domesticity. Then, framework established, we can consider the life of each writer and summarize each novel. What role does domesticity play in the characters' lives? How does it move or reroute the plot? What nuances, subtexts, values and attitudes does it reveal? How—O great unfathomable question—has it shaped their consciousness?

After treating the novels separately, we can dive beneath their separate surfaces into the sea of meaning they share. In all these works and lives, we see domesticity's power to bring order from chaos—not just physically, but mentally, emotionally and spiritually. From that center flows domesticity's ability to tie or sever connections with nature, the body, the self, the family and the community; and its ability to either damage the world or mend the soul.

The chapter titles are quick clues to the work's progression: they begin with the most basic sensory perceptions of the world, then move through bodily, emotional, intellectual, interpersonal and societal spheres, finally transcending the world itself to touch mysteries of death, rebirth and spirit. A formidable range, indeed, for a realm so often dismissed as trivial and mindless.

The conclusion will draw some tentative, reflective conclusions about feminism, spirituality, private life and social structure—not because this study gives sufficient ground to know truth, but because I want to honor an age-old feminine tradition: piecing together the whole, scrap by scrap, with care, strong stitches, and no presumption of perfection.

Two

A Woman's Place

"The labor of women in the
house, certainly, enables men
to produce more wealth...
and in this way women are
economic factors in society.
But so are horses."

from *Women & Economics,* by Charlotte Perkins Gilman

When I first planned to survey women's historical relation to domestic-ity, I thought of starting with, say, the chores and attitudes of my grand-mother's grandmother. But when I began exploring women's relation to consumption and production, order and chaos, men and children and each other, I found myself pulled all the way back to the powerful image of female domesticity at the end of the Paleolithic era. With the initial practice of cultivation, women had made the earth valuable, as fertile as the female body itself. The earliest rites of worship were indeed domes-tic rituals, clearly locating themselves on the spiritual end of meaning's continuum. The grinding and baking of bread was a sacred act, process-ing and returning the earth's life-sustaining daily gifts. Such rituals linked the life-giving earth to life-giving women, who were assumed to produce new humans all by themselves (the causal role of intercourse not having dawned on anyone). Thus archaeologists unearth broad-hipped, large-breasted female "Venus" figurines used in worship; sacred pottery vessels shaped from that earth into uterus-like vessels (Gimbutas 25).

In her description of "Prepatriarchal Female/Goddess Images," Adrienne Rich shows how daily acts transformed the spirit, as women used cauldrons, pots, vases, urns and ovens in ritual ways to ferment, preserve and nourish life. "The earliest religious activity had as its impulse not the contemplation of eternity but the struggle for survival; it was 'practical, not speculative,' as Briffault says, having to do with daily needs" (37–38).

The shift from nomadic hunting to a "settled down" agrarian life was the real beginning of domesticity: it meant a chance to acquire "stuff," live as a stable family unit and make more than one baby every four years, since women no longer had to keep the babe in arms as they traveled. When men domesticated the ox, invented the plow and took over cultivation in the Neolithic Age, women generally left farming and focused on making pottery, weaving textiles, cooking and stockpiling the necessities of daily life (Sinnigen and Robinson 19). This gave their everyday lives a new agenda, allowing a shift of priorities and methods. In her history of women's work with textiles, for example, Elizabeth Wayland Barber notes that, after the agrarian shift, looms didn't have to be portable anymore. They could be enlarged to make bigger, more elaborate pieces of cloth. Meanwhile, women could bring smaller crafts or tasks out into the communal yard, beginning a female tradition of "work parties" that combined mutual help with convivial gossip.

Textiles grew "astonishingly ornate," Barber reports, as women invested large chunks of their scarce free time to embellish the cloth into art as well as protective covering. As distinctive styles and techniques took shape, they were carefully taught to daughters, whose play was imitation of their mothers (88–91).

As a historian of textiles, Barber had few threads to follow; such artisans know their work is functional and transitory, so they leave scant records, and their products slowly disintegrate (24). The same is true for other traditionally female crafts, from fragile clay pottery to exquisite cookery. The consequences seem slight and ephemeral, thus easier to trivialize than buildings wrought in marble or laws carved in stone. Most often, women learned their crafts' forms from their mothers and taught them to their daughters, and perspective ends there. Except for a few deliberate changes—mainly practical adaptations, with the occasional whimsical detail for the sheer delight of ownership—most women have avoided the economic risks of experimentation, unable and unwilling to waste time, materials or money on failures.

Women were, after all, ordained to be helpmeets and housewives, not artists. The English word "housewifery" goes back to the 13th century, when the seedlings of capitalism sprouted a "middle class." "Housebands" worked on, and were bonded to, a house and its surrounding land. Their spouses, "housewives," drew their connection to the house from their marriage to the man who held its title. They did the usual cooking, laundry, sewing and childcare, but enjoyed a special, property-derived status in their society (Cowan 17), hence they were house-wives, married to a house, and taking their place in the social order from its existence.

Gradually the spousal home became more private and its spaces more intimate, feminized by wifely overseeing. But until the Industrial Revolution, domestic life continued to interweave itself with men's production and commerce, and with the spiritual and biological dimensions of every family member's life. Women made food, soap, clothes and candles in the same places where babies slept and nursed, children fetched and played, old people carved and stitched, men wielded tools and did trades. "Women's work" was productive and vigorous: a colonial housewife in this country, for example, might plant a vegetable garden, pickle and preserve its harvest, breed poultry, keep and butcher dairy cattle, cream butter, make cheese, beer and cider, card and spin wool, make thread, yarn and cloth, then sew.

It is easiest to judge the past by more recent standards. But in *For Her Own Good: 150 Years of the Experts' Advice to Women,* Barbara Ehrenreich and D. English point out that, busy with the list above, "pre-industrial revolution women were sloppy housekeepers by today's standards. Instead of the daily cleaning or the weekly cleaning, there was the *spring* cleaning. Meals were simple and repetitive; clothes were changed infrequently," and laundry was allowed to pile up (129).

The pre-industrial era was firmly patriarchal, with authority vested in a family's elder males, yet it was *"gynocentric:* the skills and work of women (were) indispensable to survival" (Ehrenreich and English 7). Women of this era had limited social power and freedom, but knew their role and its importance. They may have struggled with heavy burdens, but they weren't following a textbook standard of hygiene, or aping some advertising copywriter's notion of feminine excellence. Their tasks gave them autonomy and a chance to produce something tangible and necessary from raw gathered materials. The processes grew increasingly complex, requiring a store of knowledge, instinct, intuition and skills. Mom as the brainless, put-upon household drudge had yet to be invented.

The social status a woman derived from her role's indispensability, however, varied widely. Abigail Adams, for example, had plenty of household help, but put up her own preserves as a proud ritual; women of privilege knew the quiet power that lay in coordinating and sustaining their families' everyday lives. At the other extreme, African-American women held as slaves performed similar (albeit harder) tasks, but their work was forced, thus egoless and joyless.

Although most African-American women in the colonial era did not have enough control over their lives to create and appreciate regular domestic rituals of their own, meaning infused the punishing routine of their domestic work. They knew how to extract clothes dye from tree bark and berries; make soap from ashes and animal skins; fix three full meals a day for scores of people over a smoky fireplace; spin 1,200 yards of wool or thread on a single winter night (Jones 30). But instead of settling, exhausted and satisfied, into a rocker by the fire, they had to remain standing in the presence of whites, snatching a bite of food when they could, sometimes sleeping on the floor at the foot of a mistress's bed, then enduring her husband's sexual attentions. If they had a family of their own, they went home and did the same work all over again, exhausted but with more willing hands, because now they were ordering the life-world of those they loved.

In *Labor of Love, Labor of Sorrow,* Jacqueline Jones writes that, because slaveowners so readily put bondswomen to work in the fields, chopping cotton, they practiced a strict gendered division of labor in their homes and communities. Private life was an attempt to restore individual dignity and redress injustices: "Black women's attention to the duties of motherhood deprived whites of full control over them as field laborers, domestic servants, and brood-sows" (13).

Slavery's heavier oppression broke the customary tie between property relations and sexually-divided labor. Slaves did not own property, they were property, and the men had no more economic power than the women. Childcare and familial domestic chores had to be done on the sly or late at night; for enslaved women, making these chores a priority would have been a privilege, not a burden. "If work is any activity that leads either directly or indirectly to the production of marketable goods, then slave women did nothing *but* work," Jones comments acidly. "Even their efforts to care for themselves and their families helped to maintain the owner's work force and to enhance its overall productivity" (14).

The Southern white women who did depend economically on their husbands bore the ultimate responsibility for the domestic realm, thus "supervised" the slaves, instructing, cajoling, threatening and ordering. Many aggravated mistresses felt like "slaves of slaves," lashing out with domestic weapons—"knitting needles, tongs, a fork, butcher's knife, ironing board, or pan of boiling water"—whenever the inadequate performance of tasks they were unwilling or unable to do themselves (26).

Long before the Industrial Revolution, then, domestic tasks operated on multiple and often split levels. For women of privilege, they were a stable, productive, yet often frustrating arena of power. For women in slavery, they were a series of thankless, near-impossible tasks made tense by quick punishment—as well as a rebellious assertion of personhood and the right to self and family. Immigrant, pioneer and desperately poor women lived their domestic role under various constraints, some offering themselves to do others' daily work; some keeping their loved ones alive by miracles of thrice-mended shirts and pot-likker (greens and nearly-inedible scraps boiled into stock).

For society in general, the daily domestic routine confirmed and perpetuated a specific female role at the center of human life, mucky with dried gray sweat, tallow, entrails, peelings and wood ash, yet profound and transcendent. Before science dictated a rational, technological world-view, the rituals and superstitions of everyday life connected individuals to nature's larger, more enduring seasons and cycles. Menstruating women were enjoined not to bake bread, Ehrenreich and English remind us, and conception was favored at the time of spring planting (6). Women not only fed flesh, mended tears, joined breaks and swept their house into order, they also helped their families live in harmony with each other and with the world around them.

The professionalization of medicine is a textbook example of the shift away from this traditional feminine wisdom. As (predominantly male) physicians acquired surgical and pharmaceutical skills, their credentials rose in value, giving them power to restrict, specialize, compartmentalize and control the field. Midwives and herbalists were presented as dirty, unscientific and dangerous. Wives and mothers ceded the role of healer to well-paid strangers who used abstract formulae and took "heroic measures" like bleeding, dosing and cutting.

We could blame the strangers and stop there, but it is important to note what happened next. Instead of defending the rhythmic, nonlinear nature of traditional domesticity, a few legendary women decided to codify it, standardize it, and teach it as science. Catherine Beecher's legendary 1848 *Treatise on Domestic Economy* was written in the middle of the antebellum manual mania, with its urge for democratic self-improvement. "Viewing the domestic sphere as a specialized segment of modern society with a complex social task to perform, the Treatise rejected the notion that women were naturally equipped to succeed in their socially mandated work," notes Kathryn Kish Sklar in the introduction. "It urged readers to approach the female life cycle as a work cycle and prepare for it as a man would prepare for a vocation" (Beecher ix).

Readers of the *Treatise* were living different lives than their grand-mothers, who could do income-producing work at home while caring for children. Although Beecher included recipes for making candles, soap and starch, "the book assumed that 'domestic economy' consisted primarily in the judicious household expenditure of money earned outside the home, rather than the organization of economic production within the home" (x). A massive transformation had begun.

Concerned that young women might forget their role and seek a career before marriage, Beecher and other advice-givers waxed eloquent about domesticity's role in creating harmony and reinforcing the moral order. "There is nothing which has a more abiding influence on the happiness of a family, than the preservation of equable and cheerful temper and tones in the housekeeper," she insisted. "A woman who is habitually gentle, sympathizing, forbearing, and cheerful, carries an atmosphere about her, which imparts a soothing and sustaining influence, and renders it easier for all to do right, under her administration" (134). Such advice wound the bobbin tight, increasing the tension in later debates over women's domestic role.

Domestic Secession and Revolt

As the forces of industrialization began to speed and massify society, the prototypical workplace moved from farm or workshop to factory or office. The worker became a cog or drone with a set of specialized tasks constituting one minuscule piece of the general endeavor. Workplace rules grew progressively more bureaucratic, based on linear reason and abstracted as far as possible from unruly human emotions. The braid of daily life unraveled, and home and work fell into separate spheres rationalized by gender.

The division was both geographic and spiritual. Men and women now worked in separate places, on different tasks, in different ways, with different norms and values. The resulting public-private split had many implications: first, the careful mapping of the spheres placed all the most personal, intimate, physical and emotional activities of human life in the home, and declared them unwanted interferences in the workplace. Second, the values of the marketplace now dominated society, rendering the "private sphere" not only separate but inferior. The rhythms of organic life "got in the way" of efficiency, and should be closeted out of sight and mind.

The new invisibility of women's traditional arena was reinforced by the factories' absorption of a housewife's most productive tasks. Women no longer needed to stitch garments, weave cloth, preserve food or make soap and candles. All that could be done more efficiently at the mass level, in factories. Women's place was in the home. There, they produced little; unwittingly, they had switched to a service economy long before the rest of society.

The woman of the house received no wages for her services. And wages were the consummate measure of worth in an urban economy that found bartering, cooperating, counting on crop yields and stowing cash under the mattress hopelessly outdated. Wages represented the value of one's labor, thus the value of one's existence. As they moved further from the closely interwoven traditions of rural or town-based housewifery, women began doing what was more aptly called "housework"—a separate set of tasks that were, by definition, less important than men's work. These tasks had no lasting effects, produced nothing tangible, gave no sense of closure, yielded scant admiration in the powerful public arena, and brought no money to count and store away as proud consequence of labor. In a world that was simultaneously more abstract and more materialistic, housework defied conventional measures, thus was left with little to show for itself.

Invisible, segregated and trivialized, many women began to think of themselves as peripheral misfits whose work was somehow not as vital as their mothers' work had been. Yet they could not bring themselves to abandon it. "Convinced that domesticity was important even if the full responsibility for it oppressed women, the nineteenth-century advocates of women's rights wrestled with the issue," notes historian Glenna Matthews (139).

The Woman Question soon contained several questions: Why do we have to do this inferior domestic work? Who *should* do it? How do we prove we matter? A few early feminists were openly elitist, saying bright women should aspire to the public sphere and drudges should keep the home fires burning. But the majority of women were too busy silently, invisibly performing the endlessly repeated chores their gender seemed to require.

When you don't have the energy, courage and opportunity to seize visible public power, there's another option: you can become the official guardian of the invisible. Assigned truths of piety and virtue as their realm, middle-class white women became angels in the house, adherents to the Cult of True Womanhood. In order to act effectively in the world without participating in its daily commerce, they learned to deftly manipulate the moral tension between the public and private spheres, whose values were often directly opposed.

The rules of the marketplace, after all, paid little heed to compassion or obligation; they operated according to abstract forces of ordained selfishness, competitiveness, acquisitiveness and greed. Yet humans still craved nurture, romance, sentiment, idealism, coddling of their weaknesses and stern admonitions to curb their raging instincts. Following ancient female custom, women met their families' needs.

Mothers had to fill this new role, because fathers were away at work making it necessary. They, too, were scrambling for a new sense of self: the ancient patriarchal system that had given the senior male absolute authority and responsibility for the family's welfare was blunted by the new role of corporation or industry. Abstract social organizations now dictated life's standard and decisions, and they began to assume more and more of the father's traditional role in providing for the health and future of the family. (As we reorganize in another massive shift to an electronic, automated, near-workerless era, those "benefits" are again in midair.)

The patriarchal system did not crumble into matriarchy, however, let alone a more egalitarian social organization. The industrial era was stereotypically masculine, elevating Apollonian values of reason and order far above the emotional, intuitive realm. That "feminine" realm's symbol and container was now the home, and anything missing from the ruthless workplace must be accounted for there. As a rule, men came home for sanctuary, soothing, and a quick dose of truth, beauty and love. Women *stayed* home, most of them feeling unwanted in (and unsuited for) the rough, beastly work world.

In her coolly ironic *More Work for Mother,* Cowan notes that society's split and reorganization proved convenient for

> certain powerful segments of society: manufacturers who needed markets for the goods they were producing, mill owners who needed tractable workers for their factories, ministers who needed audiences for their sermons, political leaders who needed to stabilize their electorates, and the newly rich men who needed to be able to cement their status with the mortar of elaborate hospitality that only homebound wives could provide. (19)

Wives fulfilled these ulterior motives by accomplishing less and less on the concrete level. By 1900, women bought starch, bread, canned food and apparel; many owned iceboxes and easy-to-clean linoleum. "With less and less to *make* in the home, it seemed as if there would soon be nothing to do in the home" (Ehrenreich and English 129). Sharp-tongued economist Thorstein Veblen noted that, even when bourgeois housewives *looked* like they were working, their tasks were so trivial they could be counted as waste, adding points to qualify the family for conspicuous consumption and higher status.

The decorative arts offered several indices of middle-class women's new (relative) uselessness: Victorian quilts, for example, became more and more elaborately wasteful, lavish with nonfunctional satin, lace, brocade and velvet. "They became an inadvertently ironic sign of woman as consumer rather than producer.... a badge of her oppression and even an unfortunate safety valve that could delay rebellion by diverting energy" (Hedges and Wendt 19).

By the turn of the century, housework done by a privileged wife with servants had more to do with ideology than pragmatic necessity. Domestic rituals had taken on a performative, almost theatrical aspect that suited women's new role—the expression and preservation of values endangered by the rush of modernization. The home was no longer "the real world"; it was now a foil, a compensation, and more than ever before, a cultural construct.

A few brave feminists observed "that the relation between the unemployed wife and the breadwinning husband was not very different from prostitution," once women's role was stripped of skill and hung on the peg of biology (Ehrenreich and English 12). Less economically privileged women retained at least the dignity of their labor, following "women's work" into the factory system, where they helped make textiles, clothing and soap for other women's families. It was these working-class women who cleared the trail for middle-class housewives to enter the labor market decades later.

Predictably, most of the jobs open to immigrant or African-American women at the turn of the century "involved traditional 'women's work' (or rather, in the South, traditional black women's work)—domestic services performed for nonfamily members for only nominal pay" (Jones 74). These jobs included servant, laundress, cook, nurse, seamstress and unskilled laborer. African-American women were barred from peacetime factory labor (except during wartime, when their presence became convenient) and from traditional white women's clerical and retail jobs until the 1960s.

Working-class women, immigrant sweatshop seamstresses, African-American maids and laundresses worked as hard as rural or even pioneer wives. They were influenced to varying degrees by the prevailing culture, but at base level, they had neither time nor need for ideology. Their work remained essential and valuable, keeping the family's nose above poverty's swirling waters. In her documentary history of *Black Women in White America*, Gerda Lerner includes a 1912 article by a Negro nurse who wrote gratefully—too much time has elapsed to be sure whether her tongue was in her cheek—of the "service pan," cold leftover scraps the cook was permitted to take home (or took home anyway) to feed her family (229).

Lerner also includes a 1940 article about the streetcorner markets in New York City, auction blocks where employers bargained for domestic laborers. At the time, one million African-American women did domestic work for as little as $2 a week and as long as 80 hours a week. The women arrived at the blocks early in the morning and waited as late as 4 p.m., hoping to make enough money to buy supper. "They get about 30 cents an hour scrubbing, cleaning, laundering, washing windows, waxing floors and woodwork all day long," the article reported, adding that, by afternoon, the sum was a glorious 20 cents an hour (Mitchell 230).

The Machine in the Home

It would be easy to assume that new appliances and modern fuel-supply systems made the lives of at least those women who could afford them easier, more enjoyable, fuller and more stimulating. But in some ways, technology had the opposite effect. When servants were cheap and plentiful, they could haul coal and firewood, clean sooty ovens, scrub linens raw. Children could fetch and tote, empty and fill; men could do heavy regular chores; single and elderly relatives could help with cooking and cleaning. But by the end of the nineteenth century, the average size of the household had declined, families lived in tighter, more private units, and the "servant problem" had urban society eager for technological replacements (Matthews 193).

And they came. First sewing machines, then primitive washing machines, then stoves, furnaces, electrical refrigerators. Matthews points out that late nineteenth century reformers "embraced technology in an entirely uncritical fashion, making no attempt to differentiate between household drudgery and work drawing on valuable skills" (112). They shared the general society's optimism about machines and their ability to do just about anything better than human beings. "The concept of the mechanized house, the home laboratory," notes Jane Davison, "injected more adrenalin into the psychomotors of the average woman, already quivering with the imperatives of motherhood and home feeling" (88).

After World War II, automatic washers and dryers restructured laundry, removing the wringer step, eliminating piles of mending (broken buttons, broken fasteners) and making ironing easier. Then came dishwashers, trash compacters, microwaves and disposals. Unfortunately, some of the work eliminated by modernization was work men and children had done—carrying, chopping, removing ashes, stoking furnaces, beating rugs—and some was work servants had done by hand, or housewives had "sent out" to commercial services. The amount of laundry sent out (sheets, heavy linen tablecloths, men's shirts, etc.) peaked in 1929 and never returned to that level (Strasser 268).

Where women's work did indeed get easier, society's standards rose to compensate, so no hours were saved. Laundry, for example, had become a matter of sorting, pressing the "warm" and "gentle" wash buttons, shifting to the dryer and folding—but now families peeled off their clothes and threw them in the hamper after one wearing, and sheets and towels suddenly required changing at least once a week. As advertisers ranted about sparkling-clean surfaces, houses grew larger, acquiring more surfaces in need of sparkle. Each object or building material was different, many were fragile, and they all had their own special cleaning requirements. Instead of a simple array of baking soda, vinegar, ammonia and beeswax, housewives suddenly needed bucketfuls of alchemical formulae. Diets grew more varied and complex as more foodstuffs came to market and more elaborate theories of nutrition hit the stands. Newer, gentler methods of child rearing indulged picky children's preferences rather than beating them out with a wooden spoon.

The evolution of technology deskilled labor, removed some of women's control over their work processes, minimized other family members' responsibility and participation, and increased the monotony and isolation of domestic tasks. Susan Strasser uses the Westinghouse automatic washer pamphlet as an index: the pamphlet bragged about ending washday, making laundry into an "odd moments job." In actuality, the automatic washer changed laundry "from a weekly nightmare to an unending task, increasing the size of the pile, the amount of water and fuel and laundry products most households used, and possibly even the housewife's working time, which was now spread out over the week" (Strasser 268).

The pamphlet emphasized women's control over the machine, but the knobs and dials were far tougher to second-guess than one's own elbow velocity or the sun and breeze. Now the variable that ostensibly made all the difference soon became commercial laundry products, which whitened, brightened, cleaned, starched, purified, protected, softened and removed static. Instead of knowing fabrics, methods and remedies, women had to know how to read labels and directions, compare prices and replace supplies. "One gasps at the ingenuity of it all—" wrote Betty Friedan in her politically explosive classic *The Feminine Mystique*. "The housewife can participate in science itself just by buying something new" (216).

Machines could not do *too* much, however; Friedan cited a test given to 250 housewives, asking them to choose among four imaginary methods of cleaning. Rather than a completely automatic dust and dirt removal system, the housewives chose a new modern object with which she could sweep the dirt away herself (216). "Once a woman got this appliance going, she 'felt compelled to do cleaning that wasn't really necessary,'" Friedan added. "The electronic appliance actually dictated the extent and type of cleaning to be done" (217).

The more sophisticated the appliance, the more isolated and detached its user. Instead of somebody washing while somebody else wiped and the kids cleared the table, Mom usually loaded the dishwasher alone. Instead of comparing notes over the backyard fence as they hung out their laundry, women threw a load in the dryer alone in their basement. Not only were women less communal in their work, but they were pitted against each other by advertisers. Friendships foundered over different standards of perfection, marriages tensed over rings-around-the-collar, and women of different generations competed viciously to prove their very different ways superior. "'I beat my mother-in-law,' declared Mrs. Claudia Fortson in a 1980 Tide ad" (Strasser 271), and women across the country vibrated with the emotional significance of her feat.

Essayist Octavio Paz critiques the Industrial Revolution's increasing production of identical, more and more perfect utensils, until houses overflowed with "precise, obedient, mute, anonymous instruments" (55). These gadgets were truly instrumental, performing the task themselves, and leaving nothing for the human to do but buy batteries, send away for warranties, and learn to run machines.

Over the twentieth century, tools have become too complicated to repair, and elaborate service contracts or planned obsolescence have removed even that segment of human control. "Houseworkers are as alienated from the tools with which they labor as assembly-line people and blast furnace operators," notes Cowan (7). She warns us not to dismiss tools as passive objects: they reconfigure, reorganize and limit our work, following the dictates of manufacturers, salespeople, ad agencies and market researchers rather than their individual owner. Women's relation to household tools and appliances has thus changed drastically, moving from simple affection for an old stove or weary irritation with a washboard to a complex, ambivalent combination of intimidation, numb automatic use, fascination, frustrated rage, enslavement, competitive pride and escalating acquisitiveness.

The Downfall of Cooking

Glenna Matthews uses the history of American cuisine for insight into the more general impact of economic and technological change. She identifies two stages in the impact of industrialization on cooking: the first produced more abundance and more time for the housewife, improving the average household's cuisine. Then, once past the Gilded Age, industrialization began to have the opposite effect, deskilling cooking and destroying taste as well as nutritional value (105).

American cooking started out plain and simple, Paz writes, calling it "a cuisine without mystery: simple, nourishing, scantily seasoned foods. No tricks: a carrot is a homely, honest carrot, a potato is not ashamed of its humble condition." He reads this direct relation between substances and flavors as decent, democratic and sensible, a Puritanical shunning of subtle tricks and hot exotic spices (73). Catherine Beecher exemplified such earnestness when she wrote her Chapter on Responsibility of a Housekeeper in Regard to Health and Food, insisting that "the person who decides what shall be the food and drink of a family, and the modes of preparation, is the one who decides, to a greater or less extent, what shall be the health of that family" (70).

Alas, larger forces intervened to complicate the chief cook's role. In the explosive economic growth that followed the Civil War, the food-processing industry took off; meanwhile, improved rail transport and urbanization created a national market ripe for brand-name advertising. Chemical additives, factory-milled flour and extra sugar dovetailed with the newfangled kitchen range (Hess 108), which traded slow-cooked aromas and flavors for easy-bake cakes with fluffy white insides and gloppy frostings. By the turn of the century, cookbooks were flying off the printings presses, most of them in the Fannie Farmer tradition of idiot directions for noncooks. Instead of acquiring their own cookery skills, women slavishly followed other women's formulae. "No longer were taste, texture, freshness of produce lovingly discussed," wail John and Karen Hess in *The Taste of America*. "Nor would technique be sensual, and individual. From now on, things would be measured by the one-eighth teaspoon and the milligram of riboflavin. Welcome to the twentieth century" (129).

Processed foods had won. Slowly kitchens, once the busiest and warmest spot in the house, became fast-food assembly lines open 24 hours a day. The Hesses blame a middle-class that forgot how to be poor. "The history of cookery is largely the triumph of housewives making do with what the gentry wouldn't touch," they write. "Eating high on the hog meant eating the fancy marketable cuts; the poor would get the jowl, the chitterlings, the feet, the tail, and with them would make fine food." Now, everyone—from poor families who couldn't afford them to "gourmets" in the suburbs—was using canned soups, freeze-dried concentrates and boxed mixes.

By the end of the golden 1950s, Americans ate out frequently. That trend accelerated over the next two decades, with fast-food restaurants nearly tripling. Residential architects replaced the formal dining room with a greatroom and focused attention on the "entertainment center," not the dining table. Frozen food ended seasonal eating, standardized flavors, and created a veritable home supermarket. As Ben-Hur implied, the freezer could improve relationships: now "husbands could bring home unexpected guests without inconveniencing their wives" (Hess 272).

The loss of flavor can be blamed on technology, advertising and general cultural emphases. In shipping food long distances, we traded taste for "carrying quality," relying more and more heavily on chemical preservatives, hormones and radiation. Our visual culture's ads conditioned us to accept appearance as a substitute for taste, until we deliberately selected perfect apples that tasted like the wax that glossed them. The country's consumers lost their common sense. The Hesses cite a young couple observed at a supermarket in the 1970s:

> The husband was unemployed, the wife pregnant, and their cart held a sack of candy bars, a TV dinner, and a coconut pie. 'You've got to treat

yourselves once in a while,' the husband explained. As for middle-class women, most admitted that they had no idea what to do, but some thought they were being pretty smart by leaning hard on 'casseroles.' (155)

Manufacturers dictated buying and eating decisions skillfully, printing recipes that elaborated on frozen and boxed convenience foods to make women feel like proper cooks. Microwaves meant meals could be prepared at any time of the day or night, and snacks prepared during station breaks. Mom was still responsible, of course, her endless obligation rationalized by its convenience. But this kind of cooking was mindless, uncreative, a high-tech drudgery with all the credit going to Swanson's.

The Unplanned Obsolescence of Home Economics

We can also trace domesticity's changing societal role through the development of home economics as a discipline. From her post-without-pay at Massachusetts Institute of Technology, Ellen Swallow Richards was the first educator to apply science to homemaking. She advocated teaching chemistry to women as a defense against food adulteration and consumer fraud, and maintained that housewives with scientific knowledge would transform housekeeping's drudgery into productive intellectual experimentation.

At the turn of the century, science's authority was already superceding religion in mainstream culture, while management science and time management set new standards for work of all kinds. In this climate, Richards and 10 others (nine women, one man) met in Lake Placid, New York, in 1899, to baptize a new discipline called domestic economy or domestic science. The thrifty economic paradigm triumphed, and in a decade's time, the American Home Economics Association had been founded. "One of the most clear-cut themes to emerge is the importance of overruling the palate—what the family likes—in favor of nutrition—what experts deem to be good for people," comments Matthews (151). Personal preferences were far too unruly for this bureaucratic spirit, in which experts taught women to trust neither their own taste nor tradition and the advice of older women. Housewives must follow the experts' lead and take satisfaction from the achievements of husbands and children; if they did not, they were to blame for everything from juvenile delinquency to impotence.

Once the audience was receptive, Progressive Era pioneer Christine Frederick helped turn—at least conceptually—domestic labor into management science, cozy kitchens into industrial laboratories, and housewifely skills into the study of consumerism and efficiency. Frederick insisted that kitchens be "standardized," cleaning tasks "scheduled" and "dispatched," budgets "planned" and records "maintained." She instructed housewives to fill out purchasing orders, and she analyzed all tasks in terms of efficiency equipment and time-motion studies.

While Frederick was setting up sample card files, other domestic science experts advanced the Germ Theory of Disease, turning scrubbing into "sanitizing" and cleaning into a crusade against dangerous invisible enemies. Finally, there was a challenge suitable for educated and energetic women, whose foremothers had kept the world clean for centuries. New standards of hygiene paired with social pressure, until the neglect of housecleaning looked roughly equivalent to child abuse.

During World War I, the need for food conservation prompted the public to urge federal support for home economics education. By 1920, approximately 6,000 high schools offered courses in home economics (McGrath and Johnson 13). At that point, Jane Davison recalls,

> home economics was considered to be a reform movement and progressive, rather like Naderism today, and not, as I saw it in its twilight in the 1940s, dowdy occupational therapy for academically uninterested high-school students, who were shunted off from the mainstream of college preparation to sew lumpy dirndl skirts, bake carrot cakes, and memorize the Basic Seven Foods Essential to Good Health. (91)

By mid-century, the discipline had followed the general trend toward division, subdivision, specialization and fragmentation. Research was difficult, which made academic credibility elusive. Even worse, noted the authors of *The Changing Mission of Home Economics* in 1968, "although some would wish it otherwise, home economics, like nursing and elementary school teaching, is a profession largely for women. Presently only 1 percent of the college students who major in home economics are men." The number of college degrees in home ec or home-ec education had increased almost 30 percent from the early 1950s to the early 1960s. But now, as harbingers of the women's movement told girls they could be doctors, lawyers and engineers, the proportion of women in home economics was beginning a steady decline (McGrath and Johnson 17).

The story of home economics is still, however, the story of mainstream white middle-class women, and its gaps are notable. In *The Taste of America*, the Hesses note the sensible and sensual approach to food taken by African-American and immigrant women, but rarely acknowledged by the "experts." The authors complain that "a home economist trained by a textile specialist can teach their children only how to fix a carton of factory macaroni with factory cheese" (256). Concerned, the authors unearth the American Home Economics Association's original credo:

> 'Home economics stands for the freedom of the home from the domi-
> nance of things and their due subordination to ideals and the simplicity
> in material surroundings which will most free the spirit for the more
> important and permanent interests of the home and society.'

"That could be read as a defense of TV dinners," they observe dryly (257).

The Consumer's Insatiable Appetite

Perhaps the simplest way to analyze changes in domesticity over the past century is to follow the shift from production to consumption: the buildup of department stores, mail order houses, supermarkets, chains, malls and brand names; the masterful inventions of marketing techniques, market research strategies and market segmentation; the domination of media by advertising interests; the channelling of housewives' energy into acquisition.

What differences did this emphasis on consumption make? First, it redefined the job, adding infinitely expandable shopping hours to a housewife's set chores. Second, it redefined the criteria for virtue and excellence, trading old skills of needlework and cookery for coupon-clipping, bargain-hunting, money-managing consumption. In this new, product-based mode, young women were encouraged to turn their backs on their mothers' ways, casting aside traditional remedies as "old wives' tales."

By the dawn of the twentieth century, immigrants were struggling to become real Americans by buying white bread and canned goods, symbols of the new American prosperity. Women of all classes found themselves increasingly occupied by the various facets of getting and spending. This new role made them mere procurers instead of producers, and left them only the hollow victory of a successful acquisition.

Corporations, the instigators of consumption, were taking more control over workers' lives. Much of family life, it seemed, could be bought and sold: love in the form of a frozen treat for your kids, purity as a bleach, cuddling through a fabric softener. Daily ritual took its cues from the marketplace, altering the patterns of meals, laundry and cleaning according to standards imposed by commerce. In "Getting and Keeping," Nancy Eberle writes:

> What housework is mostly about is Getting and Keeping.... Getting dog

food for the month. Getting Perrier and brie for the evening.... Keeping
the medical bills in a file. Keeping in mind that the library books are due
on Wednesday, the sitter can't sit on Thursdays, the garage is taking
Fridays off in February, and you're out of Perrier. (166–167)

With all the shopping came a mind-numbing proliferation of brands,
variations and options targeted to various consumers. For all its diversity, none of those storebought, mass-made potions and appliances and
comestibles ever seemed to fit a family's specific needs. Products were
made according to pre-set goals, and until very recently, market analysts
ignored working-class women of all races, African-American women of
all classes, other minorities and recent immigrants, dismissing them as
too poor and preoccupied to court profitably. The more narrowly targeted the marketing became, the more forceful was its implicit program of
expectations—for those women positioned to achieve them. Those
excluded by circumstance had to live outside—"beneath"—the societally
prescribed role for women.

Working Two Jobs

The shift from self-reliant productive work to easily manipulated consumer behavior was a dramatic one. Even more interesting, however, was
the stability of female domesticity's patterns, even amid a technological
and social whirlwind. Why didn't men take on the running of household
machines, while women left home to work in the city? Why didn't children get carefully instructed in the gadgetry? Why didn't huge female
work co-ops form to run neighborhood laundry and cooking centers?

The answers are as complex as the questions. Ten years ago, Kathleen
Gerson published her conclusions about the feminist era's *Hard Choices:
How Women Decide about Work, Career, and Motherhood*. As background,
Gerson listed four mutually reinforcing social conditions that helped
keep women anchored in domestic roles:

1. A family system characterized by permanent, stable marriage
2. A household economy founded on a one-paycheck, male 'family
wage'
3. Limited work opportunities for women
4. Sufficient behavioral similarity among women to provide mutually
reinforcing support for female domesticity. (204)

Gerson pronounced the first characteristic the most critical. When the
Sexual Revolution overthrew assumptions about chastity, lifelong mar-

riage and childbearing, new ideas and behaviors coincided with (and perhaps helped boost) a trend toward women working outside the home. Surveying U.S. Department of Labor statistics from 1950 to 1980, Gerson found that the biggest increase in women workers occurred among married women, mothers with children, and women age 25–44.

Women had worked before 1950, of course, often in clerical and service jobs created by new urban industries. But those were dead-end jobs that paid low salaries and existed on the periphery, providing support without much intellectual and creative involvement. Gerson reports that, in the late 1940s and 1950s, most young adult women married in their 20s, gave birth soon after, and quit working at least until the children were near grown. Domesticity was the dominant model, reinforced by the example of both older women and peers. By contrast, work was a necessary evil, to be avoided whenever possible.

This was the era of "the feminine mystique," explained by Friedan as the belief that "the highest value and the only commitment for women is the fulfillment of their own femininity" (43). Alas, that elegant concept boiled down to the old role of housewife:

> Beneath the sophisticated trappings, it simply makes certain concrete, finite, domestic aspects of feminine existence—as it was lived by women whose lives were confined, by necessity, to cooking, cleaning, washing, bearing children—into a religion, a pattern by which all women must now live. (Friedan 43)

By the end of 1949, only one of every three heroines in that classic index to culture, the women's magazines, was a career woman, and the career woman was shown secretly yearning to renounce her bittersweet independence and drape ivy over a picket fence (Friedan 45). In the mid-1950s, surveys reported and glorified the unworldly housewife whose religious attendance at PTA meetings "gives her 'broad contacts with the world outside the home,' but who 'finds in housework a medium of expression for her femininity....'" (Friedan 213).

Soon these women were on Valium, diagnosed with the "housewife's syndrome" popular since the 1920s (see Abraham Myerson's *The Nervous Housewife,* published at the start of that decade). The symptoms included low self-esteem, emotional instability and fatigue—understandably so, since the housewife was now meeting industrial-level standards of cleanliness and efficiency, yet still dependent on her husband's and children's affection for any job satisfaction. A set of repetitive tasks had been knit into abstract values of love, loyalty, femininity, devotion and nurturance.

The return of the women's movement unraveled row upon row of stitches. Women began entering traditionally male professions, demanding equal wages, delaying marriage or childbirth or both, seeking alternate childcare so they could continue working. It became socially acceptable for a woman to throw herself into her work. Women wrenched acknowledgement from their male partners and colleagues, factoring their own career plans into decision-making.

The change was neither sudden nor comprehensive, and there were plenty of plateaus, backlashes and exceptions. But as Gerson points out, "the nondomestic woman, whether she combines work and motherhood or eschews motherhood altogether, is no longer a statistical, social, or psychological anomaly" (9). For the first time in history, women had multiple "options"—legally, socially, economically, intellectually. Some still chose a traditional domestic model—and found themselves forced to defend its validity and viability. Some chose career exclusively, shunning the domestic in mock horror. Some made career their highest priority and let partnerships and progeny happen as they would, taking a subordinate position to career demands. Some tried the workplace, found themselves stymied or unhappy, and began to wax nostalgic about domesticity; others tried domesticity, found it boring, isolating and unfulfilling, and began desperate attempts to segue late into the workplace. Most tried to have it all, either simultaneously or in shifts, and found themselves furiously juggling different demands, constraints, life skills and choices.

Gerson lists several triggers that continue to steer women toward a nontraditional orientation: unstable heterosexual relationships; economic pressures; dissatisfaction with domesticity; and expanded career opportunities. Unmoored, women find themselves dealing with "structural ambiguity":

> The fact of social change did not determine a uniform outcome in individual lives. These women faced dilemmas, not clear-cut choices. They had to make decisions amid contradictory circumstances, and the process was full of ambiguity and conflict. It involved development and negotiation in which women struggled with and against their employers and male partners to define and control their situations. (207)

Everything is now subject to negotiation: whether and/or when to have a child, where to live, how much housework to do, when and how to spend money. Life presents unanticipated constraints and opportunities, and because decision-making is now a constant and unstructured process, lives can be thrown into chaos on a moment's notice. Not only do external variables alter women's lives (and the lives of their families), but the way a woman defines and perceives her situation adds extra layers of ambiguity. Values and priorities are questioned to an unprecedented extent. Society must deal with the fallout.

The backlash continues, as some men and women push into uncharted territory while others stabilize themselves by clinging even more
tightly to traditional roles. Susan Faludi describes the 1988 New
Traditionalist ad campaign by *Good Housekeeping,* which set off a series of
imitation campaigns and "trend stories" in the national media:

> Grainy photos of former careerists cuddled in their renovated Cape
> Codder homes surrounded by adoring and well-adorned children. The
> accompanying text dished out predictable women's magazine treacle
> about the virtues and "deep-rooted values" of any woman who "found
> her identity by serving home, husband and kids." But this homage to
> feminine passivity was cleverly packaged in activist language, a strate-
> gy that simultaneously acknowledged women's desire for autonomy
> and co-opted it. (92)

While pop-culture makers groped for profitable answers, everybody
else sought *workable* ones. To some, the answer looked simple: women
would take on more of the traditional male role, and men could balance
by taking on more of the traditional female role. There was some hulla-
baloo in the 1950s about "new husbands" becoming feminized, and the
idea returned to the popular press in the late 1970s with a burst of grateful fuss about househusbands. But most of these articles were "written,
as it turned out, by free-lance writers and journalists who had decided to
stay home for a while with their children when their wives went back to
work" (Cowan 200).

The idea of househusbandry flew better in theory than in practice.
Rather than splitting responsibilities down the middle and muddling the
old public-private spheres, women pursued careers, delayed marriage,
had fewer children, considered divorce more often, defined themselves
with less attention to the virtues of domesticity, lived more mobile lives—
and continued doing the bulk of the housework. They were more likely
to abandon certain niceties, stop polishing or spring cleaning or baking
from scratch, than negotiate who-did-what with their husbands.

Men did take on a bit more housework in the 1980s, as public rhetoric
about shared chores rose to a pitch. "In 1987, among those working in the
paid labor force, men did 57% as much household labor as women, compared to 54% and 46% as much in 1981 and 1975 respectively," reported
Beth Anne Shelton in a 1992 social study titled *Women, Men and Time:
Gender Differences in Paid Work, Housework and Leisure.* In 1987, women
reported doing an average of 38.1 hours of household labor per week;
men reported 21.9 hours (65).

Shelton's study indicated that married women spent more time on
housework than single women (a difference of more than nine hours a

week), but marriage made no difference in men's housework hours. Since unmarried women already did more housework than unmarried men, one couldn't blame marital tyranny for the sex role socialization (104). The cause was either natural preferences or earlier parental and societal conditioning.

Schools and cultural media certainly carried their share of old stereotypes: little girls were pictured pushing a toy vacuum cleaner with "dust bunnies" inside the canister, cooking in a storybook kitchen while little boys examined leaves under plastic microscopes or pushed toy lawn mowers (Renzetti 34). In classrooms, little girls were asked to dust or water plants (Renzetti 37). The adults studied had grown up on a mixed diet of pop culture, as society struggled to reconcile traditional values with feminism, and TV struggled to please advertisers eager for housewives' dollars. *I Dream of Jeannie* (1965 – 69) and *Bewitched* (1964 – 72) had given its women magical powers men begged them not to use in the public sphere. Douglas recalls how Darrin made Samantha promise not to use her witchery: "'You're going to have to learn how to be a surburban housewife.... And you'll have to learn to cook and clean and keep house.'" So Samantha zapped the kitchen clean (129).

Unsurprisingly, Shelton found a vast gender difference in the particular tasks adults performed: men are more likely to run to the grocery store, pick up something at the hardware store, fix a faucet, take the kids to Little League or, the perennial male favorite, take out the trash. "Men spend only 24.4% as much time on laundry as women, 30.6% as much time house cleaning and 34.8% as much time as women on meal preparation," she reports, adding that men spent less than half as much time washing dishes (80). Driving and paying bills, tasks that echoed society's valuing of power, money and mobility, are the least gender influenced. And men are still more likely than women to do the less homebound outdoor work, from lawn mowing to car maintenance.

The trick to this division of labor is that most women end up doing, not only *more* housework, but the kind of housework that cannot be deferred. Unlike weeding the lawn or waxing the car, meals and laundry require daily attention, career or not. Shelton labels such domestic tasks "nondiscretionary" to emphasize how little flexibility they offer. The few that can be postponed, such as ironing, pile up and take twice as long to finish. Analysts who had set up elaborate equations converting housework hours to paid work hours had forgotten that neither was as flexible as leisure, so that's what women lost when they started working outside the home.

Ah, but they had all those labor-saving appliances. Labor-saving, that is, if you were a full-time housewife. "Not even the most efficient working wife in the world can prepare, serve, and clean up from a meal in four minutes flat," Cowan noted. The technological and social systems for doing housework had been constructed with the hidden expectation of full-time attention. These systems were far too complex, their assumptions far too deeply embedded, to adapt easily to different circumstances; indeed, Cowan takes the pessimistic view that,

> given the sacred feelings that most Americans seem to attach to meals, infants, private homes, and clean laundry—and given the vast investment individuals, corporations, and municipalities have made in the technological systems that already exist—our household technologies may never evolve so as to make life easier for the working wife and mother. (Cowan 213)

Working at Home

What of the traditional women, those who refrained from entering the workplace, and made the simple joys of home and hearth their universe? In a classic essay on "The Job of Housewife," Barbara Bergmann calls it a peculiar occupation in which one made no wage and had no employer, yet worked seven days a week on call 24 hours a day, received rewards and benefits, and could get fired or quit. As recently as 1986, "housewife" was the largest single occupation in the U.S. economy: 29.9 million women described themselves to the census taker as "keeping house" (171). As divorce rates rose and women entered the labor force, housewives' fate began to raise policy questions. Yet housewivery's association with the powerless female private sphere made it too intimate and too trivial for serious study. Impossible to quantify, it slipped through statistical analysis like berry juice through a sieve.

Modern housewives have been physically isolated from each other, socially isolated from their working-wife counterparts, isolated by technology from the camaraderie of quilt or clothesline, and isolated by gender role from their male partners. Thus the domestic world has remained self-defined and fragmented, without collective bargaining , brainstorming, advocacy or cooperative improvements.

Ann Oakley lists characteristics of the modern housewife role: its exclusive allocation to women; its association with economic dependence based in marriage; its status as non-work (unpaid and unproductive private labor); and its primacy for women, taking priority over other roles (*Woman's Work* 1). At the level of social rhetoric, each characteristic is dissolving: much is said about men sharing household duties; as women's earning power increases, marriage is becoming less and less a property relation; it is politically incorrect to say a housewife doesn't work, and must be qualified with the tagged-on phrase "outside the home"; and women now seem to spend more time apologizing for the state of their house than cleaning it. In *To Make a House a Home,* Lesley Davison actually recommends what she calls Bad Housekeeping, which requires ignoring waxy buildup and herds of dust buffalo.

Is this progress? Historians recall the "domestic feminists" of Victorian America who, by emphasizing women's personhood within a familial network of relationships, critiqued the materialism of the marketplace (Smith 119). Dolores Hayden writes of the "material feminists" of the same era, who defined a grand domestic revolution by demanding pay for household labor. These women proposed a radical redesign of American homes, culture, neighborhoods and cities, broaching housewives' cooperatives, kitchenless houses, day care centers, public kitchens and community dining clubs to break the physical separation of public from private and the economic separation of the domestic from the political economy.

When Charlotte Perkins Gilman, one of those domestic feminists, envisioned community dining facilities, she wasn't thinking McDonald's. She saw a future of hot nutritious food, cooked efficiently by a few and served in pleasant surroundings, freeing other women for more intelligent and constructive tasks. Gilman noted the multitude of professions involved in "our clumsy method of housekeeping," and suggested specialization to divide labor more efficiently *(Women & Economics 245).* She found it ironic that the revered, beloved, dainty female of the species did the world's scullery work: "All that is basest and foulest she in the last instance must handle and remove. Grease, ashes, dust, foul linen, and sooty ironware—among these her days must pass" *(Women & Economics 246–7).*

A century has elapsed since Gilman wrote. We don't use ironware anymore. And many women now divide their days, so they can work outside the home as well.

THREE

DOUBLE MISCHIEF

To be a woman and a writer
is double mischief, for
the world will slight her
who slights 'the servile house,'
and who would rather
make odes than beds.

from "Sonnet to a Sister in Error," by Dilys Laing

When we were 16, my best friend reassured me that she could, indeed, envision me cooking for a family of four: I'd have a book suspended from the kitchen ceiling, and I'd be flipping pages as I stirred the oatmeal.

If only it were so easy. Not only does the world continue to "slight her who slights 'the servile house,'" as Dilys Laing warns us, but the criteria for domestic excellence in place since the Industrial Revolution require women to accomplish the infinite, every day and from scratch, without a drop of perspiration or a hint of work-in-progress. These tasks involve muscle, memory, instinct and keen senses—not intuition, imagination and the serendipity of the creative process. As a young woman, I honed my literary interests so avidly that I forgot which cabinet held my pots and pans. But inside, I still struggled to integrate my desire to be fully female (in the world's eyes, and a man's) with my desire to create in words as well as flesh. I saw no reason why they should be mutually exclusive: both were a way of cleansing life's accumulations, straightening what had gone askew and expressing what was ideal.

My first consolation in aspiring toward both belles lettres and a beautiful house came with the realization that I'd joined a long and worthy line of jugglers, dodgers, firebrands and romanticizers. In this chapter, I will trace various women writers' efforts to reconcile the tensions of domesticity and creativity. Some of those tensions were socially induced, by husbands who resented a wife at the typewriter instead of the stove;

by mothers who warned their daughters what would be expected of them; by publishers who preferred the kind of books men wrote. Other tensions were built into the opposite natures of domestic and creative work: yes, both were ways of creating order and communicating feeling, but they required completely different states of mind and circumstance.

These tensions have revealed themselves in countless women writer's lives, opinions, language and work, telling the history of domesticity another way. Take Judith Sargent Murray, the first American-born woman to have her plays professionally produced: she wrote in 1790 that the needle and the kitchen were simply not enough to occupy a woman's mind, and being restricted to their arena was both unconstructive and degrading. She also pointed out that men blamed women for lacking the very qualities men forbade them to develop (Spender 118).

In the next century, Charlotte Perkins Gilman was blamed for *displaying* the qualities of vigor, determination, independence, intellect and talent. Her doctor advised her to "live as domestic a life as possible…. Have but two hours intellectual life a day" (Hill 149). But Gilman had never thrived on a domestic life. In 1885, after she'd given birth to her daughter, her mother had told her she'd feel better if she got up and did something. "I rose drearily," Gilman later recalled, "and essayed to brush up the floor a little, with a dustpan and small whiskbroom, but soon dropped those implements exhausted, and wept again in helpless shame" (Gilman 91). It could have been post-partum depression, but given Gilman's lifelong resentment of domestic expectations, it's more likely the chore itself depressed her.

Other women writers proved more receptive to domestic standards. By her brother's report, Transcendentalist thinker Margaret Fuller took care that her intellectual accomplishments never caused her to neglect a woman's humble domestic duties (Spender 203). Writer Margaret Walker did her writing mainly at night: "I was determined not to neglect any members of my family; so I cooked every meal daily, washed dishes and dirty clothes," she recalled (101).

Tillie Olsen, herself a veteran of years of dutybound domesticity, describes how poet Sylvia Plath found herself up at "four in the morning, that still blue almost eternal hour before the baby's cry," trying to write before a day of stirring, wringing, scraping and fetching. Olsen imagines how "the smog of cooking, the smog of hell floated in her head. The smile of the icebox annihilated. There was a stink of fat and baby crap; viciousness in the kitchen! And the blood jet of poetry (for which there was never time and self…)" (36).

Anne Morrow Lindbergh's now-legendary stay at the beach, chronicled in *A Gift from the Sea*, reminded her that the American woman's life was by and large fragmented, constantly available, open to the chaos of multiplicity: "Women's normal occupations run counter to creative life, or contemplative life or saintly life" (29). A few years ago, before taking a similarly reflective journey to learn the simple joys of domesticity from the Amish, artist Sue Bender had divided her world into two lists:

> All the 'creative' things—the things I valued, being an artist, thinking of myself as undisciplined and imaginative—were on one side, and the boring, everyday things—those deadly, ordinary chores that everyone has to do, the things I thought distracted me from living an artistic life— were on the other side. (5)

For some women writers, the imaginative and the everyday have occasionally fused. But the commingling has seldom been smooth. Anne Tyler, for example, once thought of a character for a novel while painting the downstairs hall:

> I figured that if I sat down and organized this character on paper, a novel would grow up around him. But it was March and the children's spring vacation began the next day, so I waited.
> After spring vacation the children went back to school, but the dog got worms. It was a little complicated at the vet's and I lost a day. By then it was Thursday; Friday is the only day I can buy the groceries.... (3)

That waiting, those constant interruptions, mark a life of domestic responsibility. As Olsen noted, a family's needs take both physical and emotional precedence—especially if the woman responds out of love instead of duty. Distraction soon becomes habitual, literary creation progressively more remote.

Does it have to? From the surface, housework looks easy, especially if you're home all day surrounded by modern conveniences. You simply wash up the breakfast dishes, tidy a bit, then sit down at the computer to write brilliant prose. Given the right alignment of money, children and spousal help, there may well be, technically, enough time to do both. But when Adrienne Rich went through a writing slump, she blamed it on, not only an unmeetable excess of trivial distractions, but also "that female fatigue of suppressed anger and loss of contact with my own being." Rich found domestic tradition oppressive because the woman's role was passive and constrained, urging a careful holding-back and consistent availability that left little room for intellectual self-assertion, or an artful ordering of emotional chaos.

> For a poem to coalesce, for an action or character to take shape, there has to be an imaginative transformation of reality which is in no way pas-

sive. And a certain freedom of the mind is needed...you have to be free to play around with the notion that day may be night, love might be hate; nothing can be too sacred (Spender 125).

Why didn't modern conveniences and casualness free women for creative action? Because, frozen by tradition, the "womanly" role managed to preserve a powerful body of contradictions. Even when women were carefully educated and taught to strive for perfection, getting a husband outweighed any other accomplishment. Once we married, much of what we'd been praised for in school became a liability, its continuance a trade-off. "Every book has been a baby I did not bear, 10,000 meals I did not cook, 10,000 beds I did not make," Erica Jong notes. Women writers are all divided, she adds: "In some way we identify with the patriarch—or how would we have become creators at all?" (105–106).

Because gender has been the main principle organizing the division of labor, bodies and sexually conditioned traits have had a maddening tendency to align themselves as public and creative (male), or private and subservient (female). In other words, as economics split public from private, the inherent tension between the repetitive, nurturing aspects of domesticity and the innovative, self-expressive aspects of creativity has been magnified and concretized.

The social construction of gendered reality has caused problems for both sexes; for women, it has set up frustrating contradictions between mind and body: specifically, between female identity, which is often mired in sensebound sexual and reproductive capacity, and creative, productive public achievement, which rests on abstract reason and universal ideas. In *The Visitation*, Michele Roberts captures the tension at its peak: "To write, Helen always feels she has to cancel her body out, become pure mind. Genderless, transcendent, like a man" (99).

Helen's trick works to varying degrees, depending on what one is writing. Some topics fare well drawing on only a disembodied intellect; others seem to crave the writer's flesh, bone and feeling. But no matter how successfully disembodied the writing, one must then meet the social consequences of authorship—and at that point, femaleness is tough to conceal.

Women writers such as Shirley Jackson, Jean Kerr, Phyllis McGinley and, a little later, Erma Bombeck, preferred a different route. Portraying themselves as merely humble housewives, they poked light and dark fun at their struggles, urging other housewives to laugh at the job's absurdities. "They implicitly deny the vision, and the satisfying hard work involved in their stories, poems, and plays," burst Betty Friedan. "They deny the lives they lead, not as housewives, but as individuals"—and as writers (57).

The Bombeckian, lemonade-from-lemons sort of solution grows less tenable every year, but I understand its appeal; this dissertation is itself an attempt to reconcile the two worlds. Writing is abstract, analytical and unifying, at odds by its very nature with the threads and scraps of daily life. And unless you are capable of supreme indifference, those threads and scraps have a way of taking precedence. The more tangled you become in sustenance and nurture, the harder it can be to impose cold clear ideas that threaten the safety of convention. "Listen to me," a writer insists. "Think, question, rethink, change your mind." That's an aggressive challenge, and it elicits a far different reaction than urging someone to have a second helping.

Some women writers have censored themselves to silence; some have let editors' and readers' expectations shape their work; some have found themselves barred from publishing. In her classic *Silences*, Tillie Olsen takes her cue from Virginia Woolf, who was convinced that whenever we read of women possessed by the devils or wise about life, we're on the track of a lost novelist or suppressed poet. Olsen counts as silenced Rebecca Harding Davis, whose depiction of life in the iron mills was seen as male and gloomy; she endured a nervous breakdown and several pregnancies and finally resigned herself to writing for money instead of art. Katherine Anne Porter spent 20 years getting past teaching and keeping house so she could write *Ship of Fools*; Dorothy Richardson, Hortense Calisher and Isak Dinesen published late in life. Spender says women are

> up against men's beliefs about what is proper, appropriate, and womanly in a writing woman, and to this day the problem persists. Men have a mindset about the literary efforts of women, and because it is derived from their construct of woman and not from a study of women's writing, it doesn't actually matter whether these qualities are or are not present in women's writing. (32)

In this aspect at least, women of privilege have fared worse; even before the Victorian era, society set high expectations of middle- and upper-class white women as paragons of refined virtue. These women proved far more likely to write and get published than women of darker color or fewer means, especially if they wrote novels in the privacy of their homes and allowed their husbands to mastermind negotiations with the publisher. But the emotional and artistic costs of compliance ran high.

The freedom to choose one's goals has varied, of course, with personality, life circumstances, individual talent and the tone of the decade. Serious women writers have always managed to ignore the prevailing norms and think independently—or, more accurately, interdependently. But shifts in popular culture's assumptions have made a difference in how far their ideas traveled, and what kind of reception awaited them.

When she wrote *The Feminine Mystique*, Friedan recalled her own stint as a magazine writer in the 1950s, just after women's magazines stopped including serious fiction and obsessed on "service" articles, replete with concrete, realistic, helpful little domestic details like the sudsiest soap or the freshest shade of paint. "Perhaps the new image of women did not permit the internal honesty, the depth of perception, and the human truth essential to good fiction," she snapped. Fiction would have required a heroine with an active sentient consciousness and a goal or dream. "There is a limit to the number of stories that can be written about a girl in pursuit of a boy, or a housewife in pursuit of a ball of dust under the sofa" (55–56).

In the 1960s, tired, disgusted housewives let the dust bunny run away, too angry to give chase. Annegret Ogden nicknames the result "antidomestic fiction," citing Mary McCarthy's ironic *The Group,* Sue Kaufman's aptly named *Diary of a Mad Housewife,* and Marilyn French's polemic *The Women's Room.* Powerless in the "real" world, trapped by expectations, isolated and frustrated, these heroines proved more pathetic than tragic. But by taking the risk of being judged whiny, unwomanly, selfish and neurotic, they clarified the domestic dilemma.

Only recently have novels showed "women successfully developing, learning, growing in the world at large" (Ferguson 229). The change began to gather momentum in the 1970s, as more and more women "left home" to enter "a man's world." But it took another two decades to vent enough rage for artistic ease.

Invisible Women

African-American women writers have suffered a double burden, marginalized by both race and gender; yet in Patrick Bjork's opinion, the oppression has had a paradoxical effect. Limited at every juncture, they enjoyed one freedom white women of means did not; they could become strong and self-reliant without coyly pretending inferiority to the sustaining patriarch (18).

Instead of catering to a providing spouse, however, most African-American women wound up catering to dominant white biases—and that task left little room for literary expression. According to Hortense Spillers:

> With the exception of a handful of autobiographical narratives from the nineteenth century, the black woman's realities are virtually suppressed until the period of the Harlem Renaissance and later. Essentially, the

black woman as artist, as intellectual spokesperson for her own cultural apprenticeship, has not existed before, for anyone. (31)

Nineteenth-century black women writers existed, but they spent a great deal of energy soothing their white audiences by making their black women beautiful, feminine, chaste, well-bred and as white as possible (hence the genteel tradition of the tragic mulatta made fragile and half-mad by her mixed blood) (Bjork 20).

Surely the second wave of the women's movement fixed all that weepy, delicate nonsense? Eventually, some of it. But the feminist movement boosted white middle-class women writers' lot long before it joined the cult of multiculturalism. The womanist movement particular to African Americans evolved much more slowly; there was other work to do, and African-American women had no desire to polarize themselves from men who, locked out of patriarchy themselves, were partners in the civil rights movement. When the movement did begin, its impetus came from literature rather than political theory. Writers such as Alice Walker voiced the need for a "womanism" that was fuller, stronger and more inclusive than white-girl feminism; a womanism that, while fiercely proud of females, would also commit itself to the survival and wholeness of men.

Walker has also done her part to recover the legacy of artful female domesticity. In her oft-quoted essay, "In Search of Our Mothers' Gardens," she writes: "These grandmothers and mothers of ours were not Saints, but Artists; driven to a numb and bleeding madness by the springs of creativity in them." She talks about a genius great-great-grand-mother required to bake biscuits for a lazy backwater tramp, and about a mother who "made all the clothes we wore, even my brothers' overalls. She made all the towels and sheets we used. She spent the summers can-ning vegetables and fruits. She spent the winter evenings making quilts enough to cover all our beds" (517, 520).

Another recent African-American writer, bell hooks, notes how her grandmother and other black women "made homeplace," building a safe shelter where black women could affirm each other and heal each other's wounds. This domestic work offered, in her opinion, as powerful a polit-ical resistance as literature itself: "It is no accident that this homeplace, as fragile and as transitional as it may be, a makeshift shed, a small bit of earth where one rests, is always subject to violation and destruction" (449, 452).

Like other women writers whose identity was in some way problem-atic for the dominant group, African-Americans have drawn hard on the steady generosity of their mothers and grandmothers, using domestic images and ideas to represent and celebrate their history, their life and their womanhood. "In contemporary novels, black female characters look to themselves, to their relationships, and to their communities for strength and growth," Bjork notes, adding that these novels offer an ideal unity in which every African-American has a bit of power, and no one outside the community can divide, coerce or suppress them (28). Mary Helen Washington addresses the point more fully:

> There are no women in this tradition hibernating in dark holes contemplating their invisibility; there are no women dismembering the bodies or crushing the skulls of either women or men; and few, if any, women in the literature of black women succeed in heroic quests without the support of (others). (35)

And Barbara Christian asks simply, "Who but us could lovingly present women poets in the kitchen?" referring to Paule Marshall's *Poets in the Kitchen* and other books like it (47).

American-Indian and Chinese-American Perspectives

The American-Indian literary tradition is also more receptive to the quiet rhythms of domestic labor—albeit a very different kind of domestic labor—than mainstream American literature. But like the African-American tradition, American-Indian literature has taken decades to come to fruition. Because it is less known, and therefore influential on or reflective of mainstream culture, I will use it as a point of contrast rather than a focus for explicit study.

Tribal writings began to build up during the period of white domination that stretched from the 17th to the late 20th century, and were highly influenced by that domination, as Paula Gunn Allen demonstrates in *Voice of the Turtle*. The consequent body of American-Indian work, which has exploded since 1970, focuses on cultural and psychic dissolution, its characters caught between worlds and often drawn toward alienation and destruction.

The central point for this study is that, as Allen notes, American-Indian stories and books have "certain structural features—diversity, event-centeredness, nonlinear development of story line, and transitional modes" that contrast sharply with western literary norms. Mainstream American literature has been action-oriented and straight-lined, organized analytically into beginning, middle and end, and peaking at an Aristotelian climax. The very different structure of most American-Indian works has made them more receptive to, and better suited for, topics traditionally considered "feminine" (8).

We will look at these topics more specifically in the next chapters, when we concentrate on the Ojibwa tribe of whom Louise Erdrich writes. But in Allen's quick philosophical summary, "Native people see change as the fundamental sacred process, as Transformation, as Ritual, as intrinsic to all of existence" (7). This approach opens their writing to the rhythmic, organically-ordered, physical and concrete cycles of daily and seasonal work, forging close connections between earth, individual, family, tribe.

Domestic images and ideas show themselves in Chinese-American literature, too, but their context is more often societal norms than natural rhythms, and many of the references seem ambivalent, bittersweet, upside-down. This stands to reason, if we consider for a moment the gender split and inversion of early Chinese-American history.

Chinese-American women's scarcity (men were allowed to enter the country to work in the mines, build the railroads, etc.) blocked the formation of traditional family lives. When women did arrive, they were perceived as stabilizing the men's hard-drinking, heavy-gambling "bachelor society." Meanwhile, the men cooked and did laundry for pay, and ethnic and gender stereotypes branded them effeminate. Patterns in the United States upset the genders' power balance, therefore, and reversed the devalued status of women in China, where girl babies were sometimes smothered in ashes at birth. Amy Ling points out that, as an Asian-American literature slowly formed, most of the writers were women (16).

That fact is more startling than we may realize. Ancient Chinese society may have been matrilineal in its earliest form, but by the end of the first century, "patriarchal power already had been long established and women were being trained from birth for an inferior place" (Ling 2). How did women writers break such an ancient chain of imposed modesty? "The greater the repression, the greater the force for liberation," Ling quips (16).

The earliest Chinese-American writer, Jade Snow Wong, was born in 1922, and her life exemplified the tension between domesticity and creativity. Wong depicts her family life as frugal, restrained, disciplined, with a lack of affection and praise. For this she blames Chinese culture, citing its distrust of originality, individuality and emotional expression (Kim 67). In her 1940s autobiography, *Fifth Chinese Daughter*, she says she relieved her mother, a factory seamstress, of daily household duties, then began to work in the homes of others, where she was "merely another kitchen fixture." Like other Asian-American women, Wong finds herself falling back on the sense of being "exotic"; when the meringue falls and she's ordered to make another, a humiliated "Wong attributes her difficulties to cultural differences and channels her anguish into a desire to show off her ability to cook Chinese food" (Kim 68).

In more contemporary Chinese-American fiction, such as the novels of Maxine Hong Kingston or, in this study, Amy Tan, the women crisscross and intercut time periods and voices, mixing fact with fiction, memory with event. There is a double sense of alienation: rejection by the dominant culture coupled with a rejection of parental ways, "old Chinese virtues of absolute obedience to authority, honesty, hard work, repression of anger, and sensitivity to the opinions of others" (Ling 123). Often, the younger women's rebellion plays out in the domestic arena, where something as simple as cooking can be a cursed legacy, a chance to show off exoticism, or an affirmation of life despite depression, confusion and loss.

Literary Criticism's Lag

Today, publishers are accepting novels by women of different races and sexual orientations and class backgrounds. But according to Spender, the literary criticism that consolidates a good novel's position in the canon has not caught up to the novels. She points out that, in this "postfeminist" era, many assume "that blatant intimidatory tactics designed to keep women out of the literary arena are a thing of the past." Alas, she continues, "no such improvements have been forthcoming in the context of lit-crit" (25).

Spender does add, however, that when we gave female literary critics such as Annette Kolodny and Elaine Showalter full rein, they steered us in a new direction: toward legitimating the full range of women's experience as women and as writers, and toward linking women's lives with their literature (119).

The fastest way to denigrate women writers has always been to slight their subject matter, which one of Spender's professors described as "the finer detail of the *domestic/relationship* realm" (38). As Nina Baym points out, nothing could be further from the classic American plot, which seeks individual identity in a peripatetic, adversarial, outwardly-driven series of adventures. For the American hero, "to leave behind the known and, because known, commonplace reality is to invest in the promise of finding an elsewhere that will provide a second chance for being and consciousness" (Baym 6). Even if this were a brash oversimplification—and given the tradition of venturesome self-creation in everything from Walt Whitman and *Moby Dick* to Hemingway, Kerouac and Vonnegut, that's unlikely—the perception creates a reality in which domesticity's small cozy world could not possibly serve as a catalyst for growth.

If a good solid American plot hinges on action, clearly defined and outwardly manifest, then the repetitive, often invisible processes of women's daily work don't merit a second glance. The "American Adam" strain explored by critic R.W.B. Lewis shows, in various guises, the New World's first man being initiatied, not into society, but away from it; set above the flaws of the masses, released from the constraints of corrupting civilization.

And yet, "antebellum women novelists knew that the home provided their protagonists with the most secure basis for power in an insecure and male-dominated world" (Matthews 67). The twinned birth of domestic literature and domestic feminism raised the value of home, legitimizing women writers' claims to cultural influence. These first-wave feminists succeeded so well they won themselves a backlash, however, and it included attacks by male writers on the inseparable arenas of femininity and domesticity. "If Tom Sawyer, Huck Finn, and their kindred chafed so memorably against the tyranny of the domestic ideal in the world of fiction, they must surely have influenced their counterparts in the real world—who were probably already feeling resentment about the same thing," comments Matthews (91).

Romines places the beginning of "the home plot" at the time of the Civil War, noting that women's careful attention to domestic ritual could have been influenced by American realism and by a new local-color interest in the particularities of regional life (9). From the start, this matrix of domestic ritual was ambivalent. Quoting a passage from "Minister's Wooing" by Harriet Beecher Stowe—"She shall scrub floors, wash, wring, bake, brew, and yet her hands shall be small and white"— Romines notes that Harriet Beecher Stowe "both valorizes and gently mocks the ideal of domestic competence" (5).

As soon as a woman picks up a pen to record a bit of domestic reality, she is measured by a thousand different conditions and expectations. Her prose will vibrate with the ancient tension between feminine power and powerlessness—no matter what she writes. Over the years, women writers have taken a gamut of stances toward domestic competence; the area of intersection has been, not their opinion of domesticity, but their need to evaluate their lives in relation to it. That thread runs through novels of all kinds, providing unity and continuity (and perhaps, someday, a way out of the labyrinth of domestic oppression).

When women *write* about domesticity, chores cease to be obstacles and become repositories of truths that are difficult to communicate any other way. Domestic scenes and ideas may be quiet in tone, but they are quite specific, chock full of quiddity. "Women's stories evoke distinct meanings, distinct spacial and temporal arrangements," Aptheker observes. "They have been crafted in or out of the artifacts of daily life, beckoning us to see" (45). Women using this method invest objects with meaning, using them to convey deeper truths concretely. Many, like Katherine Mansfield, have set their stories in kitchens, places of female labor, but also of light, comfort and conversation. The kitchen has been a traditional American gathering place ever since the days of fire and coal, when it was quite literally the warmest room in the house. To this day, party guests cluster in the kitchen, and family members traipse there when they're troubled. Things are said in kitchens that might never be said in the living room.

The influence of domestic ritual floats far beyond literal determinations of setting or plot. DuPlessis notes how the complex structure of Doris Lessing's *The Golden Notebook* broke form, substituting "a poetics of domestic values—nurturance, community building, inclusiveness, empathetic care." This poetics begins with ethics and relationship, and "can only be made with an immersion in personal vulnerability, a breakdown, or a breakthrough," she adds. "Since this artwork annuls aesthetic distance and is based on vulnerability and need, it is very like 'life'" (103).

Grace Paley, too, writes about the ordinary everyday details of life and its most intimate interconnections, gladly abandoning the cool, narcissistic search for abstract principles. By articulating the ordinary, she explores a very different sort of mystery, making it clear that everyday's joy is often contingent on others' happiness, rather than one's own ego. In editing their book on *Contemporary American Women Writers: Narrative Strategies*, Catherine Rainwater and William J. Scheick found such value-based choices the only fertile area of literary gender difference. Men and women tend to use the same figures of speech and rhetorical devices, but they often manage them quite differently, because they are aiming for such different goals.

Language on the Distaff Side

Much has been written by recent feminist literary critics about the sleight-of-pen required to transmit female meanings through a patriarchally developed and circumscribed language system. The masculine form is our linguistic norm, our generic, unmarked universal. Anything feminine is, therefore, a deviation, an embellishment, an other. Moving from grammatical structure to existential connections, some thinkers claim that the very notion of selfhood opposes the masculine self to the female other. Others note the insidious ways in which femaleness has been linked with everything outside the (male) subject: with uncontrollable bodies and wild emotions; with unconscious secrets and inexplicable truths. If the feminine is that which cannot be expressed, then the simple facts of women's daily lives will hang forever in midair—like misplaced socks on a laundry line, waiting to be plucked, paired and made useful in someone else's world.

According to the firmest of the feminist critics, all manner of tensions and frictions arise when you insert a female subject into a male literary tradition, then try to use male-oriented language to reveal her innermost experiences, then try to invent a new language in which to criticize the literary consequences. Juliet Mitchell goes so far as to say there is no such thing as a woman's voice; there is only the hysteric's voice, shrill and trembling because she must use masculine language to talk about feminine experience.

If we did have a feminine language, how on earth would it read? According to American critics such as DuPlessis and Showalter and French critics such as Luce Irigaray and Helene Cixous, the words and sentences would flow nonhierarchically; making an even display of elements over the surface with no point of climax; organizing the content into many centers with no subordination or prioritization. Christine Makward, an important translator of (and commentator on) French feminism, describes female language as open, nonlinear, unfinished, fluid, exploded, fragmented, polysemic, attempting to speak the body, involving silence, incorporating the simultaneity of life. Baym is quick to point out the dangerous underlying assumptions of this description:

> This open, nonlinear, exploded, fragmented, polysemic idea of our speech is congruent with the idea of the hopelessly irrational, disorganized, 'weaker sex' desired by the masculine Other. The theory leads to a language that is intensely private, politically ineffectual, designed to fail. (203)

French feminist critics spent a few fun-filled years dwelling on *écriture feminine,* a process by which the female body—the locus of difference—inscribes itself. Then they admitted it hadn't happened yet. No bodies surged into prose forcefully enough to break categories; no sentences loosed themselves from logic. Maybe they never will, at least not with recognizable purity, given the difficulty of reconfiguring language at its roots.

In *Subject to Change,* Nancy K. Miller offers another possibility: "If, however, we situate difference in the insistence of a certain thematic structuration, in the form of content, then it is not true that women's writing has been in no way different from male writing" (27). Women live within the culture, so there's no point looking for turns of speech so chaste, so uniquely "feminine," that they admit of no cultural penetration. Instead of seeking linguistic signs as foolproof as genitalia in revealing an author's gender, the new literary history consciously recreates what it describes, attending always to difference and particularity without drawing any rigidly exclusive gender lines.

Piecing the Quilt

If we want to use genuine, particular female experiences to shape our language, we can begin with the seamless garment of linguistic analogy offered by the age-old feminine pursuits of weaving, mending, quilting, sewing, knitting and embroidery. Men have done all these tasks, written about all these tasks, yet deep feminine meanings lie within them still. Penelope weaving and raveling; Beauty pricking her finger into sleep; Scheherezade spinning tales; Betsy Ross stitching the flag; opponents to slavery stitching rebellious symbols into their piecework—these are female images, and their metaphorical meanings link easily to more prosaic qualities of warmth, protection, shelter, nurture, attraction, seduction, sentiment, tradition, time, care, artistry.

Showalter, one of the biggest supporters of a female-oriented criticism she calls gynocritics, reports that "the repertoire of the Victorian lady who could knit, net, knot, and tat, has become that of the feminist critic, in whose theoretical writing metaphors of text and textile, thread and theme, weaver and web, abound" (Miller 224). In an essay on "Invisible Mending," Jane Marcus explains the impulse in the literary criticism of her collective: "We want to weave women's lives and works back into the fabric of culture, as if they had never been rent.... Penelope's shuttle, my mother's needle, and my pen are implements of order. They speak ...not of destruction and war but of the preservation of culture" (381).

Quilting is one of the most frequent feminist symbols, and it works especially well for literature. Quilts are discontinuous in process, as women's writing has had to be, creating a whole from fragments and working one bit at a time.

"I would like to suggest that a knowledge of piecing, the technique of assembling fragments into an intricate and ingenious design, can provide the contexts in which we can interpret and understand the forms, meanings, and narrative traditions of American women's writing," writes Showalter (Miller 227). She traces a changing relationship between piecing and writing: in the antebellum era, piecing was women's separate territory, a marker of a female world different from the patriarchal literary tradition. The quilt was a moral artifact, an emblem of the deliberate ordering of women's separate cultural lives. After the Civil War, Showalter sees quilts' changing designs reflecting the decline of a strong, separate female aesthetic, and their structure paralleling women writers' search for a workable form and narrative coherence. Over the next several decades, skillful needlewomen would find themselves able to achieve a certain artistic stature, as would skilled women writers of short stories, vignettes and novellas (Miller 229). Short narrative pieces that complied with basic cultural norms were easiest for women to write and publish; they followed basic patterns and traditional forms and, like quilting, could be done in one's "spare time."

Many traditional women's crafts took a back burner to the political realm in the 1960s and 1970s, just as traditional subjects left women's self-conscious, politicized writing. When those crafts returned, it was as a commentary on the *social* order. Today, they are often seen as an explicit attempt to restore wholeness, just as the AIDS quilt is an attempt to recover, share and open a traditionally female symbol on the larger scale of public life.

Food for Thought

Do other aspects of domesticity follow the richly textured pattern of needlework in literature, which opens itself to analysis at the split levels of subject, image, symbol and metaphor, as well as serving as an associative context for deeper social and philosophical meanings? As I explored the texts of the six novels in this study, two similar realms surfaced: cooking and cleaning. Both follow the basic pattern: gathering bits and scraps; rearranging and transforming them to allow the healthy continuance of life. Cooking and cleaning may seem less artful than needlework, and certainly their role in both literature and life has been examined far less frequently, but it is, I believe, equally rich in meaning.

In a study of Asian American literature subtitled *From Necessity to Extravagance,* Sau-Ling Cynthia Wong notes that "eating is one of the most biologically deterministic and, at the same time, socially adaptable human acts: a meal can be a simple prelinguistic *phenomenon* or a multivalent *sign* coded in language, manners, and rites" (18). At its most basic biological level, eating is crucial to survival, thus it embodies a universal set of significances. Those layers of meaning accrue with human responses to excess, abundance, need, starvation; take on the variety of different tastes, smells, temperatures and textures; and gather power from food's capacity to heal, strengthen, restore, seduce, wean, sicken or poison. Cooking, then, brings a meal from the chaos of raw ingredients, and it also brings shared meaning from the chaos of separate hunger.

After years of field work, anthropologist Claude Lévi-Strauss moved from the universality of cooking to a "culinary triangle," in which cooked food is a cultural transformation and rotted food is a natural transformation. On one side of the triangle, culture deliberately moves the original, raw, unprocessed food to its cooked state; on the other side, the forces of nature inevitably rot the unprocessed food and return it to the earth (478).

Lévi-Strauss's schema helps us see the high degree of elaboration in literary images of cooking, which carry the cultural processing one step further. All ways of cooking, kinds of meals, and types of foods, each with its own symbolic valence, open themselves to the writer as food for thought, signs and symbols to be manipulated into yet another layer of significance within her text. In his introduction to *Fictional Meals and Their Functions in the French Novel,* literary critic James W. Brown suggests that "appetite attests to, and even comes to symbolize, the space existing between subject and object, between 'me' and the 'world'" (Brown 12).

If that sounds like literary overreading, consider the comments of another renowned anthropologist, Mary Douglas. She described how the physical act of eating, ingestion, "mediates between self and not-self, native essence and foreign matter, the inside and the outside." This mediating relationship transforms food from an external object into a part of our body, from culture back to nature. As long as we're sated and cozy, the transformation remains unconscious. When we confront the possibility of starvation, however, we're forced to stretch our definition of food. Gritting our teeth, we prepare to incorporate anything from grasshoppers to mud to other human flesh. "Disagreeable food puts to the test one's capacity to consolidate one's self by appropriating resources from the external environment," Douglas notes (26). Survival itself suddenly hinges on having sufficient psychic flexibility to assign something in our environment an unnatural—yet supremely natural, given the body's drive to subsist—role in our life. Such a crisis marks the extreme end of a varied continuum: Jesus drinking vinegar on the cross, patients drinking barium, babies spooned spinach, Yalies gulping goldfish.

On the sweeter side of the continuum, appetite or desire signals a distance between oneself and what one wants, thus gives birth to social consciousness and communication. Language allows us to take in and assimilate information, making it our own. We ask with a grin, "Can you swallow that?"; we "choke," we "digest," we "cook up" ideas; we "eat up" pleasant words. Both eating and speaking are communicative acts that conjoin the outside world and the innermost self. Food is more than an inert substance; it is a set of processes ranging from selecting, preparing and serving to dining and washing up. These processes encode patterns of social relationship and cultural values, using variables of source, context, content, sequence, amount, type, preparation, etiquette and aftermath. (If you doubt the code, consider Thanksgiving dinner: the turkey has national and ostensibly historic significance; the recipes for stuffing and sweet potatoes carry regional and familial traditions; who carves indicates patriarchal residue; the order must conclude with pie and coffee and could not begin there without severe cognitive dissonance; and the tendency for the women to cooperate on preparation and cleanup while the men watch football puts gender roles in a nutshell.)

When we begin to decode our processing of food, the messages reveal social affiliations and power struggles; display hierarchical or consensus-based patterns; show inclusion and exclusion; indicate boundaries and the negotiated transcendence of those boundaries. Because food reflects and reinforces these social dynamics, it plays a crucial role in family life. Rituals of eating show themselves in gulped teenage breakfasts as well as formal holiday dinners—what would we think if a high-school jock sat down and leisurely consumed a gourmet breakfast, picking fastidiously at certain items, complimenting whoever had prepared it, interrupting the meal to whip up his own special Hollandaise for the eggs?

Even worse, what would we think if a mother refused to cook for her small ones? Women, especially mothers, play a central role in daily sustenance. Even today, a home-cooked dinner signals feminine devotion; consider, also, the rhetorical use of cookie-baking in the 1994 presidential campaign, with candidates' wives vying for a symbolic image that would soften, perhaps redeem, their feminist careers.

The sexual divisions, values and power relations operating in a family affect the choice of food, the amount of food provided, and the way it is prepared and eaten. Across cultures, sociologists note that "portions of meat especially are distributed unequally between family members, among whom men have a privileged position, while children and women occupy second and third places" (Mennell et al. 91). If this sounds more like a tribal culture than an American one, ask yourself who got the biggest piece of steak last Sunday.

Even attempts to "balance" meals are cultural consequences, shaped by the anxiety-producing nutritional information that reaches us via mass media and word of mouth. This helpful information/propaganda emphasizes women's responsibility for their families' health every bit as fervently as Catherine Beecher did a century ago. If Mom can "balance" her family's diet, she not only shores up their little immune systems, but she reduces her own potential guilt. She also reduces the anxiety triggered by today's overwhelming array of food choices, and by the absence of simple, widely-held norms to guide those choices (Mennell et al. 92).

The complexity of food processes begins with the overcrowded supermarket shelf, but it doesn't end there. "Complexity traces a relation between particular instances of food-related behavior and the idea of the world, such that a change in the one is accompanied by a change in the other" (Mennell et al. 26). For instance, revisions in ideal gender patterns may have prompted more men to learn to cook in the 1980s. (I am judging this trend on hearsay; my husband's specialty is fried onions and Spam with Velveeta, and has remained a constant.) Following the world's dictates, old or new, solidifies one's social ego and validates one's subjective reality (which is why many husbands barbecue so readily, and their wives don aprons in such a prettily self-conscious way).

As the circle of intimacy widens, sociologists document what we already knew: the more formal, complex and elaborate the rules of dining, the less open and inclusive one's hospitality (33). Strict rules about what is to be eaten, in what order, with what side dishes and garnishes, make large and frequent social meals difficult to organize. The easiest format is the potluck, where gathering ample amounts of food matters far more than orchestrating their tastes and textures. A home where an extra place is always set welcomes guests to take their chances, implying that the human connection is worth the gastronomic risk. A larder's bareness bears scant relation to the warmth of hospitality issuing forth; in fact, hospitality often exists in inverse proportion to wealth.

"Food is capable of symbolizing the manner in which people view themselves with respect to insiders and outsiders of society" ((Mennell et al. 86). Loaded with class, status and ethnic associations, foodstuffs bind individuals together and exclude others, reinforcing a group's identity. What would a visit to my Irish relatives be, without constant injunctions to eat more and take the leftovers home?

Sharing food with kin is at best a sign of love and inclusion, at worst a grim familial duty. Sharing food with friends and invited guests is a deliberate opening of your life, a willingness to welcome and connect. Sharing food with strangers is a sign of shared commitment, be it to a political candidate or a religion. At the point where food merges with faith, it carries the strongest valence. Interestingly enough, as organized religions have lost some of their sway and their rituals have lost some of their power, the symbolic weight of foodstuffs has dropped below consciousness. "In the sense that the whole of society has been secularized...so food has also been taken out of any common metaphysical scheme," notes Douglas. "Moral and social symbols seem to have been drained from its use" (*Food in the Social Order* 4–5).

At least, it looks that way on the surface.

The Next Best Thing to Godliness

Both cooking and needlework relate to taste and therefore subjectivity, which makes it easier to see them as vehicles of meaning. But how on earth could menial scrubbing, sweeping and dusting exist on any level other than the binary dirty-clean, twisted into a circular pattern of endless repetition?

Again, we start with the universals. Dirt is disorder, chaos, ambiguity, filth. Dirt reminds us of our flaws and limits, our inability to keep anything pristine, our childish tendency to "make a mess." When mud spatters on white ceramic tile and cobwebs soften the corner, nature has triumphed over culture. Dust and scum and mildew on the surfaces of our home, scales of skin and strands of hair fallen from our bodies signal inevitable physical decay and therefore death. The friendliest of clutter becomes unsettling as soon as it crosses our private threshhold of necessary order. A miscellany hides essential boundaries, mixes up the categories, warns us that we may not be able to act or answer promptly, because we must first "dig out."

In *Purity and Danger*, Douglas marks the subjectivity of dirt, which, like beauty, lies in the eye of the beholder. Our ideas about hygiene and health don't even begin to account for our vehement moppings and scrubbings; they exist on the symbolic, social and aesthetic level long after they've satisfied practical necessity. Human beings think in terms of "pollution," Douglas notes, which means that anything they deem out of place violates their sense of order (3). Food on china is perfectly acceptable, for example, but food sandwiched between the bedsheets is unclean. Shoes in the closet offend no one, but shoes in the refrigerator are likely to be, if you will, booted out.

The pollution concept extends to the abstract level, protecting cherished principles and categories from contradiction, ambiguity, uncertainty. In an unaccustomed observer, someone of pronouncedly indeterminate gender may provoke the same shudder as the egg on a chili slinger; neither is expected. We use our notions of pollution consciously and unconsciously, to influence each other's behavior and sanction the social code.

Once again, parallels exist between the efforts of language, which structures and orders our perceptions, and cleaning, which structures and orders the physical environment. In both the "real" world and the world of the imagination, we develop rituals of purity and impurity to unify our experience. Through these rituals, we work out and display the symbolic patterns of our culture, connecting disparate elements and giving meaning to our various experiences.

Cleaning carries heavy moral baggage; keeping a clean house has been the "womanly" way of disciplining oneself into virtuous respectability. We speak of "clean living" and pornographic "filth," setting up a not-so-subtle alliance between cleanliness and godliness. Margaret Walker, who wrote at night so she could keep up with her housework, confesses: "I have struggled against dirt and disease as much as I have against sin, which, with my Protestant and Calvinistic background, was always to be abhorred..." (101).

Why such a tight relationship between dirt and sin? "Links between housework and psyche depend on the home as the center for intimate and sensual existence," remarks Phyllis Palmer. From the start, "housework took care of those things that society found most unappealing, embarrassing, and tainted: the visible needs and evidence of fallible bodies" (145). Soon there was an inverse relationship: immaculate homes and clothing versus sexual sins, the sins of embodiment. Cleaning, after all, meant smoothing rumpled beds, washing stains from the sheets and perspiration from the clothes, subjecting the outward accoutrements of everyday life to a rigid orderly control that hopefully, ostensibly, paralleled one's control over one's own bodily impulses.

Palmer points out a split in female stereotypes: the "good" housewife is the "good" (doll-like) woman, the virtuous wife and mother. Yet as soon as she rolls up her sleeves, this "good" woman will be mucky with dirt and decay that, rigidly conceived, threaten to taint her character. She must protect her virtue with servants or supercleansers or heavy-duty machines, demonstrating her sexual purity, efficient control and pristine domesticity. Otherwise she will fall into another set of associations: the rough charwoman who defines delicate refinement by negating it; the slovenly loose woman too languorous to tidy up; or the powerful witch/midwife/healer who touches the intimate essences of human life.

If orderly cleanliness is a cultural construct with multiple, constantly evolving associations, what of chaos? When we order our surroundings, we select and discard and arrange, limiting our options with each successive step. Disorder, by contrast, is unlimited, unpatterned, full of infinite potential. Disorder destroys existing patterns, but at the same time, it contains the possibility of new patterns. Disorder, therefore, can symbolize both danger and the powerful potential of change. And ritual helps us acknowledge the power without falling into the maelstrom. "Ritual recognises the potency of disorder," Douglas notes. "In the disorder of the mind, in dreams, faints and frenzies, ritual expects to find powers and truths which cannot be reached by conscious effort" (94).

By immersing themselves in murky washtubs, scraping the peelings and detritus of food from the sink with ungloved hands, reaching deep into the drain to pull out hunks of hair and slime, carrying bowls of vomit from the bedside, women have entered life's most intimate, uncontrollable disorder. Those who have not flinched or shirked, gone numb with revulsion or frenzied in their attempt to rid us of creation's basest elements, have reemerged wiser, able to respond to need and seasonal rhythm, able not just to make but to keep a home.

Domestic Writers' Block

If the prosaic acts of cooking, cleaning and stitching can contain such lyrical significance, why has housework been such a burden? The first clue lies far in the past, when domestic chores were the source—not the dam—of art. Beginning in the late Paleolithic era, women found means of self-expression in practical, functional crafted objects, such as the pots they used to hold the food they gathered and prepared.

That early history shows us that domesticity was not always an obstacle to art; in fact, the temporariness of traditional women's work may have heightened the impulse to create. When most of your efforts go toward finding and fixing food that will vanish immediately, smoothing cloth that will rumple from the same body that evening, and washing pots so they can get dirty again, it's only natural to fight impending chaos and inevitable dissolution. You steal a few hours to stitch a quilt that will warm generations; you weave patterns so beautiful they break routine, pulling the eye, demanding an attention that cuts the ordinary passage of time.

Linking art with domesticity is startling for those who draw their aesthetic from centuries of male-dominated art, art history and art criticism. Because most men have been able to leave home and children in the care of the little woman—leave, indeed, their own health, clothing and sustenance in her hands—they've been able to keep separate. Women, meanwhile, filtered everything through their traditional role, incorporating domestic topics and approaches and chores.

The real problems, it seems, have been the extent and unbroken weight of those domestic chores, and their despised and devalued status in society. Domestic work that leaves no block of free time, no intellectual energy and confidence, does indeed get in the way. Writing is harder when everyone around you perceives it as treason to your sex and a failure to meet your obligations to society. And if we trace the outrage of women writers, it peaks at the end of the 19th century—when domestic chores trade some of their necessity for a symbolic role as angelic acts of virtue—and next at the end of the '50s, after women returned to the home to bake the apple pies of American security, democracy and prosperity. Domestic chores carry more meaning and arouse less resentment when they are necessary, vital and respected; they are the most oppressive when they serve an abstract purpose that has nothing to do with the immediacy of a family's everyday needs.

Feminist theorists have worked so hard to restore value to "women's work" that, by now, we might expect domestic ritual to carry as much weight as the Adamic quest for independent conquest, and kitchens to be as viable a setting as bedrooms when it came to revealing gritty human truths. After all, more and more women are writing and directing films and plays, writing and publishing books, and if domesticity is women's arena, it should be cropping up everywhere. Yet McHugh's comparative film criticism indicates that "'women's pictures,' despite their domestic settings and concerns, contained virtually no representations of house-hold labor" (1).

Instead of taking their audiences by the shoulders and showing them the deeper meanings behind that long tradition of "domestic/relation-ship" detail, many women writers continue to ignore the arena entirely. Eager to distance themselves from its constraints, they choose instead to do sociopolitical critiques, intense psychodramas, lush sagas or cerebral experiments with form.

Other female artists, such as the six whose novels we are about to explore, slide the domestic realm into their work quite naturally. Domesticity is omnipresent in, and crucial to, their created worlds, but they do not make its role explicit—and the critics rarely mention it. As artistic solutions go, this is excellently subtle—but unfortunately, in a society that still devalues and mocks domesticity, such nuances are often lost on the reader. The next chapter will explore the lives and ideas behind the novels, revealing the various roles domesticity can play in the creative process.

FOUR

THE NOVELS, THE AUTHORS

"Men could write about their
fears of dying by exposure in
the forest; we could not write
about our fears of being
suffocated in the kitchen."

Mary Gordon

The six novels chosen for this study resemble old brownstones rather than suburban ranch houses; different in color, shape and distinguishing features, they bear only the essentials in common. All were written by American women and published between 1987 and 1994; all deal primarily with women's lives, focus heavily on relationships and familial influences, and use the past to make sense of the present. They carry the influences of different racial, ethnic, religious and socio-economic backgrounds, they hark back to different places and times. Yet they all use domestic images to reveal their characters' social context and world-view, index their relationships, chart their growth and propel the plot.

As any informal canvas will tell us, the highly personal realm of kitchens, bathrooms, bedrooms and closets is seldom present in similar proportion in contemporary novels written by or about men. Even without gender differentiation, however, domestic imagery would be counter-cultural. The mainstream media, educational institutions and workplaces of postmodern United States rarely credit cooking, cleaning and stitching with the potential to reveal and even alter our inner lives. We have to wonder why these authors did not choose to write about their characters' politics, hobbies or interests instead of their domestic activities; why not dissect their beliefs about salvation and sex rather than monitor their cooking and cleaning?

No doubt each writer had idiosyncratic reasons for considering mundane household chores. Certainly, each novel prompts different conclusions about the domestic realm; we see it reconfigured by various ethnic, demographic and socioeconomic contexts, not to mention the accidents of individual circumstance and the whims of the creative process. Still, a number of patterns can be traced, pinned down, cut out from the novels and held up against our own lives. Unlike politics, religion, philosophy, sex or hobbies, the domestic arena stands on the common ground of necessity. Domestic forms may change with time and place, but the intimacy and significance of these acts remain constant.

Louise Erdrich and *Tracks*

Known for deftly translating American Indian culture into spare, mythically rich prose, Louise Erdrich was born in 1954 in Little Falls, Minnesota, to a German-American father and an Ojibwa mother. Erdrich combined an Ivy League education with her mother's tribal legacy and a down-to-earth miscellany of jobs. She attended Dartmouth and received her master's degree from Johns Hopkins; she worked as a lifeguard, a construction flag signaler and a psychiatric aide, weeded beets, waitressed and taught poetry in prisons. She married Michael Anthony Dorris in 1981, and until his suicide in 1997, their collaboration was both domestic and literary. Not only did they dedicate books to each other, but they jointly authored several stories and a book, *The Crown of Columbus*.

Dorris and Erdrich cared for seven children, three of whom had been adopted by Michael Dorris before they married. One of those children, Adam, has disabilities caused by Fetal Alcohol Syndrome. Dorris wrote *The Broken Cord* to tell Adam's story, and Erdrich wrote the foreword, in which she admits, "It is easy to be the occasional, ministering angel. But.... I never intended to be the mother of a child with problems.... I've got less than the ordinary amount of patience." She is often this honest, even self-deprecating, when it comes to socially expected domestic traits. Criss-crossing traditional and nontraditional lifestyles, she writes with serene conviction about her own consuming domestic role, but refers just as readily to her equal domestic partnership with her husband. In the foreword, she goes on to describe how Adam "sees Michael and me primarily in the roles to which we've assigned ourselves around the house. Michael is the laundryman, I am the cook." (Dorris xii)

There is almost a note of relief as Erdrich describes the simplicity of Adam's perceptions. She uses her children and housework for grounding, ballast against the ethereal world of intellect and *belles lettres*, prizes and conferences and book tours. She may have learned this solution from her mother; in a 1993 essay called "Nests," Erdrich praises her mother's calm patience:

When the noise and the heat of young lives overwhelm her, she still cans tomatoes. When she was frustrated, she used to press the pedal of her sewing machine flat, sending the needleinto a manic frenzy. She never lashed out at a child. That lesson was profound.

Erdrich's mother taught knitting, and she strung leftover yarn on a tree for the birds to use the following winter. Erdrich paid attention, and now her collection of birds' nests includes one woven with bits of her daughters' hair. She also made a point of disciplining herself into her mother's patience, writing prose instead of poetry by tying herself to a chair with a long scarf. And when she had a baby, she learned a new kind of patience: "I had to tie an imaginary scarf around the two of us in dazzling knots" ("Nests" 84).

In order to understand Erdrich's attitude toward domesticity—as well as the attitudes of various characters in *Tracks*, her third novel about the Ojibwa—we need some sense of her own Ojibwa heritage. The tribe whose blood runs in Erdrich's veins, and whose history informs her writing, settled along the shores of Lake Superior in the 1400s. Four centuries later, long after the French had begun trading with the Ojibwa, Americans took control of the Great Lakes fur trade. By 1854, most of the Ojibwa in the United States and Canada had been forced to move to reservations within their old tribal territory. That displacement threw their sense of identity and way of living into question. Forced into a position of wardship with the federal government, they found survival, sanity and spiritual balance increasingly, wrenchingly difficult.

Tracks takes place in North Dakota between 1912 and 1924, a time when land was easily stolen, poverty loomed constantly, and modern Western ways were beginning to compete for young people's allegiance. Old ways and new contrasted starkly. Erdrich reminds us, for example, that to the Ojibwa (often known as Chippewa) and other tribes, the American land was never wilderness, it was home. That twist doubles for the women: Erdrich once explained that the freedom of open space "is there but it's nothing that someone stays in. People aren't 'lighting out for the territory.' The women in my books are lighting out for home" (Pearlman 145).

In traditional Ojibwa society, home is a place of comfort, not oppression, because it is nature's ways, not man's, that shape and inspire everyday life. The word for "the good life," *Minobimaatisiiwin*, also means "continuous rebirth" (LaDuke 3). Time is cyclical, not linear or abstract. Space is filled with spirit-beings, even a stone is animate, and certain sites are preferred for homes. Family units are the primary source of personal identity. Food is grown or hunted, and the ethic of reciprocity demands *saymah* (sacrifice and prayer) beforehand. Sharing is expected; overfasting is considered as greedy as hoarding. "Although women had absolute control of the food supply in many societies, it did not give them license to withhold provisions from those who were hungry," notes Carolyn Niethammer. Hospitality meant an immediate offering of food, and a woman's status rose or fell with the way she distributed her larder's excess (109).

For the Ojibwa, feeling "at home" means sensing one's relationship to social, geographic and cosmic networks. But Hertha Wong points out that Erdrich is not a traditional Chippewa; in *Tracks*, the totem/family identities have already been destroyed by Euroamerican rule, and the characters are trying to reformulate notions of self, family and community (Wong 177).

Many of the displaced American Indian values were "female" in the Western European dichotomy. In traditional Ojibwa life, for example, interconnection is worth more than rupture and cooperation is better than individualism; defining oneself in relation to others is considered a realistic acceptance of the intricacies of interrelationship, not a confusion of ego boundaries or an abdication of masculine strength. Wong notes that, while Euroamerican women might write about mother-daughter struggles of will and identity, American Indians expect harmony among female relatives, and tend to attribute discord to cultural alienation and a loss of traditional family values (175–176).

To explore gender roles and domesticity in Ojibwa culture, we have to subtract the pervasive Western assumption of female inferiority and powerlessness, as well as traditional Western depictions of Indian women as virgin princesses or squaws, two-dimensional symbols of a primitive nobility. In actuality, these women are generally central to their tribe's happiness and prosperity; they often give counsel, moderate decisions or control property. Menstruating women are considered powerful, not unclean, and older women are honored for their wisdom and knowledge.

In the 1930s, just after *Tracks'* central time frame, anthropologist Ruth Landes lived with the Ojibwa. She observed that the children played "house" endlessly until puberty, with boys going off to shoot birds and bring the "game" to the girls. "The girls attend one another as midwives," she wrote, "and practice the complicated art of brewing herbs, administering massage, and preparing special diets" (*The Ojibwa Woman* 21). During their menstrual confinement, older girls learned from women who visit them to discuss womanhood and teach them sewing skills (*The Ojibwa Woman* 6).

A traditional adult Ojibwa woman's tasks dealt more with conservation than hunting, and those tasks changed with the seasons. Landes did watch women setting twine traps to catch rabbits, skinning and cooking them, then weaving their fur into robes (*The Ojibwa Woman* 124). But primarily, the women gathered rice and berries, stored food for the next season, made clothes and artifacts, cooked, swept the wigwam, cared for the children.

Frances Densmore studied the music and culture of the Ojibwa in Minnesota from the 1890s until 1957, bracketing the era in which *Tracks* takes place. She observed the women of two or three families cooperating to store rice, maple sugar and vegetables such as pumpkin or squash in pits lined with birch bark. "The cooking was chiefly done at the fire presided over by the mother of the family, who prepared and served the food, sending portions to the branches of the family" (28). Men sat crosslegged, but "the woman 'sat on her right foot' with the left foot extending out at one side. She said that in this position a woman could rise easily to 'reach things'" (30).

Housecleaning was simple but energetic: the women aired bedding daily in summer and spread it on the snow in winter; they washed dishes with lye and scoured them with sand. "Woven bags, when soiled, were brushed, pounded, and turned the other side out.... The space of hard ground between the fire and the mats in a lodge was swept clean, the sweepings being put in the fire" (47). As Niethammer remarks, "The Native American woman could see her daily drudgery transformed into the rhythm of eternity" (105–106).

Ojibwa women shared in the men's work in many ways, gathering rice as the men guided canoes through the lake's harvest, tanning the hides of the hunt or assuming men's chores in times of necessity. The tribe believed generally that, if you divided the family in work, you would tear it apart in other ways as well. When women showed aptitude for occupations culturally defined as masculine, such as hunting, doctoring and making war, they simply practiced these occupations as additional roles, and the rest of the tribe defined them as beneficiaries of the supernatural, whom their blood discharges must not have completely frightened.

With little stigma attached to androgynous abilities, marriage became far more equal a partnership than the unevenly balanced property relation experienced and criticized by Western feminists. Widows remarried with relative ease; divorce was nearly as common as marriage; women who lived alone chose the solitude and self-reliance deliberately (Niethammer 98).

We see this flexibility and independence in the male and female characters of *Tracks,* The larger story is one of a tribe slowly displaced from their land, killed by white people's diseases, cheated by a white government, and betrayed by their own young people's desire to assimilate. But in *Tracks,* that story takes highly personal form, first forging a mesh of erotic, romantic, friendship and familial relationships, then eroding or rupturing them.

The novel opens in the voice of Nanapush, an old man telling his granddaughter how he rescued her mother, Fleur Pillager, after her clan died of consumption. Nearly drowned as a girl, Fleur was one of those androgynous women skilled in male pursuits as well as female. Because she was believed to have a mystical connection to Misshepeshu, the water man, monster of the lake, men ignored her attractions and kept their distance—until a piggish drunk and his buddies lost control and raped her.

Fleur's power was one of secret wisdom, rebellious independence and sorcery. She wore men's clothes, taught herself half-forgotten medicine ways once reserved for the male Midewiwin, and carried herself with a fierce strength, laughing at the advice of old women. Even her body was androgynous, carelessly erotic:

> Fleur's shoulders were broad and curved as a yoke, her hips fishlike, slippery, narrow. An old green dress clung to her waist, worn thin where she sat. Her glossy braids were like the tails of animals, and swung against her when she moved, deliberately, slowly in her work, held in and half-tamed. But only half. (18)

An Artemis figure, filled with a self-possessed wild sexuality, Fleur hardly fit the domesticated female ideal of the Western European or the Eastern traditions. She went hunting in the middle of the night, and Nanapush was convinced that she left her body and took on the form of a bear. "We know for sure," he told Lulu, "because the next morning, in the snow or dust, we followed the tracks of her bare feet and saw where they changed, where the claws sprang out, the pad broadened and pressed into the dirt" (12).

After the rape, Fleur exiled herself in the woods, where Eli, an intense young man at ease with both wilderness and tenderness, fell in love with her. Their union was torn asunder by jealous Pauline, a plain, hateful woman of mixed blood and distorted loyalties. Pauline used her skills in sewing, cleaning and nursing to find herself a home and manipulate those around her. She was an excellent early example of the pattern detailed by Jennie R. Je and Dorothy Lonewolf Miller in "Cultural Survival and Contemporary American Indian Women in the City," when they describe how Indian girls were sent to school so they could learn skills and work for non-Indian families—and those who dared return to reservations found themselves alienated until they relearned traditional ways.

"In English, I told my father we should build an outhouse with a door that swung open and shut," Pauline said. "He scorned me when I would not bead, when I refused to prick my fingers with quills, or hid rather than rub brains on the stiff skins of animals." She told him she was made for better, and begged to be sent away to her aunt. But there, instead of learning to thread and work the bobbins and spools, she ended up watching her cousin Russell and sweeping butcher-shop floors (14). Fleur worked there too, and Russell loved the cream she spooned into his mouth. In her late teens, Pauline worshiped Fleur too. But the jealousy returned, rancid, when she was older.

Pauline's attempt to move away from the tribe into more "civilized" domestic activity, making lace as the nuns did, backfired. After an entire winter with no word from her family, who could have been ill or dead with consumption, she began to have a guilty recurring dream: "I saw my sisters and my mother swaying in the branches, buried too high to reach, wrapped in lace I never hooked" (15).

By the time she reached the household of Bernadette Morrissey, a mixed-blood widow who tended the dead, Pauline had become a pathetic Cinderella martyred to domesticity. "I told how I scrubbed the rough boards and clabbered milk, boiled salves and washed bandages, how homesick I had become," she recalled. Accompanying Bernadette as an apprentice, Pauline felt death as a grace, and she worked hard in this solitary ministry. But in her bitter psyche, domesticity's power would remain dark.

As Pauline grew more cruelly twisted, others' indifference hardened into antipathy, fueling the cycle. When she learned that Fleur was having frequent, passionate intercourse with the quiet, handsome Eli, Pauline tricked him into sex with Sophie Morrissey, Bernadette's nubile daughter. When Fleur discovered Eli's abrupt, causeless betrayal, she rose and turned from Eli. She walked to the stove, grabbed a fork to tend a pan of sizzling venison. She said nothing, but when he stepped near and laid his hand upon her arm she simply moved her arm away (90 – 91).

The venison proved more than a stage prop: even during emotional crises, the women's domestic chores continued unimpeded, forming a substratum for the plot. By tending the venison, Fleur was continuing her duty, her dignified life-sustaining role within the tribe, despite Eli's abdication. Because the wider context was one of tribal collaboration rather than individual property relations, continuing to cook was an act of independence from Eli, not of subservience to him.

In *Tracks*, the domestic world served as a vocabulary, a collection of daily objects and acts shared in different ways by the male and female characters. Power ran through the everyday, not apart from it or in contradiction to it. Hospitality was one of the book's most powerful domestic themes, which made sense given the crucial importance of sharing in

Ojibwa culture. Early in the book, after Nanapush rescued Fleur and brought her home to mend, the two fell into a grief-bound depression over the plague's losses. Only a priest's visit and the imperative of hospitality snapped them from their funk; they scrambled into action to offer him food and drink, and this opened them to hear his words and be healed by them. Later, Pauline noted that, as her own actions grew more malevolent, "Margaret ceased to greet me at the door, offered scraps and only baked a fresh loaf when I'd stayed for an hour or two" (71).

Another pattern was sorcery, accomplished through food or intimate objects. But even without magic, there was domestic manipulation: Margaret starved Nanapush into deciding his allegiance to her; Nanapush and Fleur, and later the nuns, kept Pauline's madness in control by ministering to her. Pauline sewed to set a romantic trap for Eli with Sophie; Bernadette sewed to help Pauline hide her pregnancy.

True to Ojibwa culture, the characters' gender roles were well-learned but flexible. Despite Fleur's and Pauline's pregnancies and Margaret Kashpaw's fussings over her sons, Nanapush was in some ways the book's most maternal character. He wondered wistfully how it feels to be a woman, tended Fleur, advised Eli, brooded over Lulu's delivery, agreed to rear her, and gave her long monologues of advice.

Domestic props and images layered meaning on the female characters. Approaching Argus, the town where she would be raped, Fleur's eye was drawn to the church: "Fleur saw that steeple rise, a shadow thin as a needle" (13). When Pauline despaired over her youthful alienation, she said, "In truth, I hardly rinsed through the white girls' thoughts" (15). Clouds were "witch teats" (27); Nanapush insulted Margaret and Pauline by calling them "empty bowls" (53), and Lulu was punished at boarding school by being forced to kneel on broomsticks (226).

Margaret, the oldest woman in the text, mother of Eli and eventually wife of Nanapush, was also the most domestic. Chronically irritated and headlong stubborn, she was described in terms of the food she had prepared for these men all her adult life: "full of vinegar"; "thin on the top and plump as a turnip below, with a face like a round molasses cake." Nanapush added that she had a "tongue honed keen," switching the analogue from the passive stuff of nurture to a dangerous tool of action (47). When Ojibwa land was seized by the government, Margaret used her quiet domestic role to plot their next step:

> She had been in deep thought at the stove, piercing the turnips as they boiled. She banged her fork on the burner. All of our attention clung to her and she pursed her lips in satisfaction at the plan that was growing in her mind.... Margaret's modest smile was a small neat bow that she would not untie. (175)

The tribe's efforts failed, however, and by the end of the novel, Fleur had gone off to live in isolation after trying a third time to drown herself. Eli had left her, her second baby had died, she had sent Lulu away to a government school for safety's sake. Thus Fleur ended the novel as she started it, unattached and unpossessed, wild and singular. Kind Nanapush, on the other hand, was firmly connected to himself and others—married to Margaret, parent to Lulu, a leader in his tribe.

What does Erdrich's novel tell us about the effects of domesticity? That in Ojibwa culture, it can be appropriated by males, and need not be a burden or constraint for females. That it has the power to both curse and heal. That it plays a key role as the tribespeople fight against the chaos of dissolution, oppression, treachery or disease. That it correlates with, and reflects, the state of the psyche. That it anchors hospitality, family and friendship, creating harmony and solidifying bonds. And that it links readily with supernatural forces, both divine and malevolent.

Mary Gordon and *The Other Side*

Mary Catherine Gordon was born in 1949 in the Irish ghetto of Queens, New York. Her father, David, was a Jewish scholar who could not manage to support the family; her mother was a self-sacrificing Irish American who, although confined to a wheelchair, worked as a legal secretary to support them while David stayed home with Mary. A convert to Catholicism, he swung fast and hard to the right, his fanatically conservative mind preferring the world of spirit to flesh (Robertson 4–5).

Although her father died when Mary was eight, she admits in her novels and interviews what a profound influence he had on her. As a girl, she was docile, devout and smart; she spent a great deal of time reading about saints and virgin martyrs, just as he would have wished. Then boys replaced God, and she won a scholarship to Barnard. Going to college in the '60s awoke her intellectual and social consciousness; meanwhile, on the literary front, mentor Elizabeth Hardwick coaxed her to switch from poetry to prose. After graduate school at Syracuse University, she taught English and married twice, first to an anthropologist, then to an English professor. She is the mother of two children, a boy and a girl.

"I'm obsessed with how difficult it is to live an ordinary bourgeois life," she said in a recent *New York Times* piece. "Just to keep your clothes clean, make sure you have shoelaces in your shoes, not look crazy—it takes an enormous amount of organization." Her most recent novellas contemplate the flat, obstacle-filled course of daily life: "I was interested in how a woman inhabits space, particularly domestic space, the world most women live in that is considered so unchallenging" (Hunnewell 25).

Gordon's novels reconcile the tensions of her own life: working in the world and at home; splicing Roman Catholic theology into feminism; having a mother and father so different from each other; being a wife and mother against all expectation. "I've never seen myself as a wife," she told an interviewer, "because I wasn't brought up to be a wife" (Keyishian 76). Indeed, she was brought up to be a nun, and even piles of dirty laundry could not suffocate that early-cultivated concern with philosophy and spirit. Instead of entering a convent, however, she bent that concern to the things of this world, writing about the "dangerous and messy and passionate and frightening and ecstatic" world of women, households, families (Keyishian 72).

Choosing domestic topics was quite a risk; in an essay about writing, Gordon described her perception of men's literary expectations: "Distance, then, was what I was to strive for. Distance from the body, from the heart, but most of all, distance from the self as writer. I could never understand exactly what they meant or how to do it; it was like trying to follow the directions on a home permanent in 1959." In the books held up as example, important moral issues pitted men against nature in moments of extremity. Gordon's own work was called "exquisite" by male critics, lovely as a watercolor. "They, of course, were painting in oils," she snapped. "Men could write about their fears of dying by exposure in the forest; we could not write about our fears of being suffocated in the kitchen" (Sternburg 28–29).

Gordon dreaded seeming trivial, but she was stubborn enough to pursue domestic topics, write in her natural style and accept the consequences. As for her philosophical dilemmas, she simply passed them on to her female characters. Susan Ward saw Gordon's novels commenting on the double-bind of women who, by their sex, cannot live as males, yet are intelligent enough to be coached in male values by their spiritual fathers. These women simply "are not encouraged to learn the intricacies of running households or to think of themselves as wives and mothers" (306).

Gordon acknowledged the drudgery of childcare and homemaking, but pointed out that "an extreme life doesn't breed happiness" (Keyishian 73). Current conditions and attitudes leave a lot of women starved, she commented. "Those of us who are out there in the greater world doing everything—we're so exhausted. We're so sort of overburdened. There is no place to rest" (Keyishian 75).

When Gordon talks about her own creative work, she falls naturally into one of the oldest, most primary domestic images: "My books seem to take me longer and longer to write.... There seems to be a kind of baking time that they need now" (Keyishian 82). She hungers for the capacity to enjoy the everyday, and talks wistfully about one of her characters, describing "the part of her that could have had ordinary success, ordinary happiness, ordinary self-expression...a kind of simple humanity and acceptance" (Keyishian 74).

Another source of tension in Gordon's work has been the influence of Roman Catholicism. She depicts the Church as an authoritarian, male-dominated institution dependent on bloodless abstract reason and scornful of instinct, emotion and flesh. "The word 'spiritual' suggests to me the twin dangers of the religious life: dualism and abstraction," she noted in an essay in *Spiritual Quests*. She defined "abstractionism" as "the error that results from refusing to admit that one has a body and is an inhabitant of the physical world. Dualism, its first cousin, admits that there is a physical world but calls it evil and commands that it be shunned" (27).

Gordon exhibits a traditionally female ability to find the good in nature and physical objects—clothes, melons, bowls of holly, round white arms, perfume (Ward 306). She insists on the just claims and powerful truths of the body, and she bypasses abstract principles to show the sacramental force of everyday realities. Yet she is the first to admit that a patriarchal religion shaped this sensibility; "a child at daily Mass got to observe at close range the habits of old women, of housewives at eight-thirty already tired out for the day" (Gordon, *Spiritual Quests* 27).

In *The Other Side*, Gordon scrutinized an Irish-American family across generations, marking their failed attempts at love and their rare bright triumphs. At the opening, the housewifely matriarch, Ellen MacNamara, had suffered several strokes, stopped taking her medicine and wandered from the house. Her husband Vincent had fallen trying to bring her back, and had gone to a nursing home to recuperate. While he was away trying to make sense of his mixed emotions, Ellen lay dying and the children and grandchildren gathered, bringing remnants of their childhood hopes because, as adults, they had been unable to make happy, safe homes of their own.

Cam and Dan were cousins who had both, as children, taken refuge under Ellen's strong wing. Dan was born to Ellen's favorite son, who died during the war and left a wife so timid Ellen strongarmed her into relinquishing their baby. Cam's mother, Magdalene, was an alcoholic incapable of making a stable home for her.

As Cam and Dan grew up, a family friend, attorney Jack Morrisey, steered them toward law. They reversed gender stereotypes: Cam, diverted from a Legal Aid career by her mother's cancer, became an aggressive feminist crusader; Dan, a gentle, compassionate advocate.

Cam's mother was ostensibly dying of breast cancer, but not as fast as predicted; Cam's husband lived in a separate apartment of their house, afraid to cross sexual and emotional barriers. Cam had taken a lover, who was slowly bringing her back to a freer, more whole sense of self. But she was petrified of taking the next step and actually living together, intimate in the confined space of a mutual home. Dan, too, had problems with relationships; he, too, was still groping toward an adult self.

As the novel flashes from the grandchildren's problems to the grandmother's past, we see Ellen as daughter, wife, mother and grandmother, and begin to understand the complexities that tore her apart and rippled through the family. We also learn Vincent's heart—his deep love of wife and family, his quiet sacrifices, his fears and regrets. The novel's title works on many levels, but most straightforwardly refers to Ellen and Vincent leaving Ireland and crossing to "the other side," where they met and married. Slowly we realize what a strong character Ellen had, consumingly interested in the outside world, sharp-tongued and crisp, bad at showing love but quick to anger, ambivalent toward domesticity yet allowing it to quarantine her.

She grew up in Ireland, in a cottage that was once cozy. But her mother had a stillborn baby and went a little crazy, and her father continued to seed pregnancies that ended in miscarriage or stillbirth. Young Ellen shared the care of her increasingly ill mother with a hired nurse, Anne Foley, and together they spun a domestic web of protection around the invalid.

At 18, Ellen stole money from her father, entrusted her mother to Anne, and joined a childhood friend, Delia, in the United States. Here, she worked as a lady's maid, turning the refinement of her convent school education to good use. Her room in the family's mansion could easily have been pleasant, were it not for her pride and aesthetic sensitivity:

> It was the cast-off, the raggedness that was the room's cruelty to her, and the sense that what was deficient could so easily be fixed. Nails for her clothes instead of hooks. The comforters stained, marked with the waters of who knew what life or what disaster. The mantel and the floor inadequately varnished, ready to splinter, to cause pain. (116)

Ellen managed to leave service and become a seamstress before meeting and marrying Vincent. Once they were together, she depended on him in every way, although she was far too tightly wrapped to ever let him know how insecure she was. Once, he complimented her in front of her friend Bella, saying that she had brains. "She was spooning out tapioca. She banged down the spoon in rage. Furiously, she shook a spoon of tapioca under her husband's nose. 'That's the brains of me, and not an inch above it'" (145).

Ellen kept newspapers piled on several chairs in the master bedroom (in this case especially, a misleading phrase), and stashed clippings in a box under the bed. Patient Vincent loved his wife's avid interest in the public sphere. He was proud when she walked out of the butcher shop she had patronized for two decades, sentencing them to costlier and inferior meat because the butcher criticized Roosevelt (42). Vincent also adjusted to his wife's grim determination to keep busy doing her domestic duty rather than seeking happiness. "The mention of it put her in a fury. *Happy.* The word could make her bang down pot or scissors, shovel, garbage can, whatever hard thing she was holding. Her hands were never empty" (41).

Like many women of her age, religion and station, Ellen

> secluded herself almost entirely in her house, invited no one in, went out only to electioneer—all this she never saw as withdrawal from the world. If you had told her that her kitchen was her cloister, she'd have raised her hand against you.... Although she rarely left the house, she believed herself not bound by it. (20)

Her favorite son John married Doris, a weak, pretty, kind woman who was the antithesis of his mother, and whom he could envision smiling in a kitchen. "And then the news came—John was dead—and his cruel mother became terrifying. She who was cold and perfect flew apart; her wildness made the house a danger, and made Doris fear for the child moving in her." (77)

Ellen's wildness made the house a danger—and her resolve turned it into a prison. Once baby Daniel was born, Ellen dispensed with Doris and took over his care. She "made for him a living heart and housed him there. For him alone she dug up roots and boulders, created a moist living place, and said to him: You can live here. And made a place for another child, a girl, his cousin Cam" (79). She cooked the children brown bread and stews that embarrassed them at school because they were so different from the tasteless convenience foods popular with younger mothers.

> She served the children custard, warm and liquidy in soup bowls she called basins. In the houses of their friends, they'd eaten from small cold glass stemmed dishes of chocolate pudding with black skin on the top and over that a rosette of whipped cream. (82)

Now, in sickness, Ellen, who had lived with her hands full of domesticity, had "lost the thread" (31). Stripped of newspapers, the bedroom became a sickroom, and she was no longer able to make any connection to the outside world. Her possessions had been supplanted by basins and medical paraphernalia, her sharp tongue was silenced. Like Nanapush in *Tracks,* Dan and Vincent were far more trustworthy and nurturing than the women around them. Gordon's female characters were torn into meanness, emptiness or silent complexity by their lives' limits, but Dan and Vincent managed to remain connected, wounded slightly by the women around them, maddeningly passive, but generally faithful to what mattered. Perhaps because the qualities usually styled feminine were not political issues for the men, they were able to embrace them more fully, as part of their humanity. Or perhaps their authors saw them less critically, and sanded the rough edges off their internal conflicts.

Interestingly enough, both men grew up with a woman's close care. Vincent stayed by his mother's side,

> always with her as she did the woman's work. She'd trusted him to gather eggs and help her with the milking. Together they planted the kitchen garden, and in another plot they'd both felt a bit ashamed of in front of the father and the older brother, they grew flowers. (234)

Ellen cherished (undemonstratively) Vincent's quiet, careful ways. She remembers how her friend Delia was always fetching you something: "a cup of tea, a biscuit, a cardigan. She'd open a window for you. Did you feel a draft? She'd shut the door. No stillness. Vincent was the one for that. He could be still and listen to a thing and get it right" (107).

When Vincent retired from his engineering job at Patent Scaffolding, "his life took on the rhythm of a woman's. Seasons, meals, the house itself became important." Now, with his wife dying, he found himself reluctant to return home, and only slowly made the decision to go back, see this through "in honor of the years when the house had been the center of his life. Their lives." He remembered how he and Ellen gathered apples and mulberries: "She was clever with the windfall fruit," he mused. "She loved the ease of the collection and the growth free from her care" (306).

Windfall fruit must have been a welcome change from her domestic duties, whose weight and fullness anchored her life. Throughout the novel, small domestic acts saved motherless children's lives and bound together immigrant families, but they also bogged down Ellen's brilliant mind and engendered rebellion in her female descendants. The result: a wonderful ambivalence, as tightly strung as Gordon's own life.

Toni Morrison and *Beloved*

Nobel prize-winner Toni Morrison was born in Lorain, Ohio, a middle ground that was neither rural South or urban north, and grew up in a working-class community patchworked with various ethnicities. Her educated parents encouraged her reading and shared the nurturing and providing roles equably. She also grew up with "a very strong sense of place, not in terms of the country or the state, but in terms of the details, the feeling, the mood." In a 1976 interview, she told Robert Stepto she believed in

> a woman's strong sense of being in a room, a place, or in a house. Sometimes my relationship to things in a house would be a little different from, say my brother's or my father's or my sons'. I clean them and I move them and I do very intimate things 'in place': I am sort of rooted in it. (213)

Morrison did more than her share of housework, beginning at age 13 by cleaning houses for three or four hours after school. "It wasn't uninteresting," she told Claudia Dreifus in 1994. "You got to work these gadgets that I never had at home: vacuum cleaners." She learned to take pride in performing menial, invisible tasks when her father came home and said, "You know, today I welded a perfect seam and I signed my name to it" (73).

Morrison's early novels showed interest in the chores and joys of domesticity: in *The Bluest Eye*, she writes scathingly of a white woman's neatly ordered, sterile kitchen; in describing the process of writing *Tar Baby*, two of the philosophical steps she lists are "movement from the Earth into the household: its rooms, its quality of shelter. The activity for which the rooms were designed: eating, sleeping, bathing" and "the conflict, further, between two kinds of chaos: civilized chaos and natural chaos" (Morrison, "Memory, Creation and Writing" 390).

Later, in *Beloved*, Morrison brought huge historical truths to life in the very particular, intimate context of female-driven domesticity. Slowly we learn the story's bones: after being beaten and having the milk sucked from her pregnant body (a common practice of white slaveowners), Sethe escaped and crossed the Ohio River to join her mother-in-law, now a freewoman. When the men from the plantation showed up to bring her back, she killed her baby daughter to save her from slavery. Now, the baby was a ghost they called Beloved. (Sethe had wanted the opening words of the funeral on her baby's tiny gravestone, so she traded her body in payment. The act was deemed worthy of only seven letters.)

Sethe's husband, Halle, never made it away from the plantation called, with bitter irony, Sweet Home. He went mad after white men took his wife's milk while he hid in a loft above and watched helplessly. Halle's mother, Baby Suggs, helped Sethe through her arrival and imprisonment, then died, worn out by grief. Sethe's boys fled, spooked by the domestic antics of a dead baby's ghost:

As soon as merely looking in a mirror shattered it (that was the signal
for Buglar); as soon as two tiny hand prints appeared in the cake (that
was it for Howard). Neither boy waited to see more; another kettleful of
chickpeas smoking in a heap on the floor; soda crackers crumbled and
strewn in a line. (3)

In the midst of the haunting, a man named Paul D arrived. He had
worked alongside Sethe's husband on the plantation, and hadn't seen
Sethe since they escaped. He found her living alone with her second
daughter, Denver. Paul D touched the chokecherry tree of mangled scar
tissue on Sethe's back, received her tears, listened to her story and loved
her. Slowly, by doing little fix-up tasks around the house, he asked to be
admitted to their world.

The characters' connection to deep, timeless, near-universal experience does not render them docile or predictable, however. Morrison uses
acts of domestic chaos, hostility or rebellion to question traditional roles
and expectations of daughter, wife, lover and mother. In Deo's words, she
"both plays with and works against the contemporary repression of and
ambivalence toward the maternal" (8).

Throughout the novel, invisible or insignificant domestic tasks serve
as catalysts, signposts and holding tanks for complex, memory-heavy
relationships. The book is full of symbol, image, archetypal weight and
mythic structures, but its African-American version of magic realism
stays grounded, the ghosts working alongside everybody else in earthy,
everyday reality. "Morrison has a strong sense of the existence of archetypal feminine," writes Veena Deo, "and of the authenticity and integrity
that reverberates from women's ancient values and roles as culture-bear-
ers" (7).

The characters' connection to deep, timeless, near-universal experience does not render them docile or predictable, however. Morrison uses
acts of domestic chaos, hostility or rebellion to question traditional roles
and expectations of daughter, wife, lover and mother. In Deo's words, she
"both plays with and works against the contemporary repression of and
ambivalence toward the maternal" (8).

By allowing her writing to come from the body, and often from the
soul, Morrison gains access to meanings heretofore slighted in Western
culture. The primal and mythic qualities of her writing work easily in the
intimate confines of domestic life, perhaps more easily than they would
at a larger scale. Like Gordon, Morrison uses the primary domestic image
to speak of her art: "There is no yeast for me in a real-life person, or else
there is so much it is not useful—it is done-bread, already baked"
("Memory, Creation and Writing" 386).

The character Paul D falls into the same class as Nanapush, Vincent
and Dan: a man devoid of arrogance, comfortable in a home, as eager to
nurture as be nurtured. But literary critic Barbara Hill Rigney points out
that before Paul D's arrival, and again at the novel's climax, Morrison's
women lived only with each other—and what happened then was significant. Their communal female world was erotic, sensual, wild; a world
outside history and set apart from the dominant culture. Its joy and close-

ness showed in *bas relief* how essentially alone black women have been in this country, taken from their mothers by slavery, deprived of control over their bodies by rape, kept from the men they loved for a hundred reasons. Sethe, who hardly remembered her mother, hungered for memory and identity through contact with other women. Her mother-in-law, Baby Suggs, helped heal her; her daughter Denver kept her going; and now her dead daughter was restoring her claim on the past.

Morrison's communal female world falls "outside history" in the broad sense of patriarchal tradition, but also in the subjective, Bergsonian sense that defines time as intuitively felt and lived, rather than discretely measured. "Perhaps because history as a progression has been so antagonistic," Rigney comments, "they live also on a different time scheme, without schedules, without clocks, eating and sleeping according to whim or to nature rather than sanctioned custom, thus collapsing conventional temporal coherence" (75). Other forms of logic collapse too: Rigney points out that, "After Paul D leaves Sethe's house, it becomes a veritable witch's nest, a semiotic jungle in which language itself defies convention and the laws of logic; voices merge and identities are indistinguishable" (17).

The female world is not only timeless but erotic, in the sense of joyfully intermingling physical and spiritual essences. For Morrison, the entire world is erotic:

> Eating, for example, is not merely a euphemism for sexual intercourse or an image of sensuality.... food, like everything else in her worlds, is metaphoric, diffusely erotic, expressive of jouissance. Meanings radiate, textures permeate, color illuminates. (Rigney 83)

When a man enters this world, a franker eros mingles with the domestic. As soon as she saw Paul D, Sethe said nervously, "I just hope you'll pardon my house. Come on in. Talk to Denver while I cook you something" (8). She told him they managed with no man around: she cooked at a restaurant and sewed a little on the sly. Then he remembered the dress she sewed to make her first night with Halle special. Magnetism, memory and need drew Sethe and Paul D close almost immediately, and Paul D cupped Sethe's breasts as she made biscuits, "fat white circles of dough," and touched a wet forefinger to the stove (17). Later, when she was looking forward to making love with him, we see her simultaneously planning what to cook him: potatoes, snap beans, squash, with all the emphasis on the processing of these foods, the browning, seasoning, sprinkling, frying and raising she will do (99).

Beloved's domestic imagery is lyrical, whether it's filled with love or pain. With a keen ear, Morrison describes:

the interior sounds a woman makes when she believes she is alone and
unobserved at her work: a sth when she misses the needle's eye; a soft
moan when she sees another chip in her one good platter; the low,
friendly argument with which she greets the hens. Nothing fierce or
startling. Just that eternal, private conversation that takes place between
women and their tasks. (172)

She makes vivid comparisons: a memory "as lifeless as the nerves in her
back where the skin buckled like a washboard" (6); Paul D's "peachstone
skin" and Baby Suggs' easy death, "soft as cream" (7). There are testa-
ments to female competence by the dozens, but one of the most poignant
comes during the birth of Denver. Sethe and Amy, a barefoot white
woman who chanced upon Sethe and helped her through labor, wrapped
the 10-minute-old baby in their own ragged clothing. "No patroller came
and no preacher. The water sucked and swallowed itself beneath them.
There was nothing to disturb them at their work. So they did it appropriately and well" (85).

One of Morrison's frequent themes is the black woman who,
deprived of a specific art form, creates beauty as a way to endure the
hardships of everyday life. In Beloved, we see this in Sethe's wedding
dress, assembled in stolen hours out of pillowcases, a dresser scarf, an old
sash and mosquito netting; her need to bring flowers to brighten and
claim her work; her loss of the ability to see vivid colors after killing her
baby; and her renewed desire to plant a garden when Beloved returns.
The same impulse prompted Baby Suggs to plead for color at the end of
her life. Exhausted by hurt and grief, she took to her bed, refusing to love
anymore. Instead, she turned her generous heart and keen eye on the
emotional nuances of different colors. "By the time Sethe was released
(from jail) she had exhausted blue and was well on her way to yellow"
(177).

Baby Suggs used to work on Sweet Home, too, but Halle worked
years of Sundays to buy her freedom. Even before she left, she was lucky;
the mistress, Lillian Garner, was still alive, and the two cooked, pre-
served, washed, ironed, made candles, clothes, soap and cider together.
Baby Suggs was able to preserve a sense of dignity in her domestic work:
"Even when she slipped in cow dung and broke every egg in her apron,
nobody said you-black-bitch-what's-the-matter-with-you and nobody
knocked her down" (139).

When she came north, Baby created a larger home for the town's
black community, preaching to heal their souls and cooking to stoke their
bodies. "Not one but two pots simmered on the stove; where the lamp
burned all night long. Strangers rested there while children tried on their
shoes. Messages were left there." This fusion of the domestic and the

transcendent earned her the attribute "Baby Suggs, holy" (87).

Sethe, too, knew and honored domestic work, but she had never had any way to do it in public with dignity and safety. First, she was owned. Then, after killing her baby, she isolated herself from the black community as well as the white one. After Baby Suggs' death, her private world shrank to herself and Denver, with a drudgery-filled, harshly supervised job at the restaurant keeping them solvent. At home, her everyday domestic chores continued in their own rhythm, but she had not done them lightly for a long time. Instead, she used them to knead away thinking and feeling. Paul D's arrival made her hope for a measure of relief from the work's demands, which by then she equated with all the pain and torment she had endured:

> Would there be a little space, she wondered, a little time, some way to hold off eventfulness, to push busyness into the corners of the room and just stand there a minute or two, naked from shoulder blade to waist, relieved of the weight of her breasts, smelling the stolen milk again and the pleasure of baking bread? Maybe this one time she could stop dead still in the middle of a cooking meal—not even leave the stove—and feel the hurt her back ought to. (18)

The language is interesting: "a cooking meal," passive construction, as though the meal had taken the upper hand. As indeed it had, since to seize control of her feelings would demand feeling too much pain. After this reverie, Sethe saw signs of incipient relief: the stove did not shudder, Denver did not stir, the pulsing red light of the haunting had not returned. When Beloved arrived in person, the chores of domesticity underwent an alchemy of sorts, turning wildly joyful, beribboned, vivid and carefree, as their role in Sethe's life changed.

The message was clear: Whenever home is the arena in which a woman works out her emotional problems, a layer of significance is added to everyday chores, and they take on unpredictable, transformative powers.

Marge Piercy and *The Longings of Women*

A white Depression baby, born in 1936 in a predominantly black neighborhood in Detroit, Marge Piercy grew up half Jewish, working class, and acutely conscious of insufficiency and injustice. She says she is "conscious of being very strongly in a women's tradition: an oral Jewish women's tradition transmitted to me by my mother and grandmother, first of all; second, a woman's tradition in writing; third, a contemporary community of women writers" (Walker and Hamner 148).

Biographer Kerstin Shands tells us that Piercy was very close to her mother, a housewife with a tenth-grade education whom she resembles physically, and who taught her to observe the world. A prolonged childhood illness turned Marge from a street tomboy into an avid reader (3), and at age 15, when she finally got her own room, she wrote her first poem. She promptly decided to become a writer—an unsurprising goal for someone of vivid imagination and reflective intelligence who had grown up feeling like an outsider. First in her family to attend a university, she received a scholarship to the University of Michigan, then left for graduate school at Northwestern University. Once there, she decided that she would never become a writer if she stayed in academe, so she promptly left.

She now lives with her second husband, writer Ira Wood, who assists in reading her manuscripts. Piercy gardens, cooks and enjoys nature and their four cats; she and Wood keep "a very lived-in house" in Wellfleet, Massachusetts (Pearlman 65).

Critics place Piercy within socialist and radical feminist traditions because she questions—with burning intensity—the institutions of capitalist society and their effect on women. She defends all kinds of feminists, from radical separatists who want to create their own culture to classic liberal feminists who want to broaden the existing culture.

Piercy links her work in the women's movement with her creativity, using images of bread-baking, gardening and quilting as political acts as well as hierophanies. Her poems present everyday objects in existential glory, as crucial components of the real world that influences us. Her novels are feminist narratives that break the boundaries of the traditional romance; Shands lists their central themes as the patterns of power and the principles of healing, connection, creation and *tikkun* (a Hebrew word meaning repair of the world). Piercy examines women's ability to create feminine spaces and structures within that broken world. In *The Longings of Women*, Leila is likened to a caryatid, a Greek statue which serves as a column holding up the structure of the building. In the eighteenth century, Shands points out, caryatids were chimney pieces bracketing the hearth, symbolic guardians of home's nurturing warmth (160).

When Piercy received the Sheaffer-PEN/New England Award for Literary Excellence, she read from her poem, "The fecund complain they are not honored." The poem describes how "the driven work," writing in buses and laundromats "while clothes/flash by, and somebody steals their socks" (Pearlman 70).

As you read more of her poems, Piercy's attitude toward domesticity unfolds, mixing with wilder nature images. In "The common living dirt," one of the "elementary odes" in *Stone, Paper, Knife*, she writes of dirt "rich in the hand/as chocolate cake," and how she places the seeds, "careful as stitching" (123). In an overview of Piercy's work, Walker quotes her assertion of "knowing with the teeth" as well as the brain, and credits her with a capacity to tolerate "uncertainties, mysteries, and doubts, without any irritable reaching after fact and reason" (140).

In *The Longings of Women*, Piercy unfolds the stories of three very different women and lets them cross, affecting each other's destiny. All three women have been to some degree deceived or abandoned by a husband, and each finds her own way to survive.

The first, and in many ways central, female character is Leila Landsman, an associate professor who accepted her publisher's assignment to research a murder. Living on the elegant side of middle class, Leila was the wife of a theatrical philanderer and the mother of a son away at college. Her best friend had just died, and she would soon learn that her husband was having yet another affair. The master bedroom was

> cool, even cold at night. While Nick was away, she slept under a feather quilt her mother Phyllis had given her when she had set up housekeeping. While Nick was with her, she threw the quilt over a chair and slept under a blanket.

The house was cold—without enough steady love—and Leila still needed cozy nurture, either from her memories of an ineffective mother or her proximity to her faithless husband. She lived contingent on other's demands and gifts. When Nick, who was directing a play on Broadway, flew home unexpectedly, she felt herself "shifting from one economy, one set of demands to another," and like a good wife, she immediately begins to plan how, "in the morning, she would put together a special breakfast to seduce him" (10). The aphrodisiac she selected was a honey cake made at Rosh Hashanah by her best friend—who'd given her a more loyal intimacy than her husband (11).

The second woman in the novel, Mary Burke, was one of countless displaced housewives cast adrift by divorce after years of cooking, cleaning and child-rearing. Mary's selfish children, a grown son and daughter, lived out of town; she had not even told them she was homeless, cleaning houses for a temporary agency and sleeping wherever she could. Staying furtively overnight at the house of a client who was away, she revealed her domesticity, a mixture of habit and exigency:

> She had bought milk and a half pound of hamburger meat the night before and a head of lettuce. The rest of her supper she had put together out of leftovers and items she dared appropriate.... Any dishes she used, she washed at once. (15)

Mary had done her laundry the night before, folding it neatly into her carryall; now she indulges in a refugee pleasure, making a mug's worth of coffee with a tiny Melitta insert she found at a church rummage sale. She carried the filter along with her fork, spoon, serrated knife and can opener—remnants of what was once, no doubt, a fully-equipped Sears & Roebuck kitchen in harvest gold or avocado green.

The third woman was Becky, daughter of a Portuguese fisherman and a cleaning woman. Becky was sick of crowded, filthy poverty, yearning for a bourgeois life. She went to the mall for privacy, and in the midst of beckoning consumerism, she daydreamed about a fairy-tale future. Chores got in the way of her intended self-realization: "If she tried to think about anything at home, Mama would give her a task to do instantly. Go to the store and get two pounds of hamburger for supper. Wash out the tub. If the water's hot, run a load of laundry for Gracie" (28).

Becky went to school then work, all the while planning her strategic exodus. Sure enough, at work she met Terry Burgess, a clean-cut, self-centered, painfully middle-class young man come to organize their computer system. Becky instantly fell in love with the future he could give her. She flirted with him in the best way she knew: "Maybe you'd like a cup of our terrible coffee. I could make it fresh, which helps." When Terry looked surprised, she decided "he must not have a bunny assistant to fetch and carry for him" (138). For her, however, the coffee-fetching was a bid for power, not a token of inferiority.

Soon Becky went to Terry's house to meet his parents. The Burgess ranch-house was on a marsh, not on solid ground—but the azaleas were mulched. Inside,

> the doors of the television were shut and the carpeting was white and spotless. Everything in the room was white or blue. The dried flowers had been purchased dyed blue, although the marshes outside were full of naturally dried grasses. (63)

However contrived and derivative, the domestic artifice only seduced Becky, who wanted success before refinement. Eager and anxious, she took no clue from the rigidly gendered, stylized behavior of her future husband's parents, noting only that "Mr. Burgess did the talking, while his wife sat upright on a colonial wing chair that matched the couch and wrung her hands" (64). Mrs. Burgess wasted no time telling Becky her cleaning woman was "one of the local Portugee," and showing her shocked disgust at the news that Becky's mother cleaned houses herself. Loyal and proud, Becky flinched, but contented herself with a quick dignified reply. Despite the family's chilly bias, she was determined to make this slipper fit.

At work, no one thought of Becky as warm and maternal (137). She'd frozen that aspect of domesticity, throwing her energy into more materialistic goals. "Becky was a furniture snob," carefully studying her friend's fringed lamps, knobby tables and tufted sofas. "She never gave up studying How Things Should Be, in case she ever had a crack at making something nice in her life" (136).

Leila, too, grew up poor and intellectualized her future. She was more nervous about the nurturing that would be required, however. She chose good Oriental rugs effortlessly, but "when Melanie had given her an African violet nine years ago, she had immediately read two books and a botanical garden pamphlet. Before David was born, she had read thirty books on child development" (77). It seemed a sign of both disorientation and growth when, alone and lonely, she brought home a cat for company and realized with a jolt that she had forgotten to buy, not only the proper feline accoutrements, but a food bowl.

Leila's friend Jane, a lesbian, reminded her that, "for the last two thousand years, spinsters were far more apt to get something done, including spinning, than married women" (95). But the witticism gave scant consolation; Leila had grown up with a harum-scarum mother who couldn't cook, and had spent her adult life hopefully living the myth of the ideal wife and mother. The domestic realm exerted a strange pull on her. Planning for Thanksgiving, she mused that "she had cooked no feasts, no real dinners in the last month. She wondered why a day of cooking made her feel like a good woman" (115).

When Leila decided to divorce Nick, she threw herself into work researching the case of a woman—Becky—who murdered her husband. In the course of her research, Leila met the gentle veterinarian Zak Solomon, uncle to the lovesick teenager who helped Becky perform the fateful deed. Slowly, in fits and uncertain starts, surrounded by the macabre and by their own lives' confused baggage, Leila and Zak fell in love. And it was in Zak's bachelor house, where "apple cores had been forgotten, desiccated among the books," that Leila learned the most about him. Teasing him about his hideous drapes, an unwanted gift, she said, "Why don't you throw them in the washer? A man isn't expected to know what's washable and what isn't." And he replied, "I don't want my washer to break again" (205).

Zak and Leila joked about stereotypes without feeling the need to fulfill them. Mary Burke, on the other hand, did fulfill her stereotypical but perfectly valid dream of household usefulness. She wound up helping Leila's divorced sister with a houseful of hungry, messy children. And Becky ended up in prison, an interior she never appraised.

Each of these women in some way transgressed, broke free from, or was thrown from, the boundaries of idealized domesticity, and its images riddled the plot. Leila admitted, "I have trouble with anger. I just sit on it like a big hot egg," cheerfully casting herself as a fat clucking hen (222). Her son David "had a slightly hunched look, a starchless way of standing in contrast with his father's massive presence" (110). Becky's sister Laurie once wore a chlorine mouthpiece, and "now she had alarmingly white teeth that looked like so many well-scrubbed washbasins" (106). Women's duties were everywhere, and beneath their innocuous details lay a sinister message: performed blindly or obsessively, these roles could lead you to murder, homelessness or betrayal.

Jane Smiley and *A Thousand Acres*

Like Mary Gordon, Jane Smiley was born in 1949, but in Los Angeles instead of Queens. She grew up in St. Louis, surrounded by language's craft; both her mother and great-grandfather had held newspaper jobs (Green 59). Smiley was an only child, living in tandem with her divorced mother until a stepfather joined them. She remembers being very scared about the Cold War, then thrown head-first into an ideology of rebellion in the '60s, deeply concerned with ecology (Smiley interview). She loved her years at Vassar—she even found a boyfriend who was 6'7", which for a girl of 6'2" was a blissful feat. She graduated in 1971 with a B.A. in English literature, then went on to the University of Iowa for a doctorate. Married before finishing school, she worked, whimsically enough, in a teddy-bear factory.

Now married for the third time, Smiley has two daughters. She teaches creative writing at Iowa State University and lists her politics as "skeptical," her religion as "vehement agnostic" (Lesniak vol. 30). *A Thousand Acres* won a Pulitzer Prize for fiction in 1992. Its imagery came from Iowa's farmland and the domestic order within the farmhouses; its destructive power from a patriarch with the stature and befuddlement of King Lear, but a far more wicked past.

The original *King Lear* identifies women with nature and wildness and, in the case of the malevolent sisters, Regan and Goneril, with evil. "I don't believe in evil," Smiley once told reporter Martha Duffy, "but I do believe in anger. I wondered what made them so angry" (91). Smiley linked her exploration of patriarchal power and oppression with issues of land ownership and use because "women, just like nature or the land, have been seen as something to be used" (92). She sees the two kinds of exploitation as inextricably linked, with modern agriculture's machinery and pesticides transcending nature just as patriarchy elevated male principles over female. "There has been so much special pleading for the father," she concludes (90).

Smiley once asked her grandmother what life was like on the family's Idaho ranch, and the woman replied, "I don't remember—I was too busy cooking" (Duffy 91). Two generations later, Jane Smiley is a staunch feminist who manages to expose all sides of domesticity in her writing—and in her personal life, delights in baking bread. Her approach to writing is organic: she told Duffy that, to her, "Plot is like the leaves and stalks on that rose bush. It grows and grows and then in just the right place here and there you find a blossom" (91).

Ginny, the dubious heroine in *A Thousand Acres*, was the eldest of three daughters. She was 36, married to a nice stoic farmboy named Tyler, skilled in the wifely arts but unable to bear a child. Her sister, Rose, had two, Pammy and Linda, whom Ginny adored. But that adoration was as bittersweet and envious as her sisterly love of the self-possessed, strong-willed Rose. Their baby sister, Caroline, whom they reared after their mother died, was the only one who had enough confidence to leave their rural life for a career in law.

The plot centered in the Midwest's isolated heartland, on a large prosperous farm in fertile green Zebulon County around 1979, as corporate agriculture began to take over the small family farm and its traditional ways. Its primary conflict opened with Lear-like family strife after the father decided to deed his vast acreage over to his daughters. Caroline spoke her mind about his foolishness; Ginny and Rose had learned better. Customarily passive, docile and conciliatory, Ginny hoped Caroline would come to her senses and obey their father's wishes—but it was Ginny and Rose who lost their father's trust, perhaps because their husbands had modern plans for the land.

A tyrant landowner looking at a future he cannot control, the father went half mad, calling Ginny a barren whore during a raging storm. In a matter of weeks, the family spiraled out of control. First Ginny betrayed her husband by sleeping with Jess Clark, newly returned to the county and free of its muddy weight; then she learned that her father had abused her sexually. Her marriage crumbled. Rose, who was battling breast cancer, also fell in love with Jess, and her passion was reciprocated. Her husband killed himself. The father disinherited Rose and Ginny and cleaved to undomesticated Caroline; meanwhile, Ginny threw herself even more feverishly into her domestic duties after a lawyer advised her, Rose and their husbands to behave as conspicuously clean, decent citizens, fit stewards of their delusional father's property. The flurry of activity covered Ginny's dark jealousy, as Jess and Rose entwined their lives.

In the end, Ginny tried to murder Rose in absurdly domestic, diabolically passive fashion, by poisoning a sausage and sauerkraut concoction no one else liked, canning it and hoping someday Rose would eat it. Meanwhile, Ginny left the farm, her marriage and her shadow of a self, went to the city, found work as a waitress, got an apartment and bought herself a microwave, jettisoning all the domestic accoutrements of her former life.

The context for the book's central conflict is thoroughly male: backbreaking manual labor, strategic planning, territoriality, status and farmers' pride. The women's roles were that odd traditional blend of peripheral and crucial, as they worked to maintain, sustain and perpetuate lives lived off the land. From childhood, Ginny knew that people's worth was measured in terms of acreage, financing and agribusiness, and that those standards underpinned even cooperative female work. While the farmers of Zebulon County appraised each other's land, buildings and equipment, their wives inspected each other's houses, checking for cobwebs, smeary windows or sloppily inefficient methods. They, too, checked out each other's tools:

> Farmwives are real connoisseurs of household appliances: whole-house vacuum cleaners mounted in the walls, microwave ovens and Crock-Pots, chest freezers, through-the-door icemakers on refrigerators, heavy duty washers and dryers, pot-scrubbing dishwashers and electric deep fat fryers. (120)

Both Ginny and Rose learned their constant domestic activity from their mother, who "fit in" with her female neighbors by baking pies and trading dress patterns, and who spent more time monitoring her daughters' household chores than showing them affection. Ginny learned to see the larger issues of her world through the filter of domesticity, noticing how "the rows of just-sprouted corn fanned into the distance like seams of tiny bright stitches against dark wool" (62).

As adults with their own households, both women responded to an emotional crisis with a tornado of domestic activity. Upset after the first flash of family crisis, Ginny escaped emotion by carrying plastic plates and forks into her host's kitchen. Jess joined her there, startling her with his sudden, vehemently male presence, and drawled, "There's something missing in this kitchen, and now I realize what it is. It's the cylinder of bull semen. I used to eat with my foot up on it" (21). This tells us how Ginny will perceive him—as the man who can interrupt her stifling domesticity and make it possible for her to bear a child.

After Rose's mastectomy, Ginny responded predictably, "feeding her, cleaning her house, doing her laundry," baking banana bread and ginger snaps for the girls (8–9). Not only did the baking give Ginny a chance to feel like a mother, but feeding Rose and cleaning her usually impeccable house gave Ginny the upper hand for the first time in their sisterly relationship.

After their father's clash with Caroline, Ginny again found strength by following prescribed routine:

> When it was my turn to have Daddy over for supper, the Tuesday night after the property transfer, I cooked what I always did for him—pork chops baked with tomatoes (my third-to-last quart from the year before), fried potatoes, a salad, and two or three different kinds of pickles. (47)

Why the detailed menu? Perhaps to show that Ginny had learned certain fixed ways of pleasing her father. She was far more interested in peace and ease than in discovering the range of his tastes, surprising him, asserting her own preferences. Ginny was a careful manager of her stores, counting what she had set by the previous year and meting it out. She gave the meal a sense of abundance by dishing out two or three different kinds of pickles with rural largesse, but there was a hint of her real feelings in the way she made do with leftovers for dessert, the point at which the cook often presents, with a flourish, a special treat prepared just for a beloved guest.

When Ginny, Rose and their husbands decided to fight the father's decision and win back his land, the lawyer instructed the women to "wear dresses every day, and keep the lawn mowed and the porch swept." The old double-bind: dressing so formally that you are constrained, ill-clad to perform the expected work.

In the car, Ginny—with her work cut out for her—asks what time it is, and Ty tells her it's about 4:30 p.m. "Already? It seems like I just made dinner," she exclaimed (285). The work arrived before she was ready to perform it; the chores set the pace, controlling her life instead of being controlled by her.

When Rose's husband drove his car into the lake, Ginny was "upstairs making the beds, so I didn't see the sheriff's car go by." When she went outside to hang blankets, she saw Rose stumbling up the road toward her. Rose asked her to go to the girls, an interruption that took immediate priority: "I dropped the blankets in a heap and ran toward her house." When she arrived, the girls were still asleep, so she returned to domestic work: "The milk and eggs and butter were in the bowl of the mixer," so Ginny finished the muffins (287). The cozy world of the kitchen did not allow her to escape from the crisis, however: she found herself staring at a "Pete's Joe" coffee mug, filled with water in the sink (288).

After Ginny methodically prepared and delivered her sister's murderous liver sausage, she returned home clear-eyed:

> Usually, I didn't take in my place as a whole. I focused on a chair I'd just

shampooed or a picture I'd found at the antique store in Cabot, or a corner that looked presentable or welcoming. Tonight I came back to my
house as a stranger, and I remembered a friend of Daddy's who told me
once about when rural electrification came through.... The mother's first
words of the new era were, 'Everything's so dirty!' Those could have
been my first words of our new era, attesting to how strange and far
from home I felt taking meat from my refrigerator and salting it with my
old red plastic saltshaker and slapping it onto the broiler pan I'd used
for seventeen years. (328)

Ginny did not return to the comfort of unquestioned habits. Her world
was now alien to her, and familiar objects had the strangeness of a word
repeated into absurdity. She moved into her automaton state, preparing
dinner with routine motions, "running an inch of water in an old pot,
piercing the bottoms of the sprouts with a fork" (329). Her husband
walked in, stepping out of the boots that represented his work outside the
home. Their typical, almost idle domestic conversation soon erupted in
conflict, and as if to mirror Ginny's anger, steam rose from the boiling
potatoes, and she remembered to check the broiler. "The contained roar
of the gas and then, a minute later, the first sizzling of meat juices, took
on the volume and weight of oracular mutterings, almost intelligible.
With a feeling of punching through a wall, I said, 'I need a thousand dollars.'" Instead of protesting, Ty blurted the coincidence that he had a
thousand dollars in his pocket, rent on his farmstead. Ginny held out her
hand for the money and got the car keys, "and with the meat broiling in
the oven and the potatoes and sprouts boiling on the stove," she walked
out of her life as a housewife (330).

Amy Tan and *The Kitchen God's Wife*

Amy Tan was born in 1952 in Oakland, California; her father was a
Baptist minister and electrical engineer, her mother a nurse. Tan received
her bachelor's and master's degrees in linguistics from San Jose State
University, then worked as a switchboard operator, A&W carhop, bar-
tender and pizza maker, language development consultant, copywriter
and freelance business writer before beginning serious literary work,
inspired by the writings of Louise Erdrich.

In 1974, Tan married tax attorney Lou DeMattei; they live with their
Siamese cat, Sagwa, and Yorkshire terrier, Bubba Zo, in the bottom
duplex of a post-Victorian row house on Sacramento Street. When
Mickey Pearlman arrived, "she was baking cookies for our interview and
for her writing group, which was meeting there that evening. We sat

drinking tea in the comfortable living room" (Pearlman 15).

Tan's first book, *The Joy Luck Club,* published in 1989, was nominated for the National Book Award and National Book Critics Circle Award. Her second novel, *The Kitchen God's Wife* was a 1991 Booklist editor's choice (Trosky vol. 136), praised for its poignancy, bittersweet humor and exuberant storytelling. Much of the book was tight-focused and domestic; Tan once compared the techniques and effects of male and female writers to those produced by a movie camera:

> 'Men pan the whole scene and describe a wide panorama; their world is larger, but the sense of intimacy is not there. In my fiction and that of many women, the focus starts close-up, then the world pans out.... The mind is connected to the heart.' (Pearlman 19)

When I interviewed Tan in November 1995, she mentioned the layered contextual definition of "yin" as femaleness and darkness, and "yin eyes" as the ability to see the invisible. "Women are known for being more intuitive and able to see things that may not be apparent to men," she said easily. "The semantic linkages are not accidental." She sees strong gender differences—but does not necessarily live according to stereotype. "I'm the sort of cook who pours water into dehydrated things," she chuckled, explaining the importance of food in her novels as pure nostalgia.

Tan resists the scholarly probing multiculturalists have given her work : when she saw *The Joy Luck Club* in CliffNotes, her first thought was, "But I'm not dead yet!" Many a scholar has explicated her use of various symbols—incorrectly. "I'm not that clever," she laughs. "Symbols to me occlude meaning; images clarify emotions." She also resents the constant questions about how her Chinese and American cultural backgrounds intersect. She is writing about human nature, not Chinese-American nature (Tan interview, 1995).

If we zoom out from her work, however, to the general question of women's domesticity, we must briefly consider the Chinese-American experience. Both men's and women's roles swung toward the "feminine" when Asian immigrants arrived here. The men were often perceived as less than macho; the women as ultra-feminine and exotic. Shirley Geok-Lin Lim and Amy Ling see this femininization as "an index of the entire group's marginalization and its function as the 'good natives' in American cultural myth" (122). While the sexes remained differentiated, the men were more likely to launder or cook for pay than American men of Western European descent. The conditions awaiting Chinese immigrants shaped their work and family life; those experiences then reshaped gender roles. Such shifts are unsettling, as "masculinity and femininity prove to be contingent, mutable, provisional—products of historical particularity" (Lim and Ling 117).

Lore and superstition saturated *The Kitchen God's Wife* as thoroughly as the supernatural filled *Beloved*; like Morrison, Amy Tan grew up surrounded by this transrational perspective. Her mother explained her great-grandmother's death to her by saying: "'One day your grandmother went into her mother's room (your great-grandmother was very sick) and cut a piece of meat off her own arm and put it in this soup, cooked it with some herbs, but the soup didn't work and she died that day'" (Pearlman 19).

In both *The Kitchen God's Wife* and *The Joy Luck Club*, Chinese mothers showed affection, not with kisses and ticklings, but with delicacies like duck's gizzards. In China, the kind and amount of food one ate was considered crucial to one's health. In *Food in Chinese Culture: Anthropological and Historical Perspectives*, K.C. Chang pointed out that "food, therefore, is also medicine" (9). The interconnected principles of yin and yang organize both bodily functions and foods, so the Chinese endeavor to balance these forces by orchestrating an equilibrium of hot and cold. "The other concept is frugality," Chang continued. "Overindulgence in food and drink is a sin of such proportions that dynasties could fall on its account." Unlike the Ojibwa, who relished an abundant sharing and partaking, the Chinese ideal was to end each meal 70 percent full (10). The Chinese assigned some foods symbolic meaning (noodles signaled longevity, candy sweetened life) and favored "tonic foods," such as wildcat and snake. They used banquets to cement group relationships.

In *Reading Asian American Literature: From Necessity to Extravagance*, Sau-ling Cynthia Wong held that alimentary images excised from various texts "symbolize Necessity—all the hardships, deprivations, restrictions, disenfranchments, and dislocations that Asian Americans have collectively suffered as immigrants and minorities in a white-dominated country" (31). She traced the bizarre motif of "like devouring like" (chicken scraps going into chicken feed, humans reaching into monkey skulls) in several Asian-American works that explore familial relationships between first- and second-generation immigrants, suggesting that "necessity might have taken a peculiar and acutely distressing form in Asian American immigrant families" (31).

In *The Kitchen God's Wife*, most of the food-related deprivations and dislocations take place in wartime China, their influence reaching this country and the next generation by way of memory, ritual and scar-tissued habit. The book opened with Pearl, who, like Erdrich's Lulu, was the intended audience for the history about to unfold. Pearl had her own secret: she had been diagnosed with multiple sclerosis. By the end of the book, she would be able to confide this disturbing news to her overprotective mother, Winnie Louie. Born Jiang Weili (Weiwei) in 1919 China,

Winnie was abandoned by her mother; married a man prone to violence and mania; endured the deaths of her first three children, her hated first husband and her beloved second husband, Jimmy Louie.

Winnie had the traditional Chinese woman's attitude toward domestic responsibilities: she cooked with skill and cleaned with energy, performing these duties to prove worth, win love, forge security, show affection. Pearl, on the other hand, had a career, a feminist husband and a modern attitude toward housework: she and her husband were constantly playing catch up, dropping their children off with Winnie on pretext of a business trip, so they could go home and do all the chores they'd let go (10).

In the novel's first crucial scene, Pearl and her husband were leaving an overnight stay with Winnie to attend Grand Auntie's funeral. She told them Grand Auntie had left them a farewell gift, which she'd stored in the laundry room. Pearl conjured up images of a vinyl ottoman or a set of indestructible Melmac dishes, then caught sight of the gift sitting on the dryer. It was a Chinese shrine, an altar for her good-luck god. Pearl's husband carried the ornate red lacquered altar from the dryer to the kitchen—again, an appropriate room, for the god is the Kitchen God.

The altar's wooden panels had gold Chinese characters representing different kinds of luck; inside, the man in the picture frame was "almost cartoonlike. The man is rather large and is seated in regal splendor, holding a quill in one hand, a tablet in the other. He has two long whiskers, shaped like smooth, tapered black whips" (58). Unimpressed, Winnie informed her daughter that he was a lesser deity, nothing like Buddha or Kwan Yin, the goddess of mercy. "Maybe he was like a store manager, important, but still many, many bosses above him," she explained (59).

Winnie has had lousy luck all her life, and she spent several horrendous years with a violent man, so no god with whiskers like whips was going to appeal to her. When her granddaughters clamored for the story, she told them about the origins of the Kitchen God. Zhang was a rich lucky farmer blessed with abundance because of his hardworking wife Guo. Greedy and unsatisfied, he flirted with a pretty, carefree woman, forcing his good wife to cook for her. Eventually, the wife was cast out of her own home, and Zhang's mistress—devoid of domestic virtues of thrift, prudence and discipline—helped him squander his fortune.

Reduced to beggary, Zhang fainted and woke up warm at the hearth of a compassionate woman, realizing with a guilty jolt that she was his former wife, Guo. He jumped into the kitchen fireplace to hide, "and his ashes flew up to heaven in three puffs of smoke. There, the Jade Emperor made him kitchen god, for having the courage to admit he was wrong. It is now his role to watch over everyone's behavior, deciding who deserves good luck and who deserves bad" (61). "You never know," Winnie shrugged. "Sometimes he is in a bad mood. Sometimes he says, 'I don't like this family, give them bad luck.' Then you're in trouble" (61–62). She proposed they take the altar without the kitchen god, and she would find them another god to put inside.

Winnie's life story revealed the nuances of being lucky or, as she felt, unlucky. On a grocery shopping expedition, her friend "Helen picked out a flat fish, pom-pom fish, she called it, only a dollar sixty-nine a pound, bargain bin," and Winnie warned her about it. "Look at his eye, shrunken in and cloudy looking. That fish is already three days old." Helen saw nothing amiss, so Winnie let the fish's body slide between her fingers to prove how long ago he had died. "Helen said it was a good sign—a juicy, tender fish!" Winnie told her "the sweetness of its meat had risen to the skin and turned stinky-sour in the air," but she inhaled the fish's odor and pronounced it "a good pom-pom smell." When Helen prepared and served the fish, she won compliments from her husband and son and smugly urged Winnie to try some. The fish was so sweet and tender that Winnie wondered if Helen had gone back to the Happy Super to exchange it. Then she remembered that Helen was not smart, she was lucky. "Over the years," Winnie sighed, "my luck—just like my prettiness—dried out, then carved lines on my face so I would not forget" (67–68).

At the novel's end, the episode repeated itself in different form. At a wedding celebration, Helen asked, "Who didn't eat this last scallop? This is too good to leave behind," and pressed the scallop on Winnie, who stubbornly refused to taste it. When Winnie finally blurted that it was not fresh, Helen popped it in her mouth, turned to Pearl and whispered, "Your mother is a good cook.... That's why it is hard for her to appreciate other good things'" (521). Winnie had pushed herself so hard, she had lost the ability to enjoy life.

Hospitality was a strong virtue in *The Kitchen God's Wife*, but a more burdensome sort of hospitality than, say, the Ojibwa custom of sharing, or the community feast in *Beloved*. "My mother hands me a cup of tea, waving off my protests," Pearl said, Winnie doing the usual womanly insisting: "Already made. If you can't drink it, I only have to throw it away" (60). She sent Pearl's family away with the usual heavy care package (63). She recalled, with a touch of self-pity, her simple homecoming meal: "spinach with one little black mushroom chopped up for taste, and egg custard with pork, fried strips of yellow fish, and a fish-head soup. That was all, three dishes and a soup, for four people" (492).

Food affirmed individuals' worth and their collective life, keeping the senses vivid even in the midst of catastrophe. At the Chinese marketplace were "rows of tables covered with buckets of tofu and weighing scales, piles of sweet potatoes and white turnips, baskets of dried mushrooms, pans of live fish, freshwater soft-shell crabs from the south, and wheat, egg, and rice noodles." People lined up "in a stream as long as a dragon," happily thinking about the evening meal. Hulan and Weiwei followed the sweet smoke of roasting chestnuts until Japanese planes attacked, shattering the peace (267).

The raids continued, intercutting the women's domestic routine. On one occasion, an anxious Hulan cooked herself a big meal to calm her fears; on another occasion, Weiwei was bathing her baby in the kitchen when Hulan screamed an alarm (365). One morning they ventured out to find glasses for Hulan's failing eyesight, and at market she became "a big expert" on mushrooms, pointing out every bruise, broken stem or soggy spot. Weiwei was planning how she would cook these carefully chosen mushrooms, spicing them with blackened hot peppers, when sirens signaled a bomb scare (370).

When a bombing finally did take place, the women murmured how lucky they were to get good bargains at the marketplace afterward and decided to celebrate their survival with "a big meal and lots of rich-smelling tea" (370). Gleeful in their relief, they laughed over domestic absurdities: how the servant spilled the chamber pot when the bomb exploded, leaving "the whole floor, bombed with this smelly disaster!" Auntie Du told how she was chasing a chicken with her cleaver when the bomb dropped, and the next thing she knew, the chicken was chasing her (370). The jarring change in scale, shuttling back and forth from instruments of death to the small tools of daily life, revealed the enormity of the former and the sweetly familiar, concrete immediacy of the latter.

Slowly, the women learned how to factor war into their domestic tasks, making sure no pots were left burning when they left for a bomb shelter, and letting go of things gently, remembering where they set them (371). When the time comes to evacuate, Weiwei instructed her servant to bring out the rest of her clothes, her husband Wen-Fu's radio, and her little black sewing machine, which she ceremoniously bestowed on Wan Betty, who bravely planned to stay. Wan Betty solemnly promised to use the sewing machine to make a good living for herself and her baby. The moment was intimate, intense, an intersection of two lives. The appliance was an instrument for, not only economic survival, but the realization of a woman's dream (279).

At the novel's end, Pearl learned that her father was not Winnie's beloved second husband Jimmy Louie, but the evil Wen-Fu. Once this burdensome secret was lifted from Winnie's shoulders, the two women could connect. Winnie had just heard that Wen Fu was dead, and she told her daughter, "Now I don't have to worry. For so many years I thought he was going to fly out of a closet, or jump out from underneath my bed" (509). The other secret—Pearl's struggle with multiple sclerosis—was shared; Winnie scolded her daughter for wearing a thin dress and urged her to see an herb doctor, her motherly care is firmly in place, to be steadily transmitted through her domestic concerns with food, drink, healing, warm clothing and family ritual.

For Winnie, and so many other women, such concerns warded off the chaos of fear, illness, guilt, emotional distance, loneliness and powerlessness. Quite a feat, for such trivial pursuits.

FIVE

ORDERING CHAOS

"Ah done been in sorrow's kitchen
and ah licked de pots clean."

Gulla proverb

Odd, for someone as disinclined toward domesticity as I am to come home exhausted after a trip and feel compelled to, as my grandmother would say, "tidy." Yet invariably I find myself unpacking, straightening, starting a load of wash, checking the refrigerator's contents. Like many of the women in the novels just summarized, I consider home our safe place, the base from which we enter the world and to which we return for renewal. If its daily routines are violated or its boundaries uncertain—if the dirt and confusion of the outside world have penetrated—our safety is in question. Home contains the food we need to live; if the shelves are bare and the milk has spoiled, our very survival is in question. Home contains the clean clothes we need to interact in civilized fashion with the outside world; if egg dribbles down my husband's tie or perspiration stains my linen dress, we are unfit for commerce.

In the novels, domestic rituals intersect all forms of order and chaos, mediating between them. This is far more than a literary device: domesticity has been part of Culture's arsenal for civilizing Nature since the first four walls rose from the mud. The rituals of the home tame us, making us predictable to our fellow human beings. As soon as we stake out our home turf, we must protect its boundaries, sweep it of nature's decaying filth, remove vermin and insects that could make us ill, and set up routines by which we can bake and eat our daily bread, keep ourselves clean and warm, clothe ourselves.

All this is basic survival, but as the layers of cultural practice deepen, the rituals take on symbolic significance. Remember the elaborate permutations of plot in the novels, the delicate correspondences of domestic acts with internal states? There is solid ground for such interpretations. Rabuzzi notes that the changes in texture effected by cleaning—from dull, dirty or fuzzy to shiny or smooth—satisfy an inner need to transform the physical world (110). We tidy our surroundings to order our thoughts; we feed our bodies to soothe emotional hunger. Sensing these correspondences in each other, we learn how to manipulate our house-mate's psychic state with domestic weapons, destroying equilibrium or restoring harmony, showing love or withdrawing compliance. Our behavior within the home reflects our agreement with, or rebellion against, society's norms. Or the norms of the previous generation. Or the norms of the subdivision. (Here in South St. Louis, our postage-stamp zoysia lawn must be trimmed within the quarter-inch.) We all, in one way or another, fend off the chaos of homelessness—the up-in-the-air anomie of not quite belonging anywhere—by feathering a cozy nest.

Bringing domestic order from chaos has, in the end, far deeper mean-ing than scrubbing the floor or fixing dinner. When daily domestic rhythms are interrupted, the results can distress us disproportionately. Common wisdom predicts divorce when an already fractious couple rehabs a house, and tension rises if houseguests extend their stay. There have been screaming fits over wriggling washing machines; horrors verg-ing on child abuse when mud or jam smears a newly washed floor.

Deconstructed, the novels diagram many different kinds and levels of order: the linear, compartmentalized sort so clear to Western rationalists; the hygienically clean, chemically composed order prescribed by science; the social order of family or community; the intuitive order of emotional attunement; the physical order of nature; the aesthetic order of grace and beauty. Chaos, too, comes in different brands: the social chaos of poverty, insufficiency or inadequacy; the emotional chaos of grief, confusion, anger, fear or frustration; the interpersonal chaos of divorce, abandon-ment, alienation, illness, murder, death. Even our sense of mortality, our fragility and indeterminacy is a form of chaos, setting unwelcome *thanatos* against the dream of eternal life.

The plots also show us how a woman's ability to create domestic order can define her; how economic conditions can swing a family toward chaos; how the gendered responsibility for order can affect rela-tions between the sexes. In *The Longings of Women*, for example, Becky cast a critical eye on her fiancé's family habits:

> The boys were spoiled. They never picked up after themselves. They never volunteered around the house. They seemed to feel that food mag-ically appeared and dirty clothes or spilled coffee drifted away into the great beyond, bringing cleanliness and order to areas they had aban-doned to dirt and chaos. When they were married, finally, she would have to change Terry's attitudes. (177–178)

She did try, but ended up murdering him instead. It was a drastic solution to a disproportionate share of housekeeping. Devoid of both love and maturity, the marriage turned into a game of nagging and manipulation, and Becky realized she was in danger of being divorced and sent back to economic square one. Piercy used Becky's lack of foresight to both condemn and excuse her, presenting Becky's obsession with domestic order and security as the consequence of a sharply ambitious, rapacious nature whose growth was stunted by poverty.

The character Leila, meanwhile, used domestic styles to explain the tension between herself and her younger sister: "Looking at her, what did Debbie see, except a busybody dull hausfrau who counted every penny and measured every response. She found Debbie chaotic and Debbie found her controlling" (336). Debbie had become, in one of her customary emotional upheavals, a single mother, and her household was falling into crisis. When Leila flew out to California to rescue her, she found a suburban ranch house surrounded by rural trappings, dead vehicles and an upended tricycle, failed technology rusting in the garden (350). The house was painted a nontraditional pink and faded to boot—rebellion topped by negligence. Everything in Debbie's world offended Leila's sense of deliberate, measured control. And yet, Leila was fair: Debbie had always been the better mother when it came to baking cookies and stitching Halloween costumes (355).

The tradeoffs between living in the present and planning for the future are familiar to anyone who has balanced a budget, made a spiritual journey or made love—and those tradeoffs are just as sharply defined in the domestic sphere. For these sisters, order came at the price of creativity, spontaneity, playfulness and pleasure. Leila spent her time earnestly trying to do things properly, by standard and textbook expertise. Her sister's friendly clutter left room for freedom, for the creativity that chaos makes possible.

Chaos allows us to embrace the moment, freed of categorical imperatives, loosed from structure, careless about time's burdensome ticking. We no longer follow the societal dictum to impose one's will on time, dominate it, subdue it by ordering it to hold still. Nor do we practice the vigilance of Catherine Beecher, whose nineteenth-century treatise on housekeeping urged the reader "deliberately to calculate on having her best-arranged plans interfered with, very often; and to be in such a state of preparation that the evil will not come unawares" (137).

Chthonic Chaos

In just a few lines of her poem "Dust," Ingrid Wendt gives us a sense of the dark, irrational forms of chaos we stave off with domestic labor, calling dust "indiscriminate as sin" and describing how it clings, greaselike, to everything—including "the edge of anger" (Hedges and Wendt 130–133). Those are strong statements for particles as innocuous as dust. Even if you put its bunnies under a microscope and magnify the pointy-nosed mites alive inside, they hardly seem sinister enough to challenge both Eden and the Enlightenment. But we live in a culture that draws heavy lines between male and female, clean and dirty, rational and irrational, right and wrong, body and soul. In *Ordinarily Sacred,* Linda Sexson points out that, "in a secularized yet dualistic culture, women are still charged with being unclear and unclean, irrational and nonlinear, mad and bloody" (85). Paradoxically, it is women who have been charged with cleaning the world, straightening up its chthonic mess.

Women are trained assiduously to first clean up their own chthonic mess, then the world's. When Leila in *The Longings of Women* finds out her husband has spilled his seed elsewhere, she felt "the same sense of shame and secretiveness her mother had trained her to feel toward her sanitary napkins, that must not go into the family garbage, that must not be flushed down the toilet lest they clog the pipes" (25). Throughout history, the females who have energetically scrubbed both house and body have been credited with holy virtue—usually the only official reward for such thankless tasks. This is why, after centuries of conditioning, Wendt can link dust with sin and anger and know her readers will understand.

In *A Thousand Acres,* women struggled constantly to keep the chthonic realm of nature from invading the farmhouse. After spending an entire morning shampooing the carpet in the most civilized, citified rooms—living room and dining room—Ginny explained that

> no matter how careful you are about taking off boots and overalls, the dirt just drifts through anyway. Dirt is the least of it. There's oil and blood and muck, too.... Farm women are proud of the fact that they can keep the house looking sparkling and starched, that the carpet is clean and the windowsills dusted and the furniture in good shape, or at least neatly slipcovered. (120)

Why tread water in a maelstrom? What gave Ginny such a superior tone when she mentioned women who cop out and get linoleum, proud that it's ersatz parquet? Because sparkling clean order implied that human beings were capable of taming the wilderness; it was an inroad of civilization, an *hommage* to both urban sophistication and our foremothers' backbreaking standards.

Later in the novel, as Ginny grew more disenchanted with the tight confines and hollow, temporary consequences of her wifely domestic role, she began to focus on chaos instead of order:

> The house looked somewhat better, thanks to my obsessive work, but
> the furnishings were old and mismatched, the carpeting and vinyl dark
> with stains that simply didn't respond to the products available for
> removing them. Shit, blood, oil, and grease eventually hold sway in
> spite of the most industrious efforts. (328)

After the impeccable Rose died, Ginny acknowledged, with emotions so
mixed they'd gone flat, the triumph of dirt and decay. "The white siding
on the western face of the house was dark with grit," she noted. "Rose
would have washed that down" (365). By now, Ginny had deliberately
distanced herself from housewifely compulsions, becoming the neutral
observer of what Rose would have done, rather than what she herself
should do. Rose's habits were predictable; Ginny once shared them. But
now she saw the dirt and sins of the father who abused her, as well as the
ruthlessness of her vying sisters and the fiercely competitive agribusiness
industry. In this new ironic awareness, any effort to maintain appearances seemed hypocritical.

In *The Kitchen God's Wife*, the chthonic realm surfaced in war and
homelessness. Traveling away from the military zone, Winnie and her
companions had to stay at a hotel that was "primitive and dirty," with
only a spot on the ground to serve as a bathroom.

> They used any kind of thing for a mattress—dirty straw with little rocks
> still clinging to it, old feathers and things you did not want to imagine.
> The cloth holding all this in was thin, had never had hot water poured
> over it to tighten the threads. So it was easy for bugs to hide inside the
> mattress—just walked right in as if the door were open. (285)

Well-trained and indignant, Winnie pinpointed the slovenly housekeeping that allowed the intrusion of nature. There was wit in her outrage: she
tried not to laugh aloud when bugs crawled over the hated Wen Fu's
back. This was not, after all, Winnie's own domicile; she was not responsible for this sordid state, and rocky straw was preferable to violence.

When Winnie and Helen were sent to a muddy air force base in
Yangchow, Helen ordered her manservant to paint a mixture of egg-
whites and mud onto her floor. Then she made him cook a sticky porridge of rice and mud and throw it on the wall. "Said it was cooked just
right," he reported mischievously (245). Appalled and curious, Winnie
trooped over to Helen's house, and lo: "Her floors had baked shiny-hard
like porcelain, so no dust rose up. And her walls that once had been
crumbly like ours—they were smooth and clean with new mud, not one
insect marching across" (246). Helen then helped Winnie secure her own
quarters against dirt, as any good female friend would.

The next infested mattress waited in a rooming house, where Winnie fled with her son Danru to escape Wen Fu's cruelty. This time, she was even more cheerful about the chaos: she promptly began to claim the space and teach her son how to live. "I used my chopsticks to pluck bugs out of the mattress," she said. "Danru would chase them, smashing them flat with the bottom of a bowl. We did that until there were no more bugs, until we had changed our world, dirty to clean" (396). She seized the power to order her world, first emotionally, by leaving Wen Fu, and then both practically and symbolically, by ridding her new home of dirty bugs. She enlisted her son in the effort, making him her partner in their new life, and when they finished their plucking and smashing, she congratulated him for their victory.

Tracks showed no similar conflicts and orderings. The Ojibwa lived in harmony with nature, and saw its rocks, feathers and insects as soulful and significant. There was no need to drive nature back, as Smiley's farmwomen did, or smash living creatures, as Tan's Chinese did. Domestic order had tremendous meaning for the Ojibwa, a tribe of family units, but none of that meaning came from a clash between inside and outside or nature and civilization. Furthermore, women may have received spiritual power through their menstrual blood, but that blood did not relegate them to a chthonic realm separate from men's rational world. Women may have taken responsibility for much of the home's cleaning and keeping, but that did not mean they were dealing with filth and mess spurned by their men.

Gordon's Irish-American novel, by contrast, held a strong sense of dualism and an ambivalence toward frail flesh and natural processes. As a girl, Ellen sat, lonely and despairing, by her mother's sickbed, and she "would hold the hand that had been lively, clever, magic in its ministrations, dead now, fat, the flesh growing over the wedding ring so that the gold was barely visible" (98). Perhaps it was this sense of physical decay and domestic uselessness that later drove Ellen to constant busyness. In any event, the flesh growing over the wedding ring showed how easily the body, disordered and dysfunctional, could overshadow society's rules and ceremonies.

Earlier in the novel, we saw Ellen's own aged hand—"claw, paper, bone"—through her grandson Dan's watchful eyes, as he recalled

> her apron over her flattened breasts.... The smell of her, he was unable to forget that she was physical, unlike the mothers of his friends. Those mothers of the fifties were corseted even for housework; they wore scarves around their pincurls and their housedresses were not like Ellen's; on theirs you smelt detergent and felt the fabric stiffened by starch. His grandmother wore dresses limp from washing. (73)

Ellen's body had begun to sag and loosen, but her sense of self had never hinged on the consumer ethos of the younger generation. Their clothes and products concealed the body's true nature, erasing its smells, constricting its billows, ceremoniously (and ineffectively) hiding its cosmetic efforts; sanitizing and starching its clothing into a mechanical, always-new perfection.

The Longings of Women gave us two very different examples of women fighting chthonic chaos. Bourgeois Mrs. Burgess kept an immaculate house by hiring a cleaning woman; she lived at the surface, never engaging deeply or physically enough to let the house reflect her. When Leila inspected the house, her nose detected nothing more human than the odor of furniture polish. The guest bathroom was small and sterile, its towels perfectly embroidered, its rosebud soaps dusty (64–65).

Dinner at the Burgesses was processed into a pale tasteless imitation of food, beginning with half grapefruits mortally wounded, a "deadly red maraschino cherry in the bull's-eye center." Next came a white fish smothered in so much cheese sauce that Becky, a fisherman's daughter, could not identify it. Civilization had killed all recognizable nature; all Becky knew was that, "whatever it was, it had been dead awhile." The rest of the meal was equally corpselike: white rice, white bread, and a grace note of artificially green peas. "The food tasted as if it were made of magazine pages," whose recipes had surely inspired it (168).

Mary the homeless cleaning woman, meanwhile, found salvation in ordering the household of Leila's sister. Mary stepped into utter chaos: stinking laundry, rotten lettuce and spoiled tofu and a few open cans in the refrigerator. Nature was this refrigerator's only saving grace, yielding goat's milk and eggs to keep the family healthy. Immediately, Mary began shopping, cooking and cleaning, tending to the goats and chickens and horses. She responded to the household's messy organic demands with willing energy, nurturing nature instead of killing it and substituting artifice. And because she was both strong and grateful, she loved the way there was always something to be done, the animals and children and bored bedridden Debbie all needing her attention (413). In a matter of hours, Mary was involved and engaged in this household in a way wealthy, silly Mrs. Burgess had never known.

Social Chaos

Beyond earthy chaos lies social chaos, the cacophony of conflicting lives orchestrated by law and ritual into orderly community. Domestic chaos—spills, broken dishes, disrupted meals, filth, disease, insufficiency—often reflects social chaos, alerting us to tensions beneath the surface. Domestic rituals, on the other hand, remove or at least subdue this chaos; they anchor marriages and families and neighborhoods, signaling hope for a stable future.

At the social level, the characters in *Tracks* did confront chaos, as the Ojibwa underwent the poverty and regrouping that followed white domination. Nature could not unsettle them, but society certainly could. The two clearest incidents occurred in the home of the mixed-blood Morrisseys, who teetered between old tribal ways and an amoral, opportunistic assimilation. First we saw Bernadette driven out by her grandchildren's domestic mischief:

> They put their feet through the wicker chair seats, devoured the soup in the kettle before it had boiled, poured sugar straight from the sack into their mouths. But it was not until she went to the cellar the next morning and found every pickle jar empty, that Bernadette packed to leave. (179)

The children's disrespect heralded a new era, one that allowed Bernadette no security. She packed her belongings and moved to town, closer to the white world that was splitting them apart. A few weeks later, at her children's house, "no smoke came from the chimney, but from inside could be heard the clank of pots and the shrieks and accusations of feeding children." The hint of poverty, hunger and a cold rebellious hearth started the Morrisseys' downfall. "They lost status as the years went on," their domestic chaos reflecting increased alienation from the community (182).

The Longings of Women repeated, in very different circumstances, the same linkage of marginalization, poverty and chaos. Leila, who grew up in a slum herself, had studied her way into the middle class. When she visited Becky's poor Portuguese family, she excused herself to sleuth, and "from the bathroom she learned there were many males in the family who aimed at the toilet and missed, there was still a baby in diapers, and she would use a convenient McDonald's on her way to her next interview instead" (61).

No wonder Becky hated her mother's *National Enquirer*, which added even more sensationalized social chaos to their lives. Becky preferred "the clean tidy space of the evening news. Those people had never seen a roach or a brown rat. Those people had never had ringworm or scabies. Their underwear would be new and crisp as fresh lettuce" (53). Her longing for this kind of order propelled her into a shallow marriage, entrance prize a condominium that had already depreciated when Leila visited. There had been just time enough "for the decks to begin to sag, paths to be worn across the skimpy grass, plastic to start cracking and aluminum to warp out of shape, the trim to cry for paint it was not getting" (62).

For Becky, that condo had been paradise—until, of course, they moved to a nicer one in Falmouth 16 months later. Again, newness bought her brief paradise: "She regained that sense she had enjoyed right after marriage of things being perfect, unworn, unsoiled" (208). By then, she had grown to hate visiting her family home, with "the smells, the utter chaos, the inevitable decay and disintegration caused by eight people living in a small space" (198).

Domestic order reflected economic security, and poverty meant social and domestic chaos. Leila gave us a slightly different picture: she grew up poor too, but the source of chaos was not crowding or insufficient resources, but a lack of care. She survived "a childhood of haphazard meals and half-empty refrigerators with nothing more substantial than open jars of pickles and maraschino cherries and ketchup to satisfy the hunger of an oversized and rapidly growing girl child" (115). We could attribute that to a single mother working, but the same hint of insufficient love and reassurance showed up again and again in Leila's adult musings. What she experienced was a different kind of poverty, one with more emotional overtones, and it left her determined that her life would revolve around a loving family, and their holiday tables would groan with "way too much food" (115).

On Thanksgiving, "Leila, whose meal was under control and on schedule, basted the turkey and prepared the pie," using her carefully established domestic order, ritual and sufficiency to ward off the social chaos of her husband's affair, her son's absence, her mother's lesbianism and her best friend's death (119). Thanksgiving Day she was traditional Leila, using habits of many years' standing to cope like Hera with a wayward Zeus. When she received Nick's note about his affair, however, the domestic consequences *reflected* the chaos:

> She heard the crash and saw that she had taken up the Imari plate he
> had given her three years before and smashed it against the table. The
> table had a visible scratch and the plate was in fragments at her feet. (24)

The marriage she once thought beautiful was in pieces, too, her regret overshadowed by long-suppressed rage. Leila used the table and plate, props of everyday life, to give her emotions physical form and consequence.

So did Mary, when she remembered her past naïveté. She had planned to be a perfect wife and mother: "To her loving faceless husband, she would bear two children, a boy and a girl, and live in a nice house where she would cook good meals for her family and care for them. Until she turned forty-five, her life was just that way." Now, however, all the rules had been broken, her safe world destroyed, her very survival thrown into question. Her imagination found the perfect image: "She had been swimming in a big pink aquarium and she never thought that somebody would come along with a hammer and break it until she was gasping for her life and everything she had taken for granted, for permanent, was gone" (86).

Mary comforted herself by observing her clients' houses and thereby their lives. "Mrs. Landsman's house was a mess," she noticed sharply. "Why did she call this Mrs. Landsman's house? Probably Mrs. L. thought it was hers" (86). Mary assumed—incorrectly—that Nick was the breadwinner, and her own traumatic experience left her ready to extend a patronizing sympathy.

More similar to homeless Mary than anyone in the middle class might want to admit, Ginny in *A Thousand Acres* cooked and cleaned to endure a childless marriage. Then a series of psychic jolts loosed social chaos—incest, an affair, familial and marital strife, a lawsuit—and she could no longer sublimate her emotions into domesticity. When she left home, we finally heard her true feelings, soaked in ironic nostalgia. "A certain type of man reminds me of Ty," she commented, "and when I think of him I remember the ordered, hardworking world I used to live in, Ty's good little planet" (370). It was never Ginny's planet; she survived by following someone else's rules.

In *The Other Side*, social chaos invaded at the outset, when stroke-bemused Ellen wandered outside in her nightgown, violating all propriety. Vincent tried to follow her and fell. Lying helpless on the floor, he had to shatter his own windows with keepsake figurines to attract help. The paramedics' cavalier attitude made the disruption of home and memory even more painful: "'It's a shame there's so much furniture,' one of them had said" (40).

At the novel's end, likable Dan stands in the hallway of Vincent and Ellen's home realizing how deeply "he believes in human frailty. He sees the wholeness of all life, the intricate connecting tissue" (349). He remembers the broken figurines, "but there is Franklin Roosevelt, intact" (350). Domestic order has survived

Domesticity can stall, escape or outlive social chaos; it can also bind people into a community. In *The Kitchen God's Wife*, Winnie tells us the men liked Wen-Fu for his generosity as a host. A good wife, she obligingly "made dinner for fourteen people. Hulan offered to help me shop and cook. And with so much to do, I protested only a little, before agreeing I could use her extra hands." Winnie accepted friendship and support to create a wider community, and she used her dowry money to buy the food—money given to her by her family on her wedding day, as passage from one social bond to the next.

Why did Tan emphasize her free choice, her deliberate generosity? To show how urgently Winnie wanted to create a domestic center from which she could reach out to the world. She bought and cooked extravagantly because the pilots' planes might be shot down the next day; like the maid in *Babette's Feast,* she was determined to make life's value sacramental. "I decided also to include a few dishes with names that sounded lucky," she added. "These were dishes I remembered Old Aunt had cooked during the New Year" (247). She was applying family tradition to a social crisis, using domestic ritual to bring hope and joy.

Something similar happened when Winnie left Wen Fu. Not only did he refuse to divorce her, but he held a gun to her head and raped her. Helen told Winnie, "We must think about what you should do, where you should go," then immediately walked over to her sewing basket—feminine symbol of self-sufficiency—and pulled out money. Auntie Du sighed, accepting the inevitable, and walked into the kitchen, where she "found dried fish, mushrooms, noodles, and tea, then wrapped each of these things in clean paper" (396). The food represented a loving wish for Winnie's survival, and paradoxically, its motherly gift inaugurated her independence.

Psychic Order

Chaos and order tug at each other rather obviously on the physical and social levels; they tug less visibly, but just as powerfully, at the psychological level. Housekeeping's concrete forms often correspond to an economy of order and chaos inside our heads and hearts. Home is a state of mind, a residence for all our images of protected intimacy, nurture and restoration. Home is somewhere we belong, somewhere they have to take us in. In Hebrew, Rabuzzi notes, "home" and "family" and "house" are all the same term, *het.* That word is used about 2,000 times in the Old Testament, and in Ruth 4:11 it is a verb that means producing a family (44).

If the concept of home has wide, deep associations for us, then what we do to create, order and maintain our home will reflect them. Home occupies symbolic as well as actual space, and when we sort, straighten and tend, we act on our psychic as well as our physical environment. Our internal need for order—and our capacity to create order—spend themselves externally. Just as Pauline, in *Tracks,* tended the dead to soothe her psychological sickness and alienation. Just as Winnie in *The Kitchen God's Wife* tried to clean away her shame and fear after learning that Wen Fu had died on Christmas Day. At first, when Helen told her to "sweep your floors, sweep him out of your mind," Winnie resented the facile advice.

"What does Helen know about sweeping? If you looked at her kitchen floor, you would see—dust balls as big as mice, black smudges polished smooth in every corner, twenty years' worth, all the disappointments she thinks I can't see" (90). But the basic psychological equation between disappointments and dirt ran deeper than Winnie's resistance.

She was frightened because if she told the truth about Wen Fu (Pearl's real father), she would feel shame and cause her daughter pain. So she responded in classic feminine tradition: "All night long I cleaned my house to forget. I shook my curtains, beat my sofa, dusted my tables and the rail going up the stairs. I wiped down the TV set, wiped the picture frame on top, the glass, looked at the picture underneath: Jimmy." He was her second husband, the one she adored. Reminded, she went into the bedroom and changed the sheets on "the same bed I shared with Jimmy, the curve of his body still sunken in." It was a chance to touch and cleanse the bed, the marriage, the memories. Still in emotional upheaval, grief for Jimmy mixing with the horror of Wen Fu and the hardships of the past, she went into her son's old room. There she found plastic airplanes he had made, Japanese and American bombers, "the little soldiers running away on his desk." Just as she and Helen had tried to run away from the war; just as Wen Fu had run away in cowardice (93).

Earlier, Helen had told Winnie she was bad for thinking (hoping) that her husband would die in the war. "When I no longer wanted to hear her words in my head, I searched for something to do," she recalled. "I opened a drawer and took out some cloth given to me by New Aunt, a bolt of cotton made by one of our family's factories." Winnie remembered the cloth perfectly—pale green cotton with small gold circles—and she already had the pattern in her memory, copying it from a dress she'd seen on a carefree girl. Hoping to sew her way into a more ideal state, she imagined herself blithe, admired, perfect.

> But then I saw Hulan criticizing the dress, saying in her too loud voice,
> 'Too fancy to wear after a husband has just died.'
>   Right away I made a mistake—cut a sleeve hole too big—that's how
> mad I still was. Look what she did! Affected my concentration. (241)

Helen would use the same method later, after an epidemic killed both her husband and Winnie's son. At first, bewildered, she resisted the news. "Then she became very busy cleaning her house, washing the walls and the floors with turpentine. Only when she finished could she bring herself to write Winnie with news of little Danru's death" (472).

In *A Thousand Acres*, Ginny used the same time-honored method:

> The shades were drawn, and the whirring sound of the machine was like

> a den I could curl up in, safe from my father's vagaries, Caroline's furies,
> and Rose's vigilance. And I was not immune to the accruing virtue of the
> clean, richly colored swathes in front of the cleaning head. It was like
> combining a field, except what you left behind seemed deeper and more
> fertile than before, rather than the other way around. I cleaned without
> a break, and when I turned off the machine, I had worked myself into a
> rather floating state of mind, abuzz with white noise, effort, and sweat.
> (121)

Euphoric in her chore-altered state of mind, she stood, stretched with the
proud ease of a woman whose hard work is well done, and "pushed
through the door into the kitchen," assertive in her own sphere. She was
still carrying the reservoir of dirty water; the relief from tangled worries
is always temporary. In the kitchen, Ginny found Jess Clark "standing in
the middle of the floor," anchored and confident, smiling at her. She
jumped, startled out of her safe private world, and the dirty water
sloshed. When Jess invited her out for a walk, she accused him of appear-
ing suddenly; he told her she was oblivious; she got irritated. But the psychic order she had just created bought her instant relief: "The irritation I'd
voiced floated away under the influence of the buzz and the virtue" (121).
    She had to use the same method less happily later in the novel. After
she gathered her courage to tell Jess she loved him and he said, "Oh,
Ginny," she went home and, after untold agonies, grimly started to wash
the breakfast dishes. Then, when her marriage began to disintegrate
noticeably, it was signs of domestic chaos—"dirty plates in the sink,
chicken bones in the garbage can, and the coffeepot warm on the burner"—that told her of her husband's movements in and out of the house.
He had eaten and left; Ginny did neither. "I couldn't eat, so I began
straightening the house up. It didn't take long—it was the one thing I still
knew how to do" (253).
    As the summer of discontent wore on, she honored the lawyer's
admonition to be respectably domestic, cooking big meals for all the farm
help. Rose helped her, but they didn't talk much: "The kitchen was like a
steambath, too hot for getting worked up." Again, an external mirroring
of internal chaos that in some mysterious way eased the pressure. Finally,
one Sunday afternoon, Ginny was "basting a turkey for supper and
washing dinner dishes"—good wifey—"when Ty came in the back door
and threw some dirty rags on the floor." Not such a good little wifey after
all: the rags were the nightgown and underwear Ginny had buried after
she tried again desperately to get pregnant, miscarried and hid the evidence (255).
    After Jess gave Ginny hope by blaming her infertility on the well
water, domestic tasks regained a pleasantly dreamy cast: "I thought

about such things all afternoon, basting the turkey, peeling potatoes and carrots, snapping beans, icing the applesauce cake Rose had baked, putting a jug of sun tea in the deep freeze to cool" (256). Chores offer wonderful cover for seething emotions: they can distract someone suffi-ciently to let her think risky thoughts, or open and drain a painful wound. In *Beloved*, Sethe worked by old habit while summoning the nerve to tell Paul D what happened to her on Sweet Home:

> Sethe took a little spit from the tip of her tongue with her forefinger. Quickly, lightly she touched the stove. then she trailed her fingers through the flour, parting, separating small hills and ridges of it, looking for mites. Finding none, she poured soda and salt into the crease of her folded hand and tossed both onto the flour. Then she reached into a can and scooped half a handful of lard. Deftly she squeezed the flour through it, then with her left hand sprinkling water, she formed the dough.
> 'I had milk,' she said. 'I was pregnant with Denver but I had milk for my baby girl.' (16)

The white men stole her milk and whipped her, and once she worked her way through to that confession—instead of using household tasks to sup-press those memories—a slow healing began. But the old lessons were well learned, and when Paul D returned the confidence, talking about the tobacco tin buried in his chest where a red heart used to be, she rubbed his leg steadily:

> She hoped it calmed him as it did her. Like kneading bread in the half-light of the restaurant kitchen. Before the cook arrived when she stood in a space no wider than a bench is long, back behind and to the left of the milk cans. Working dough. Working, working dough. Nothing bet-ter than that to start the day's serious work of beating back the past. (73)

Housework soothes; after years of practice, the actions come by rote, and the mindless, habitual nature of the work—which at fresh creative times can drive you crazy—quiets you. In *The Longings of Women*, when Leila's adored but unfaithful husband Nick was off in New York agoniz-ing over the opening of his play, she stayed home, "straightened her drawer of pantyhose, placing blacks with blacks and reds with reds. It momentarily soothed her. She sewed a button on her black silk blazer. She mended the pocket of her raincoat. She put her earrings together by pairs" (96).

If such tasks were as easy as Prozac, however, more men might do them. A chore's medicinal effects are circumscribed and not always reliable. When moral Mary was tempted to steal a sleeping bag from Leila, the chaos of desire clashed with conditioning, so "she cleaned the downstairs at a breakneck speed, scrubbing furiously, bashing that vacuum to and fro like a speeded-up video. Before she let herself touch it again, she cleaned the master bedroom and its bathroom" (190). Then she stole the sleeping bag.

For young Denver in *Beloved*, the internal chaos was the loneliness she felt before her sister's ghost came to live with them. She craved Beloved's "look," her recognition, affirmation, connection. So Denver did whatever she thought would elicit that look, which included keeping up a running stream of commentary while they worked around the house:

> No given chore was enough to put out the licking fire that seemed always to burn in her. Not when they wrung out sheets so tight the rinse water ran back up their arms. Not when they shoveled snow from the path to the outhouse. Or broke three inches of ice from the rain barrel; scoured and boiled last summer's canning jars, packed mud in the cracks of the hen house and warmed the chicks with their skirts. All the while Denver was obliged to talk about what they were doing—the how and why of it. (120)

She was explaining life to a baby in an adult's body, using ordinary work as a textbook.

The joy of a newly-forged family entered the domestic sphere again when Sethe, Denver and Beloved went ice skating. They shared a gleeful, interwoven fun that turned cozy when they returned home to warm themselves with cocoa and crawl into bed. The next morning, Sethe tiptoed around the kitchen, "happy to have them asleep at her feet while she made breakfast. Too bad she would be late for work—too, too bad" (182). The joy and security of family finally outweighed the work she'd done to survive and forget. She beat eggs into hominy cakes, fried them with luxurious pieces of ham, and went to work late, "wrapped in a timeless present" (184). Her sense of security lasted: "Sawyer shouted at her when she entered the kitchen, but she just turned her back and reached for her apron" (188). She, like Debbie in *The Longings of Women*, had found Rabuzzi's "positive face of chaos: a letting go into the possibilities that freedom from externally fixed routine allows. This face of chaos allows you to be one with the moment," receptive, freely responsive, independent of "all the shoulds and all the fixed structures" that constrain our daily lives (153).

Housework can reflect either positive or negative chaos, either positive or negative order; it can represent constraint and oppression or release and redemption. In *Domesticity and Dirt*, Palmer notes that "links between housework and psyche depend on the home as the center for intimate and sensual existence. Housework took care of those things that society found most unappealing, embarrassing, and tainted: the visible needs and evidence of fallible bodies," and its nature depended on the housewife's relation to those bodies. Housewives, or their domestic alter egos, prepared the food to sustain bodies (transforming other living things into dead forms for people to ingest) and cleaned up the detritus left from meals (145).

In *Tracks*, after fretting for days about her son's doings in the woods, Margaret finally secured information about Fleur from Pauline. Relieved and triumphant, "for days after their conversation, Margaret cleaned and swept with new vigor" (54). In *The Longings of Women*, by contrast, Mary divined Nick's abandonment from the surface chaos: "Usually the Landsman house was messy rather than dirty, but this week it was a sight...a foul mix of dirty laundry and things fallen off hangers" (42). After surviving her husband's infidelity, her rage and their marriage's severance, Leila eventually reached a sense of wholeness. Mary sensed the change: "The house had not returned to its abandoned air. Mrs. Landsman seemed to be eating regularly and keeping things in reasonable order" (149). Soon Leila's future partner, Zak, would study her ordered home and say, "'It's hard for me to imagine, looking at you in your own setting, how you could drum up much real empathy for women who are poor, disorganized, confused, impulsive—for people with sloppy lives'" (160). Inside *and* out.

Safe Home

Domestic activity—or its absence—can reveal chaos, but in general, home represents safety, security, sanctuary from the outside world. Its sheltering walls and solid lockable doors carry meaning in direct proportion to the harm that can befall us *away* from home, which may be why only one image of safe shelter emerged in *Tracks*. The Ojibwa were perfectly comfortable in the woods: they built and inhabited houses, but their utmost concern was losing their land. The single image of shelter was rudimentary, almost primitive: Margaret found pregnant Sophie paralyzed outside, "hopped four poles with her hatchet" (using the four-cornered orientation common to most of the world's homes) "and pounded them into the soft earth around the girl. She draped the oilskin over this, made a rude little sagging shelter with Sophie beneath it, wet and wretched and still" (90). Sophie was unmarried, pregnant, of mixed blood, hexed and ashamed; the image showed her helpless, cast out of the civilized community.

Domesticity did provide Ojibwa women refuge in other ways, however. They used their skills to work magic, heal and sustain life, keeping each other safe. Both Fleur and Margaret continued cooking at times of crisis, and Pauline, shamed by Margaret's sexual innuendo, "crammed the corner of her apron into her mouth" (53).

There were no strong images of safe home in *The Kitchen God's Wife*, either; most of Winnie's recalled experiences took place traveling through a war-torn country. Her father's home, her original place of safety, had fallen into a disrepair linked with his betrayal of his country. Similarly, the house in *Beloved* began as a safe haven for Sethe, but after the white men invaded that refuge, she did murder there. The house became haunted, and her magical thinking trapped her in an ambivalent love of the place. When Paul D urged her to leave the place, she recoiled in a domestic self-defense, loyal to her own need to connect to beautiful surroundings:

> This house he told her to leave as though a house was a little thing—a shirtwaist or a sewing basket you could walk away from or give away any old time. She who had never had one but this one; she who left a dirt floor to come to this one; she who had to bring a fistful of salsify into Mrs. Garner's kitchen every day just to be able to work in it, feel like some part of it was hers, because she wanted to love the work she did, to take the ugly out of it, and the only way she could feel at home on Sweet Home was if she picked some pretty growing thing and took it with her. The day she forgot was the day butter wouldn't come or the brine in the barrel blistered her arms. (22)

In *A Thousand Acres*, Ginny's great-grandparents ordered a house by mail. The Chelsea kit came with every board, joist and nail, and they proceeded to construct a civilized abode amid acres of farmland. Two generations later, Ginny's home nearby was more trap than sanctuary. She quietly buried her miscarriages outside and never even contemplated leaving this fertile part of the world. Watching the pine trees, listening to the hogs clank their feeders, she thought, "It was the same calm and safe vista that was mine every night.... it suited me, and it was easy to let it claim me every night" (27). She passively accepted the place's hold on her—which was, of course, linked to her father's hold on her.

Domestic work still retained the power to make Ginny feel safe, however; after informing her that their father had sexually abused them, Rose returned to the sewing machine, and "the methodical way she assembled her pieces, transformed them into a pair of tan slacks, was reassuring enough" (274). Even Ginny's own kitchen was a safe and pleasant place, as Jess commented when he came over for supper. When Henry the minister showed up to pry in pastoral guise, she took refuge in domestic activity, using it to regain control of the situation. "I couldn't tell whether I mistrusted his office or him, but either way, there would be no confidences," Ginny recalled. "I set my coffee cup on the table, stood up, and went to the sink, where I wrung out the sponge under a stream of hot water." Smiley magnified every detail for us, as the habitual actions became a ritual of self-defense. "I began wiping the table. I said, 'Lift your cup.'" No please or thank you, no deferential murmur of hospitality. Just a peremptory, "Lift your cup," and it worked. "He lifted his cup," Ginny recalled with satisfaction. Then, contenting himself with the admonition that she should at least come to church on Sundays, he departed (267).

In *The Other Side*, domesticity was even more of a stronghold. Vincent and Ellen were immigrants whose primary task was to anchor themselves in America and make a home for their family. The entire book took place in that home, and we learned each character's attitude toward the homestead and the concept of home. The matriarch "had clever fingers, she could do things with the rough, unpromising material, quicker than the others"—whether that material was her friend's coarse hair or her family's flawed lives (111). Her granddaughter used to lie that everything was fine at home, that her mom made her breakfast.

> In truth, Cam walked two blocks every morning to her grandmother's and headed for the kitchen, where she'd watch her grandmother's clever hands, deft but bluntly molded: their padded fingertips, their pinkish palms. She would watch her crimp pastry, fill it with fruit, shut the oven door angrily, hard, bang down her pots, chop violently, stir deliberately, slip silently to Cam a nip of pastry, a tender carrot, or a spoon of soup.... By the time her grandfather came to the kitchen, washed his hands at the sink, Cam's cramped limbs had relaxed. (44)

Her grandmother's hands *did* things, performed the tasks a mother should have been able to perform. Despite Ellen's "violent" chopping and political curses, she was tender in giving Cam little tastes, acknowledging her presence without asking her to carry adult burdens. Cam "had been set free by her absorbed, purposeful grandmother. And Ellen had been in turn set free by her own skill, and her consuming tasks" (44–45). She accepted her responsibilities matter-of-factly, taking control of every domestic situation. "Dad, it's lunch now," she called, not "I've fixed you some lunch" or "Would you like lunch now?" but "it's lunch now," invoking a divine order of necessity with which she only cooperated.

Pathetic Magdalene, by contrast, never grew up; she even fantasized a burglar hurting her and Cam coming to her rescue. "She touches her hair and feels patches of sticky drying blood. She's helpless until Cam comes home. Cam sees her and starts crying. She unties her, bathes her, dresses her in nightclothes, puts her to bed" (315). Magdalene craved the mothering she was unable to give.

Ellen's own childhood home was safe and happy in the beginning. "All day in school she longed to be running up the road, from chalk, back to the heaven of the room she lived in with her mother, to hear the sure click of her thimble, the wooden spoon against the pot side" (90). That "sure click" had the competence Ellen later developed; it allowed her to use her domestic skills first to support herself, and then to fashion a haven for her family.

She decided early in life that home mattered tremendously, both as socioeconomic index and existential validation. Comparing herself to girls from "better homes," Ellen "curses them all, their sense of gratitude and having been well situated. WE ARE OF THE HOUSE. WE ARE THE HOUSE. *We count for something, as the house does; we weigh, as it does*" (114).

After repeatedly impregnating Ellen's mother, her father hired a woman named Anna Foley to help with the housekeeping.

> So they created between them, Ellen and Anna, a shelter for the mother. Anna, unhoused, the middle girl of a dreamless family, called up a romance from some hidden part of her and pressed it down: a lozenge of devotion that expressed itself in furious domestic passion. To the linens lately bought through the father's prosperity, the crockery kept from the first day of marriage, the white curtains, the long table where they took their meals, she paid the homage she would once have paid to the person of the mother, whom she counted herself blessed to serve.

Anna was "unhoused," therefore eager to do someone else's work, as was Mary in *The Longings of Women*. Anna saw no reason to live if she had to work only for herself; she was instinctively domestic, eager to nurture and even to worship with religious devotion (Gordon 91). Fortunately, she "had her work cut out for her. It was important work. She understood it perfectly and did it well. She saw herself the solid prop that held up the abode of two superior creatures" (92).

When Ellen came to the States, the early days were hard and lonely, and she went to her married friend Delia's house for the comfort of "the old food, the soda bread, potato with butter and a drop of milk, the stirabout, the meat cooked black, the dense, muffling comfort of the sweets: rice pudding, trifle, custards, sago," with Delia heaping the plates time and again (138). It was the kind of repetition that makes a mantra soothing: if she could still taste home, she could still feel its safety.

Once Vincent and Ellen had their own house, it became the sanctuary.

Ellen went through the same experience Ginny had in *A Thousand Acres* every time parish priests came to the house: "One, threatening her with hellfire, in her kitchen, told her of her melting bones to come" (148). Set off in apposition, the "in her kitchen" adds a feisty note of indignation; the kitchen was clearly the woman's domain, and not even a man of God dared threaten her sway.

Cam, too, found early shelter in the domestic but, freed by a different sort of marriage and a shift in societal expectations, did not even bother to make a home. In *The Longings of Women*, by contrast, Mary sought the security of homebound domesticity with every breath. Toward the end of the book, she had picked up the unlikely language of a street person, and instead of noting how clean or messy Leila's house was, she told herself gleefully, "This was going to be a cozy squat. Mrs. L. always had plenty of food in the refrigerator and the cupboards, and she did not keep a tight inventory. There were comfortable places to sit and draperies to draw" (343). Yet the transition back to earlier values and attitudes happened just as inevitably:

> Every time she washed dishes in the kitchen that was sort of hers, she remembered what it had been like never to know where she would lay herself down that night, never to have enough sleep, never to have more than she could carry with her at all times. (425)

Washing dishes is a proprietary act; it's hard to initiate the dishwashing in someone else's kitchen. Do they use a squeegie or a scrubbie or a Handi-wipe? Do they pour boiling water over and air-dry, or rinse each dish as they wash it, or save water and rinse them at the end, or just let the soap dry? Is there a trash compacter, can the remains of noodles go down the drain, do they compost? Stupid questions become urgent when a highly procedural task is owned by someone else.

Consider how delighted Becky was that "she had dishes that matched, they had a kitchen with tiles and appliances she kept without a fingerprint." She told us about her condominium as though it were a church: "The bathroom was sanctified by cleanliness and smelled of pine disinfectant, after shave and lilac bath gel.... Every evening after a day at work, she tried to do one good thing for this precious sanctuary from noise and dirt and squalor." The condo structured her life, alpha and omega: "Every morning she woke and looked at the beautiful unmarred ceiling and the curtains with the blue and white pattern of perky sail-boats and she sighed with pleasure." Like a dutiful acolyte, "she kept the windows and mirrors clear. She scrubbed the burners and placed over the heating coils pretty covers with daisies" (232). In the evening, "she floated around the condo, picked up a stray sock of Terry's for the hamper, gave a little spray of polish to the coffee table. It was the time for her to make love with the condo she adored" (255).

Despite their transcendent ambiance, Becky's efforts had a great deal to do with societal approval: "No matter if Mrs. Burgess peeked in her drawers and in her corners, never did she find dust bunnies." When all that virtue went unrewarded by the temple high priest, the foundation of her faith, hope and charity crumbled into bitterness. "I am a good wife, Becky told herself, and he doesn't appreciate me" (232–233). Meanwhile, Terry lost his job—and when the tithe disappeared, chaos invaded the sanctuary. "Now the condo was never neat. His golf sweater flopped over the back of the chair. His clubs fell over when she opened the hall closet. Wrappings from a fast-food lunch lay on the counter and something sticky had spilled on the floor" (255).

Ghosts, Illness, Death and War

In many of her books, Toni Morrison has inverted the usual order, in which houses were stable vertical enclosures that shelter their inhabitants from chaos, and the outside world was horizontal, constantly shifting, always threatening. In *Beloved,* for example, the house became haunted, an invasion of the horrific that disrupted domestic routine. Denver needed extra help to grow up safely in such a house, so "after the cake was ruined and the ironed clothes all messed up," Grandma Baby gave her a talisman, telling her she was "charmed" (209).

Illness lacks a ghost's cachet, but it, too, can disrupt domestic order. Conversely, loved ones often use domestic acts as a vocabulary for tenderness. Poet Kathleen Norris, for example, wrote an essay titled "It All Comes Out in the Wash," in which she described how it felt to do laundry for a friend dying of ovarian cancer. The friend's husband had been washing the clothes unsorted and cramming the machine to its rubberized brim. Norton gladly offered to help,

> thinking of my own husband's disrespect for the sacred rituals of laundry, rituals that for the next few days would provide me with great consolation. Sorting and washing dirty clothes was a way of providing order in a world turned upside down by marauding cancer cells; hanging them on the line gave me time alone under the sky to grieve, and gathering the clean clothes in, smelling the sunlight on them, was victory. (16)

The nurses who tended Ellen around the clock in *The Other Side* were cooler and more impersonal, but took pride in their prevention of bedsores, their routine changing of the linens. The invalid's house had

shrunk to the four sides of the bed, and the chores radiated like spokes
from its heavy anchor.

When Ellen's daughter Magdalene developed breast cancer and Cam
bluntly informed her that she was dying, she came home from the hospital and redid her bedroom in purple, then "bought herself a bed fit for a
dying queen, a purple velvet spread, lavender sheets" (20). At that point,
Cam dutifully began doing her mother's domestic work, but with far less
tenderness than Kathleen Norris or even Ellen's nurses. Years went by,
and Magdalene failed to die. She stayed in her purple suite, hardly leaving the house, and her meals were either sustenance or party food.

> Last year she installed a microwave. In one lavender cabinet she keeps
> her foodstuffs: Cup-a-Soup and Noodle-roni. Waverly Wafers. Swiss
> Knight cheese. Every week she gives her daughter a list of food to buy,
> a list of liquor for herself and guests, handing the piece of paper to her,
> holding it at arm's length, holding it with her fingertips, as if they were
> distasteful to her, all these bodily needs. (47)

We move from illness in *The Other Side* to death in *A Thousand Acres*,
and the domestic realm comes with us. After Rose's husband drowned,
via either suicide or drunken accident, the grieving widow called her sister Ginny over in the middle of the night and offered her vodka.

> The living room was immaculate, the real Rose. Apparently she had
> been drinking and cleaning. She saw me looking around and said, 'You
> should see the kitchen cabinets. I wiped all the jars with soapy water and
> put down new shelf paper. Edged in black for widows. The funeral
> home has a concession. Shelf paper, drawer liners, inflatable sweater
> hangers, dusters made from raven's feathers, everything for the house-
> wife-widow. (296)

Housewife-widow had become Rose's new persona, courtesy of a consumer economy. She saw the irony, but continued nonetheless. Drunk,
she made Ginny help her move the couch out from the wall, so she could
uncover its secret dirt. (Remember that Rose was having an affair with
Jess—a different kind of secret dirt—at the time of her husband's death.)
"There was no stopping her," Ginny sighed, heaving the couch:

> Rose got the Electrolux out of the hall closet and plugged it in. After she
> vacuumed behind the couch, we tilted it onto its back and she vacu-
> umed dustballs off the underside. We pushed it back. Over the grinding
> roar of the vacuum cleaner, she yelled, 'Let's pull the stove out and I'll
> clean behind there.' (298)

Rose was yelling like an industrial work supervisor, urgent in her need for activity and absolution. But when they pulled the stove out, the floor was actually fairly clean. Still in need of catharsis, Rose made herself another drink. She must have been some of the guilt, fear and compulsion that plagued Becky in *The Longings of Women*, after she and her young boyfriend murdered her husband. When Detective Beaumont stopped by, Becky was scrubbing the bathroom (396).

Becky's work served two purposes: eliminate evidence and prove yourself a good wife. Plus, she seemed genuinely worried about the contamination of her clean home: "She had scarcely had a good night's sleep since they had shut her out of her condo. It really was a mess. They had taken some of the bloody bedding, but the carpet was stained. She had cleaners in and they charged her a bundle." Unbelievably, she was eager to resume sleeping in the bedroom, her only concern the "bad smell" from her husband's bloody death. "She was going to have to do that room over," she thought, noting that "the bedspread was gone, the curtains she had sewn herself had been torn and the bedside lamp broken in the struggle" (397). Paradise had been damaged, but it could be fixed. When Captain Edelson stopped by, "she followed him obediently up to her condo. It was neat and clean. He would not find anything out of order" (400). It was now "her" condo, and the most deviate, disordered human act had not stopped her from tidying it.

Multiply the murder exponentially but make Becky a helpless onlooker and you approach what happened to Winnie in *The Kitchen God's Wife*. She used domestic images to master the chaotic events:

> Suddenly machine-gun bullets hit a whitewashed building in front of me—and a long line of holes instantly appeared, just like stitches when the thread is yanked out fast. The piece of the wall underneath those empty stitches crumbled away, and then the rest of the wall on top fell down, like a big pile of flour that had lost its sack. (375)

The homely similes made war's apocalyptic agonies approachable, almost intimate. Winnie was comprehending the war in her own terms. After the gunfire, she opened her eyes to see a woman standing before her. "She held a poor straw broom in her hand. She was staring up at the sky, her eyes as big as eggs" (376). Her child had been killed in the bombing. Winnie looked around slowly, taking in "bits of blankets and stools, a bicycle wheel, a cookstove and pot, and torn pieces of clothing—only it was not just clothing, but a sleeve with a bent arm, a shoe with a foot, and things I did not want to recognize" (376–377).

Once the war was over, they left again, this time better equipped for domestic comfort. "We even had our own quilts with oilcloth bottoms,"

Winnie said, "just in case we needed to spend the night in a place without proper bedding" (403). They drove to her father's house, and she saw the front gate smashed, statues knocked down, the house painted in mismatched colors. Inside, the upholstery was worn, papers scattered everywhere. Seeing her shock, the servant "rushed ahead and swatted a sofa pillow, sending clouds of dust into the air. 'I've been busy with so many other things,' she said with a little laugh. She swept the hem of her sleeve across a dirty table" (412).

Winnie told the servant not to worry; war caused great suffering and changed everything—in other words, disrupting proper domestic routines. But a few sentences later, Winnie told her daughter, "So you see, our homecoming was very strange" (412).

Six

THE HOLLOW WOMEN

"My mother's in the corner
knitting a chicken."

Woody Allen, *Monologue*

My mother must have counted on me marrying money, because the only domestic lessons I remember were to iron the collar first and to open the rag and grab all the crunchy slimy dirt from the floor, rather than circle over it with a neatly folded square. At 25, I was suddenly taken with envy for women who knew their grandmother's methods of kneading bread, polishing with beeswax and soaking lemon oil into the furniture. No one ever *told* me, I wailed, checking household hints out of the library.

Or maybe I just wasn't watching.

McHugh describes transmission of domestic knowledge and skill as "mute pedagogy, knowledge passed on by a miming of the mother, by a wordless exchange" (9). That wordless exchange is a powerful one: housework is the first human work most of us observe. And since mothers are still the most frequent caretaker, and much of a home's inside work is still done by women, most children see the most influential person in their lives performing these tasks every day from infancy. For female children, especially, that performance sets up an equation between gender and domesticity—one we either fulfill or reject or, as is usually the case, keep trying to meet halfway.

"How often and in what subtle ways do we, against our best interests, conform docilely to circumstances no longer relevant (if they ever were) to the realities of our daily lives?" asks Jane Davison. "How often are we keeping someone else's house?" (22). In *The Fall of a Doll's House: Three Generations of American Women and the Houses They Lived In,* she traces her attitudes to the family matriarch: "She instilled, at least in this susceptible granddaughter, a deep sense of home as a woman's domain, as matrix. One definition of *matrix* is 'womb,' another is 'a binding substance such as cement in concrete.' Both definitions apply" (27).

Juxtaposed, "womb" and "binding substance" express some of the powerful ambivalence that lies within this generational transmission. Acts and perceived responsibilities that travel through a family's female members bring a sense of nurture, shaping, belonging, burden and complicity. They help a woman place herself within (or outside) the domestic feminine stereotype. They encode a list of expectations she must choose to honor or ignore.

In the second half of this century, those expectations have become increasingly problematic. The second-wave women's movement that started in the 1960s threw an acid-yellow spotlight on the domestic role, convincing women to make themselves at home in the public sphere instead of the kitchen. Feminist ideology clashed with early lessons, however. In 1971, Carol Eisen—casually claiming her husband the psychiatrist as her credential—analyzed her contemporaries' tangled attitudes toward domesticity. "You feel conflict between the desire to do what you want and the desire to do what you think you should. Making a bed, then, may bring up the conflict because it forces you to decide between doing what you want to and doing what you've been taught" (19).

Or, making the bed forces you to decide between doing what you want to and doing what the new feminist ideology says you should do; the knife cuts both ways. Once being a housewife ceased to be a laudable, logical role, women had to make conscious decisions about how many of their mothers' and grandmothers' overt and covert teachings they would follow. Those decisions formed part of the core of their feminine identity. But even if they identified with the traditional image, they might have refused to act it out. In Oakley's opinion, the degree of continuity between identification and orientation often hinged on the mother's behavior and attitudes, since "both imitation and rebellion are essentially aspects of the same identification process" (*Sociology of Housework* 185).

Is the determining factor how much a daughter loves her mother; how much she strives to be like her mother; how like her mother she is already in terms of values or disposition; or how happy the mother seems to be with her own role? In *Hard Choices*, Gerson points out the complexity of the influence. "Mothers may feel ambivalent about their own choices and their own children; they may also present ambiguous images and provide double, or even negative, messages to their daughters" (48).

To further complicate matters, once a woman begins keeping a house, she assumes the care of herself as well as its other inhabitants, becoming in that sense her own mother (Rabuzzi 135). That does not mean a simple echoing or mimesis. Gerson notes that "childhood experiences provide the context in which personal conflicts are formed, but they do not determine how, or if, these conflicts will be resolved in adulthood" (37). The wider social milieu plays a role, as do overlapping belief systems and accidents of personality or circumstance. We become our mothers, but never perfectly; we imitate them, modify them, react against them, rethink them. Along the way, we "develop structurally incompatible goals, needs, and capacities," remaining ambivalent even about those traditional expectations we choose to fulfill (34).

In *A Thousand Acres,* Ginny and Rose both learned domestic skills (and obligations) from their mother, who sewed and baked dutifully. Then she died, and Ginny and Rose took on the rearing of their baby sister, Caroline. They gave her the best start they could, doing all the housework themselves, and confining themselves to aspects of child raising they knew best: "sewing dresses and doll clothes, baking cookies...enforcing rules about keeping clean" (63). They did not make the tacit assumption, as their mother had of them, that Caroline would inherit their domestic obligations. Unsurprisingly, she was the sister who left home, choosing a law career in the city over domestic work on the farmstead. She also, perhaps not coincidentally, ended up the only sister independent enough to speak her mind to their father.

In *Tracks,* Pauline received many doses of domestic training, first in traditional Ojibwa ways by her family; then in the niceties of refined stitching by the nuns at the convent school; then in caring for the dying by Bernadette. Pauline's instincts did not include the nurturing that so often underlies domesticity, however. She used the power of her acquired skills to harm others and vindicate herself. Fleur, on the other hand, was untaught; the tribe's awe of her supposed relationship with the god of the lake had curbed any impulse to socialize her. When Fleur cooked or fed or tended, she did so because she wanted to, and it came naturally. Shorn of ambivalence, her acts carried tremendous creative power to heal, protect or save the land.

In *The Other Side,* Irish-Catholic Ellen felt constantly torn between the life of the mind she coveted and the life of the homemaker she felt was her duty. Her mother had fulfilled that duty until she became ill; like Rose and Ginny in *A Thousand Acres,* Ellen assumed domestic responsibilities early. "She hated the fine lace, the covered buttons, the exact folds, the silk ribbons, veils, false flowers, the embroideries, the small stitches: she knew the blood of slaves went into them. And yet they were her province" (117). More than once, Ellen "cursed her training at the Presentation convent," which focused on needlework, cooking and the painting of china, and feared ideas (125).

Ellen had plenty of fears herself, but ideas gave her strength to face them. Thus she did her duty as a housewife and savored serious information on the side—in stacks of papers on a bedroom chair, in files under the bed. Her daughter Magdalene rebelled against this example, choosing to work in a frivolous place, a hair salon, and drinking instead of cooking. In the mornings, she dropped young Cam off at Ellen's and hurried away, refusing even a cup of coffee on the pretext that the child had dawdled and now she was late. "The truth was that she didn't want to be detained for a second longer than need be in the domestic world her mother's house embodied" (210).

When it came time for Magdalene to mother, cook and serve, she played best friend instead:

> Sometimes she could catch her daughter off guard by making some warm, female nest, not womanly, but girlish: a lush refuge where two equals could retreat and settle. The two of them could sit on Magdalene's bed with its varieties of pillows and watch the Late Show and eat foods of great comfort and pleasure with no nutritive value at all.

The plan backfired: "As Cam grew older, she took on her grandmother's asceticism" (213). Severed from any female lineage with which she could comfortably identify, Cam ignored both her mother's girlish hedonism and Ellen's taskbound wifeliness. She chose instead to live the unlived life of her grandmother, shunning domesticity and immersing herself in ideas full time.

In *The Longings of Women*, Leila tried for the best of both worlds, combining her successful academic life with rituals of shopping, cooking, baking and serving. She, too, had a mother utterly uninterested in traditional domesticity: "Their apartment had been cleaned sporadically by whichever of them could no longer stand the dirt. Supper was slapped together by whoever was hungriest. When they had enough money, they got takeout." When they didn't, they ate the great American standbys: tuna casseroles and cream soup over something. As an adult, Leila was impressed by Mary, her shy poor cleaning woman, because "she knew how to take tannin stains from teapots and how to fix a sticky drawer" (103).

Becky, like Leila, was desperate to make a bourgeois home, but her struggling, overworked mother did not have the time or refinement to transmit the necessary skills. Objects took the place of apprenticeship: In the first weeks of her marriage, "the sheets had no stains, no history of sickness and pain.... The shower curtain had cute penguins on it. Everything was clean, everything was new, everything smelled fresh" (195). She took hope from the pristine objects, as young women have for centuries, tucking items into their "hope chests" to magically induce a happy future; registering for every piece of silver, china and crystal they can think of, as well as some whose purpose they don't even know. These are the grown Girl Scout's preparations for every contingency of domestic life; the dependent female's charms and spells and talismans.

Alas, when Becky tried to prove herself to her in-laws, she failed miserably. At the obligatory Sunday afternoon dinners, "she was expected to help Mrs. Burgess clean up, while the men took out the boat or just sat and watched a game on TV." Mrs. Burgess could have become the polished, gently instructing mother Becky never had; instead, she played the judge:

> 'Becky, put the pickles back in the jar. On the counter. Wrap the roast beef. No, Becky, not in aluminum foil. In plastic wrap. How am I supposed to see through foil? Becky! Think for a minute now and then. No, Becky, don't save the salad with the dressing on it. It gets soggy. If you wish to save salad, you must wash off the dressing gently and then dry it just as gently. That's the correct way to save salad. You have a great deal to learn about running a house properly.'

To make matters worse, Mrs. Burgess had rigid, superhygienic ways of loading the dishwasher, storing the knives and restocking the shelves. "Becky was used to her family's kitchen where everybody stuffed things where they would fit" (211).

Hoping to fare better on her own turf, Becky agreed to host her in-laws for dinner. Overwhelmed by options at the supermarket, she decided roast beef would be simplest, and—as young wives have for centuries—called her mother for advice. Mama was prompt and precise: "I put it in a pan with a little leftover wine, some tomatoes and onions and garlic and celery." Becky did her best to follow that recipe. Meanwhile, her tactless husband was inspecting the table: "Where's the fork for the appetizer.... Where are the flowers?" (213).

Information had followed the prescribed generational path, handed down from mother to daughter—but it was the wrong information for this social class. "Half an hour later, the only sound was knives grinding against china. The roast was tough and Mrs. Burgess openly laughed. 'Oh, Becky, poor thing, you've destroyed it. Did you start cooking it yesterday? You serve roast beef rare. That's the civilized way to treat a cow'" (214). Mrs. Burgess was *so sure*, so absolutely authoritarian in her domestic knowledge, that she was able to dismiss Becky with pity as a "thing."

If only Mary Burke had been there to help Becky! "A standing rib roast had been one of her specialties," Mary reminded herself sadly. Now everything had changed: "there were dishes none of her ladies ate that used to be common, like carrots in orange gelatin and vegetables in lemon, and the frothy gelatin desserts" (223). Why was Mary so disconsolate about the changes; why wouldn't a repertoire of new entrées delight a good cook? Because the change was one more reminder that everything she had learned was now useless.

In *The Kitchen God's Wife,* Winnie was desperate for such learning. Her mother had abandoned her, and her aunt was only interested in teaching her own daughter, Peanut, how to put a house in order. "New Aunt did not consider these were skills I should learn too," Winnie said bitterly. "But I watched. I learned without anyone telling me what to do." She noted the pulling and beating of the quilts' cotton batting; the oiling of the table legs; the shifting of furniture before dusting. She watched Old Aunt in the kitchen, using a hybrid of superstition and scientific precision:

> She lifted the lids on jars of peanut oil, soy sauce, and vinegar, smelled each one. She counted the number of fish swimming in a wooden bucket.... She scolded a cook's helper for letting too many clouds of fat float in the chicken broth, scolded another one for cutting strips of squid the wrong way: "Stupid girl! They must curl up into a lucky ball when cooked. The way you've done it, they'll look like leftover strips of cloth. Bad luck."

Winnie noted all the superstitions, arts and sciences that folded into domesticity. It became her responsibility to sort through the family's clothing, "mending anything that showed unlucky signs of prosperity coming apart—a loose thread, a little hole, a torn spot, a missing clasp or button." She came to womanhood knowing that in order to last and give you good memories, "everything must look good, taste good, mean good things" (136–137).

By the time Winnie was preparing her trousseau, she knew she needed two sets of everything. San Ma, one of her father's wives, accompanied her on the ritual dowry-shopping excursion, instructing her in social niceties and necessities. First, she would need 20 quilts to keep all her future children warm. Interesting, how this domestic motive changed Winnie's attitude. Usually modest, withdrawing and insecure, she came to spirited life and "chose good, thick quilts—all Chinese made, with lots of fine-weave banding around the sides. Inside, they were filled with the finest cotton batting, the most expensive, beaten many times until it rose up high."

They shopped every day for a week, mimicking the seven days of creation. "On the sixth day, we bought all my things for entertaining guests and honoring ancestors," she recalled. "On the seventh day, the last, we bought all my dishes and silver" (183–184). From those dishes, she would serve food that would sustain human life and keep her marriage divinely happy. At least, that was the plan. Even though it failed miserably, she still tried to teach this world view, this cosmic-practical body of knowledge, to her daughter. But Pearl found it all boring and far too much trouble, and was infinitely more interested in eating Big Macs.

The Housewife Trap

In Ingrid Wendt's poem "Dust," women who clean know it's what "you could order your life/around:/getting dressed to eat breakfast/for strength to finish the cleaning" (Hedges and Wendt 130–133). The daily, weekly and seasonal cycles of domestic work weave and unravel like Penelope. They can be a mantra or a trap—or both, as they were for Ginny in *A Thousand Acres*, after the lawyer told them to be respectably domestic if they wanted to keep the farm.

> I did what he said. I swept the porch, mowed the lawn, weeded the garden, canned tomatoes and pickled peppers and onions, mopped and swept and washed and dusted, and wore housedresses in the heat rather than shorts. I served up meals at six and eleven-thirty and five on the dot as if Ty were a train coming into the station.

After so many emotional upheavals (her infertility, her sister's cancer, her father's rage, her attraction to Jess), she enjoyed the structure: "It was like going back to school or church after a long absence. It had ritual and measure. Tasks proliferated." Soon she was compulsively nesting spoons and forks in a freshly lined silverware tray; using every vacuum attachment; repeating tasks two and three times. She surpassed obligation and started to think in terms of possibilities:

> Even though you had washed the supper dishes as you were cooking, you could jump up from the table when a serving dish got emptied, and wash it and dry it and put it away before finishing your beans. You could follow your husband from the door to the sink, and sweep the dust from his boots into the dustpan and throw it away before he was finished washing his hands, and then you could take the towel he had dried them with and run it downstairs to the washing machine while he was sitting down to his food.

That litany made Ginny's priorities as clear as an ammonia-washed window. Doing the tasks immediately and thoroughly had become more important than the reason for doing them, which might have meant keeping a happy, orderly home they both could enjoy. "I was amazed at what I didn't have time for any more," she noted, her tone both panicked and proud (285–286).

Ginny's mother had tied herself to chores in a similar manner, canning or cooking with Mrs. Ericson while their daughters sewed doll clothes. "Mrs. Ericson had a welcoming manner that my mother appreciated but couldn't master," Ginny recalled. "She always said, 'When I'm home, I've got to get things done, even if there are visitors. Elizabeth knows how to relax in her own house.' And then she would shake her head, as if Elizabeth had remarkable powers" (46).

For many women, the routine of domesticity quickly becomes overwhelming, or so addictive it dominates the rest of their lives. "In what sense can a housewife who has very high standards and extremely repetitive routines be considered 'pathologically' obsessed with housework?" enquires Oakley, describing the "houseproud" woman who is so emotionally involved in housework that her guilt, worry or anxiety does indeed suggest obsession (*Sociology of Housework* 108). Eisen tells her readers cheerfully, "You'll never get it all done because IT'S INFINITE. And being infinite, unstructured and undefined, it provides a remarkably fertile area for you to express your own hangups" (3). In other words, we live the myth of Penelope at her shuttle, weaving again and again because she unravels what she has woven every night. A woman's work is never done, simply repeated.

In *The Longings of Women*, when Mary Burke was married, she was consumed by domestic work, and it turned her into a servant. "She was a serviceable chauffeur for children needing to be taken to ballet lessons, basketball practice: she was a capable delivery boy bringing suits to the dry cleaner's and bags of groceries home" (148). When Mary was not schlepping children and objects, she was waiting—passive, dependent, reactive, locked into the mode of patient Griselda or of the goddess Hestia, keeper of the hearth. "A housewife didn't give much weight to boredom," she thought to herself, "because whether she was waiting for a husband to come home or a baby to be born or a load of clothes to dry or a roast to cook, she spent a lot of time exercising her patience." The days unwound from task to task, crisis to crisis, filled with small worries—"the driveway cement is cracking and the dog has to go to the vet for his shots and is it Ed Vickers or Ed Simmons that Dr. Caldwell can't stand at the dinner table with him?" (86).

When Mary lost her home and began cleaning her clients' houses instead, she kept her old compulsive habits, perhaps because they let her continue to feel safe and virtuous.

> Anything of theirs she used, she washed at once: compulsive, but part of her daily discipline. She had always been a mad housekeeper who never left dishes in the sink or beds unmade or dust under the couch. Besides, she owed it to the people whose houses she borrowed to return them at least as clean as she found them. Third, she had a policy, leave no traces. (129)

Even after Mary collapsed with pneumonia, she forced herself out of bed to clean the kitchen. Leila said crisply, "This is silly, Mary. Don't feel you have to be scrubbing everything." Mary replied, "I like to be useful," and Leila snapped, "That's the problem with both of us" (388).

In *The Other Side*, Gordon gave similar examples of compulsive housewives, including the Irishwomen, who, fearful of being thought slatternly,

> seemed, Dan thought, to have been taken up by an obsession with concealment, or protection, by impermeable plastic.... He watched the furious, the desperate, the anxiety-filled cleaning of the Irish women who had taken paying guests. He saw that there was nothing natural about their cleaning, nothing learned in childhood, practiced over the years. The cruel, expensive vacuum cleaners (Just doing a bit of Hoovering, so) set the rhythm of the day for these genuinely nice women and their families. (161–62)

The "genuinely nice women" cleaned because they were slaves to bias and machinery; Dan's ex-wife had no excuse. Later in the novel, Dan's daughter, Darci, told him she wanted to come live with him because her mother didn't want her around. "With me gone, they'll be happy as clams," she added. "Up at six in their jogging suits cleaning the bathroom tiles with toothbrushes and bleach" (355).

Cleaning house compulsively answers many needs: to feel virtuous; to distract oneself from less concrete problems; to obey parental or societal injunctions; to be needed; to feel one has validated one's existence. Yet another motive is pain: the housewife is emotionally wounded, thus anhedonic, forgetting about pleasure or denying it to herself. Thus Morrison's Sethe did years of guilt-driven housework before healing interrupted her. "She had been on her knees, scrubbing the floor, Denver trailing her with the drying rags, when Beloved appeared saying, 'What these do?'" The returned baby girl was holding a pair of ice skates, representing a playfulness Sethe had nearly forgotten. "On her knees, scrub brush in hand, she looked at the girl and the skates she held up" (173–174). That exchange led to the most joyful scene in the book, when Sethe abandoned work and went with her daughters to the frozen pond.

The grind of compulsive domesticity, by contrast, can leave its victim dependent upon others' approval or circumstances; helpless; empty; hopeless; anxious; bored; angry; apprehensive; passive; paralyzed or depressed. It can also breed a volcanic resentment. When Vincent asked his daughter to play the piano for him after supper, "he'd hear the angry banging in the kitchen: Ellen furious that Theresa had got out of drying dishes, knowing it was her job. It was Ellen's time to read, while the girls did the dishes" (Gordon 251). When Vincent walked through the house at night turning off lights and smoothing pillows, he realized he cared more about their furniture than Ellen did. "She said it was simply that he got away from it all day. By six o'clock, she said, the furniture became her enemy" (257).

Jane Smiley's Ginny had the same testy, martyred tone in her voice when she recalled her sister's bout with cancer: "All through the gloomiest April in years, I was cooking for three households.... My morning at the stove started before five and didn't end until eight-thirty" (7). Marge Piercy's Leila admitted how often she had envied her husband, "who seemed to have little need to do what he did not want to. As if she had ever been in the mood to cart David to the dentist.... She was forever doing things she felt had to be done" (201).

A constant sense of responsibility—and a constant perceived demand for responsiveness—make the rewards of housework contingent upon the human relationships within the household. And contingency means the rewards rise and fall with uncontrollable variables, making them as solid or as fragile as the family matrix itself. As more of modern life automates, accelerates, abstracts itself and splinters into fragments, the slow necessary repetition of intimate, mundane tasks and services becomes harder for many of us to accept and enjoy. If all conditions are not right— if one's husband ceases to be appreciative or one's children turn cranky— everyday chores quickly change from a mantra to a curse.

The Insufficient Rewards of Dreck

In *Working It Out*, Sara Ruddick notes how persistently, how automatically, women have been charged with domesticity, "this activity of world-protection, world-preservation, world-repair—the million tiny stitches, the friction of the scrubbing brush, the scouring cloth, the iron across the shirt...the invisible weaving of a frayed and threadbare family life" (xvi). Unpaid, women have been presumed to act out of love, instinct or devotion. The problems have begun as soon as love died, instinct faded, devotion was thrown into question.

Once again, *Tracks* yielded no examples of disillusionment with the private sphere; the Ojibwa had no private sphere. The white women in *The Longings of Women*, however, inherited the private sphere's divisions and expectations. Piercy gave us three very different examples of women who, betrayed in some way by their husbands, lost their grip on the household. Leila relaxed into messy abandon, then fell in love with someone different and started cooking again. Mary lost her home but kept the compulsive, careful, almost frightened aspect of domesticity as a way to salvage dignity. Changing clothes in a lavatory stall, she reviewed her wardrobe: "She had three blouses, two skirts, a wool dress and a sweater, each rolled and held with rubber bands.... She must wash clothes soon" (49). Mary continued to pride herself on her "fiber." And she remembered—as a measure of despair—information that was now useless:

> Jim hated his eggs runny. He wanted them fried until the yolks were solid and the whites, rubbery to her taste. His toast had to be close to burnt. On the other hand, she cooked her own bacon longer than his.
> She would go to the grave remembering exactly how Jim had liked his sirloin broiled, the barbecue sauce he favored, the way he liked his shirts lightly starched, the kind of ties he would wear. (263)

Becky fantasized her domesticity before experiencing it; when she met the rogue professor Ted Topper, "she saw herself laying a beautiful table for him with a perfect rose from the florist beside his plate" (69). Then he spurned her, just as Mary Burke's husband had, except that Mr. Burke "treated you like a piece of cheese that had turned bad" (83), while Ted treated Becky like a "dessert" that gave itself up gladly for his pleasure (71).

By the time she met and married Terry, Becky was prepared to be disgusted. And he did not disappoint her.

> Terry needed taking care of. He tossed his clothes when he undressed, and she had to pick up his socks, his briefs, his tees from the floor and the chair and the top of his dresser. He never thought about laundry or dry cleaning. He considered his clothes a self-enclosed system that functioned automatically: dirty clothes off, then the next morning, clean clothes appeared. (199)

Becky soon grew bored with running that closed system. She hated hauling heavy bags up the steps, and Terry never grocery shopped with her (200). She felt no inclination to cook when she got home from work, and they had traded in their domestic wedding presents—"two blenders, an electric knife and an electric mixer"—for a VCR (196). So, rather than bolster Terry's unemployed ego and win his worship with domestic excellence, she chose to murder him.

In *A Thousand Acres*, Ginny, the housewife *par excellence*, first began to see her marriage fall apart in the interchange at meals. The morning after the epic storm, she asked Ty, "How about a couple of fried eggs and some of those sausage links?" and his assent was cool, distant, unfriendly (197). Slowly, their relationship began to reconfigure itself. Weeks later, when Ginny cooked for the farmhands, they praised her cooking, and she turned to Ty hoping for the same warmth. "I said, 'Ty, honey, you look really beat,' and the man from Kansas started exclaiming about how much they'd gotten done.... I looked at Ty, but he was looking out the window. His plate was clean, so I said, 'Sweetie, you want anything more?'" (205). That night, Ty was asleep by the time she came to bed. A few nights later, *she* was in bed first, reading *Good Housekeeping*. With a housewife's practiced ear, she heard him eat a second helping of cake and rinse the plate. When he walked into the bedroom, she was staring blankly at an article about strawberry desserts. Again, she tracked his motions with the sonar some husbands jokingly claim is a uterine device:

> He threw his socks and underwear in the hamper, his work clothes in
> the work clothes bin.... When he went into the bathroom, I turned the
> page to 'New! Quick and Easy Strip Quilting.' I heard the shower go on.
> The first line of the article was, 'Love to quilt but hate to cut those pieces
> out one at a time?' I read it over, concentrating on each word. None of
> them made sense. (257)

Ginny did not meet her husband's eyes, and could not tell whether he was seeing her, because she was staring resolutely at the wifely rulebook that served as both protection and burden. As the wedge between them widened and cooled, the rulebook turned to nonce.

Amy Tan offered yet another disillusioned wife looking back on hollow domesticity. "In those days, I was still trying to please Wen Fu, to act like a good wife, also trying hard to find my own happiness," Winnie recalled. "I was always ready to cook a good meal, even though the men usually returned home without telling me ahead of time" (249). By the time she left Wen Fu, however, this eager hostessing was well behind her.

For these women, disenchantment was inevitable, because motivation was tied so tightly to the marriage. In *Tracks*, Fleur continued to cook and function whether Eli was around or not, but in cultures where the wife is cared for only by her husband and not by the entire tribe, her daily work has a more specific exchange value. Sequestered in private households, married women become isolated from each other and from the larger world. Arlene Rossen Cardozo analyzed her own and other women's experience in the 1970s, when, "with extended-family ties weakened and old friends scattered, loneliness became a way of life." Absentee husbands gave their time to work, leaving women alone at the helm of their suburban ships (2). Writing in the same time frame, Adrienne Rich commented, "The privatization of the home has meant not only an increase in powerlessness, but a desperate loneliness" (53). Thus in *The Longings of Women*, married Becky "tried to shake herself out of her funk. After all, if she was home, what would she be doing? Her old home.

Doing housework. Doing laundry, just like now. But at least there was always someone to talk to" (200).

Housewives' isolation made them tough to organize or politicize. As Oakley notes,

> The 'fit' between socialization for domesticity, adult performance of the housewife role and the other social arrangements in which housewives are often implicated (marriage and motherhood) makes for a particularly complete encapsulation within the world of traditional femininity. The more closed the system, the fewer the possibilities of seeing beyond it. (*Sociology of Housework* 193)

In other words, traditional housewives were cut off from their husbands, from extended families, from other women, from the larger culture and from alternative ways of life. That isolation lent inertia to the domestic sphere, even in a century of radical change. Surfaces changed, as new appliances and foodstuffs came to market, but domestic rituals retained many of the norms of the previous century.

Writing about ritual in general, Bell observes how easily we mistake a grudging, minimal consent by the participants for an underlying harmony and unity of purpose (210). Until recently, only women as strong and opinionated as Charlotte Perkins Gilman dared voice their discontent with domestic ritual. According to the physicians who prescribed all that Valium and psychoanalysis (see Abraham Myerson's *The Nervous Housewife*), many women in the 1950s, 1960s and 1970s were as depressed and unfulfilled as the "neurotic," suicidal poets, such as Sylvia Plath and Anne Sexton, who actually wrote about their plight. But every time a chorus of voices began to rise, domesticity was sentimentalized, the magazine industry made much of househusbands, a new trend made extra work fashionable (superhygienic bathroom tile; making your own pasta), or appliance manufacturers dazzled us with something that looked so fast and easy we could not possibly feel burdened.

Such trends are imposed rituals, if they qualify as rituals at all. True domestic rituals intersect with biology and necessity to regulate our common lives. And when they lose their power, Driver writes, we feel "a pervasive sense of anomie," a doom-filled directionlessness (140). In other words, we suffer an existential despair remarkably like the feeling many American housewives experienced in the decades after World War II. The 1950s attempt to make, preserve and bless a happy home prompted all sorts of ritualistic behaviors, but they clashed hard against many women's individual truths, and then they clashed against the resurgence of the women's movement. As Bell observes, "if cultural and sociological categories are experienced as discontinuous, the ritual which mobilizes these forces fails. Successful rituals are those in which these terms or forces are perfectly congruent" (34). Sunday dinner fixed at leisure in a happy, loving family. Weekly wash done by someone who takes it as her unquestioned, unresented duty, has the time to do it well, and treasures the skin those fabrics will drape, warm and protect.

When second-wave feminism insisted that women enter the public sphere and implied that homemaking wasted their abilities and kept them in drudgery, the ideas that had shaped a feminized domesticity began to grate against each other. Rather than expand existing definitions of maleness and femaleness, activists simply reversed them, urging the male success ethic on the not-so-happy homemaker. "Women's liberation, which originated as an attempt to fill the void, did not support the woman at home by helping her to alter the causes of her boredom and loneliness, but rather stated that she required freedom *from* home *for* 'something else,'" notes Cardozo (92).

The problem with inviting the private sphere into the public was that the shift often increased modern women's alienation instead of easing it. If part of women's discontent came from unsatisfactory family relationships and part came from isolation, deserting the traditionally female sphere entirely did nothing to restore its meaning, and juggling the traditional with the nontraditional only intensified the exhaustion and the loneliness. Ruddick points out that if women try too hard to fit the male model, if "we split ourselves off from the common life of women and deny our female heritage and identity in our work, we lose touch with our real powers," individually and as a community (xvii).

Judging by the resentment and panic that float through letters to *Ms.* and covens of Wiccans, many women have either lost touch with those powers already or are in immediate danger of doing so. Housework grows progressively less meaningful; when a ritual fails to overcome social alienation, it dissolves into mere routine. Routine does not participate in the sacred or the timeless; it is soul-deadening, uncreative, mechanically efficient, perfectly suited to an overbusy world with neither time nor sensitivity to heed its own gestures.

In *Tracks*, housekeeping remained powerful for every character except Pauline, who was alienated from the tribal community and could not define herself by participating in its wider meanings. In *The Kitchen God's Wife*, Americanization turned Winnie's traditional domestic rituals into Pearl's burdensome, never-finished routines. The same pattern marked *The Rest of Life*, as daughters and granddaughter either rejected or obsessed on domestic chores that, for Ellen, were stable rituals. In *The Longings of Women*, the loss of meaning came with the end of relationships: Becky felt burdened by domestic routine when she grew disillusioned with her new husband; Mary Burke began a life of alienated drudgery when her husband left her; Leila stopped cleaning and cooking when she discovered her husband's infidelity. In *Beloved,* by contrast, Sethe's and Denver's alienated domestic routine took on deep meaning as they opened their hearts and their lives, ultimately rejoining the community.

Thankless, Mindless and Endless Chores

Even if the marriage that inspires and justifies domestic work stays stable; even if lawyers and doctors dare to trade meatloaf recipes; even if they belong to a community (most probably a church group) that actually honors their domestic work, modern life can *still* make it seem tedious and unrewarding. Back in 1958, Hannah Arendt pointed out that "the daily fight in which the human body is engaged to keep the world clean and prevent its decay bears little resemblance to heroic deeds; the endurance it needs...is not courage, and what makes the effort painful is not danger but its relentless repetition" (101). Today, relentless ordinariness is even less tolerable, as media and computer technology accelerate us into an adrenaline-risky, caffeine-charged state of constant electronic stimulus.

Even if you're not "on the Net," even if you practice Zen Buddhism and shun TV, the temporary nature of housework can frustrate you. We have reached a time in which many of us have leisure—or at least the expectation of leisure. We want space in our lives for purely recreational pleasure; for hobbies that craft something permanent; for knowledge that deepens and grows. When we cook, "pretty or not, the handiwork is always eaten," notes Rabuzzi. What we have done is immediately destroyed, consumed, obliterated. Then we clean up, trading tangible dirt and mess for "a negative state, generally understood as an absence of disarray and filth rather than as a positive presence of order." We build sandcastles of food; we bail dirt from leaking dinghies.

In *The Other Side,* Ellen sensed from girlhood that a life concentrated on domesticity would be unrewarding and unserious. Her mind yearned for a larger arena, but exigency demanded that she make a living by sewing. One day another seamstress, Bella Robbins, revealed her own intellectual life by confiding that she was worried sick about a war:

> Her words were a knife slicing the thick air of the room of women sewing. Women stitching fine, beautiful stitches, women ignorant as dirt, skilled women, making things for other women who need do nothing for themselves, the unreal dreamwork of the dresses of the period. Bella's sentence let in life, breath, pulse, the whole world of ideas. (126)

Ellen and Bella became fast friends, talking, attending lectures, dreaming of large public rooms rather than cozy parlors, bedrooms or kitchens. "They stripped their dreams of the domestic with a devotion that was female in its thoroughness, as if they stripped a house for a spring cleaning" (131). They took union membership cards to sewing shops, where they set them on old dark tables "among the mix of threads, scraps, scissors, tissue papers" (132). The contrast was clear: the determined political symbolism of the hard-edged white card, set against the dark wood of female oppression and the multicolored, chaotic fragments of domestic work.

Ellen's daughter, Theresa, would have been more comfortable sorting those fragments than introducing union cards. "Theresa liked collecting, then discarding. Keeping straight. She'd come behind her mother, cleaning where she had just cleaned, reproachful." Because the two women's value systems barely overlapped, the reproach was ineffectual. Ellen simply turned around and snapped, "If you'd an idea in your head, or an interest worth a shilling in the world, you wouldn't have the time to be behind me with a dustcloth" (224).

Ellen's spirit was far more kindred to the stalwart domestic feminists who preceded her, and the second-wave feminists who succeeded her. She might have functioned more easily as the mother of Sara Ruddick, who writes bemusedly of the Woman's Life Plan she never found sufficiently clear, constructive and purposeful to follow. Ruddick deplored the schism Ellen took for granted. Rather than alternate between the public and private worlds, preferring the public but obligated by the private, Ruddick wanted to interweave them. She resented the assumption, when domesticity and other "feminine" concerns entered academe, "that the problems we need to examine are trivial, unscholarly, nonexistent. We are urged to separate the 'personal' (our entire existence as women) from the 'scholarly' or 'professional'" (xvii–xviii). After years of debate on these issues, Ruddick saw (as did author Mary Gordon) how important the ideas underlying domesticity could be. Ellen, on the other hand, accepted the societal definition of domesticity as intimate, temporary, small, mindless, trivial, feminine and inconsequential.

Ironically, Ellen's domestic life proved powerfully influential; her cooking and cleaning steadied the forlorn lives of Cam and Dan, centered and anchored Vincent, and provided the entire family with a homestead where they could gather to scrutinize their lives. The domesticity of Dan's cousin Sheilah, on the other hand, was pathetic. Because Sheilah had not succeeded in forging strong relationships—she was critical, unpopular and nitpicky—she burdened her domestic achievements with too many emotional needs, and they sank under the weight. Her work in the kitchen, preparing for the family gathering, illustrated this pattern.

First, she looked forward to a compliment from kind Dan, hoping "he notices how she's arranged the cold cuts, carefully, beautifully, she thinks, fanning out from the cherry tomato in the center like a star" (32). But

> even Dan, with his merciful eye, looks at Sheilah and sees failure. He sees the plate of cheese and cold cuts she has arranged to fan out like a star from the cherry tomato at the center and does not think, as she had hoped, how original, how pleasing. He notes with pity that this simple infantile arrangement took his cousin an hour and a half to effect. (34)

Sheilah couldn't help but see the ridicule in Dan's eyes, and it affected her deeply. First, she was crushed, and decided everything she had ever done or felt was ridiculous. Then she turned angry and blamed him for making her feel this way. That anger spun into fear and bitterness and took final shape as superiority, a haughty grudge against the women of her family. None of them would have bothered to arrange the food so attractively, she decided. "They'd have put it any old way, horrible, disgusting how they would have put it" (35). The more absurd and disproportionate the incident grew, the more it revealed about Sheilah's past, present and relationships. Several chapters later, Ellen railed, "There is no reason for Sheilah to use an electric knife on a block of Muenster cheese. It is a useless gesture, a misuse of power: it will get her nowhere, it will open her to ridicule, create a mess" (62).

Ellen's domesticity never opened her to ridicule; it created order from messes and established her power. But Sheilah spent too much time on the trimmings, hoping for attention. A law of domestic karma would have told her that necessary acts done for the family's sake yield untold rewards, but trivial acts done for reward yield only scorn.

Like Becky, Sheilah held a distorted view of what mattered in life, found it hard to love others, and had exceptionally little self-worth. Still, *any* woman who sets out to build an identity from domestic work, especially in modern America, will run into obstacles. Housework in a modern era is an endless manipulation of machines, bought goods and chemical solutions, and the housewife's role is devalued and disrespected. Spender summarizes the larger psychological trap: "It's the sense of injustice, the recognition that one's work is demanded but not rewarded, that it is necessary and yet invisible, which can undermine the existence of women: Is there in men's experience any such pervasive and pernicious equivalent?" (132).

No doubt there is; one thinks of the male clerks or schoolteachers who do unsung, painstaking work each day, harboring private dreams of glory. Or the blue-collar workers dulled into vain hopes of lucky lottery numbers as they manipulate widgets on the assembly line. Or the road crews dodging angry traffic to make the rest of us safe. Domesticity is just one more way to be invisible, because it has so often been apotheosized as unfulfillable angelic virtue or degraded as drudgery.

In *The Longings of Women*, for example, homeless Mary Burke went into a laundrette to use the bathroom. The others "barely registered her presence," and "Mary sat there as if she were a pile of laundry," reduced to a domestic object (16). Later, she ran into Leila's husband Nick while cleaning his house, and he said peremptorily, "Who are you?" She found the question insulting; true, "they hardly saw each other, but she'd been cleaning for them for a year. But she wasn't real to him. She wondered if he thought the house cleaned itself every Wednesday" (83). No doubt he did. It is so much easier to take for granted the work someone else does for us—or treat it as an overnight gift from the elves—than to remain sensitive, aware and constantly grateful for such an intimate service.

The lot of the service provider, meanwhile, spirals into drudgery, and if that person needs the job or marriage desperately, the expectations silence and enslave her. After Thanksgiving, for example, Mary walked into the Mafekings' house and found "burnt fat all over the oven, runover sauce on the stove, a mess of dirty pans in the sink. They had an old dishwasher that couldn't handle pans. She resented having to scrub pans from two days before, but she didn't say anything. It would be too easy for them to complain" (128).

Becky's "sweet and long-suffering and hard-working" mother was equally invisible. Becky always knew their house was "a dump," but she expected her new husband to honor her mother's domestic virtues. Instead, he showed his mother-in-law only an awkward resentment (197). In *The Kitchen God's Wife*, when Winnie visited her father's house after the war, a servant answered "wearing plain working clothes. She was not at all like a servant who would answer the door of an important house," Winnie noted scathingly, invoking the age-old domestic hierarchy. "She looked more like someone who cleaned things when no one was looking" (410–411).

When a homeless person, a poor person, a lowly servant or a cleaning woman is invisible, we nod, unsurprised. But Leila, too, felt she was or should be invisible. When she walked through their elegant Cambridge house, she noted the socially prerequisite Oriental carpets, "paintings by friends and acquaintances, David's attempts at art photography, photos and mementos of Nick's past successes" (24). She saw nothing that represented her. After her laborious Thanksgiving preparations, she won criticism from her son—"There's too much food"—and a reminder from her husband: "Leila, you've forgotten to change." She suddenly realized she was still wearing the old clothes she had cooked in all day. But instead of a healthily narcissistic bolt to the bedroom, she said, "Oh well. Nobody comes to look at me" (119).

In *The Kitchen God's Wife*, Winnie was anything but invisible: she was so domestic and so solicitous, she drove her daughter and son-in-law half crazy. She offered them tea, instant coffee and orange juice, the hospitality so persistent they went to bed in self-defense. She trotted after them, calling, "Enough blankets, enough towels?" They answered politely, turned off the light and waited five seconds. "Too cold? Heater can be turned up," Winnie exclaimed. Finally, Pearl heard her mother's slippers "slowly padding down the hallway, each soft shuffle breaking my heart" (38).

Winnie was accustomed to the thanklessness of domestic care. Her old friend and nemesis Helen was never grateful to the servants; "she went looking for spots of grease on the floor, found them, then said, 'Ayo! Look here.'" When Winnie invited Helen and her husband to dinner, "she would eat lots, then say, 'Very good, but maybe the meat stayed in the pan too long'" (304).

Unfortunately, domesticity is not its own reward.

SEVEN

HOME TIES

the greens roll black under the knife,

and the kitchen twists dark on its spine

and i taste in my natural appetite

the bond of live things everywhere.

from "cutting greens" by Lucille Clifton

Whether she's the queen bee, the angel in the house, Mother Superior or Marmee in *Little Women,* the reigning female has long held an almost mystical authority within a homeplace, binding its inhabitants together and anchoring their daily lives. If we look at isolated acts of housework—which is difficult to do, since the various systems and chores immediately weave themselves into a tight web—we see that each act is in some sense an act of connection. Knitting, mending, knotting; removing filth to restore a surface's integrity; spooning food into the mouth of a baby or a lover—when we perform each day's domestic acts, we are reaffirming our links to the earth, our senses and our bodies, our family, other women past and present, civilized society.

We are dealing, after all, with the most basic of elements: earth tracked onto the linoleum, water splashing across it, air whooshing through the vacuum, fire searing the pot roast. When housework functions as ritual, creating home symbolically as well as literally, it does what Driver predicts of all ritual: "It not only brings people together in physical assembly but also tends to unite them emotionally." Often there is a feeling of "loss of self" in the best sense: a loss of the hard boundaries of separation, a merging into the liminal state of union with others (152).

In *The Voyage In,* Abel uses the psychological theory of Nancy Chodorow to suggest that literature's typical heroine defines herself by identifying intimately with others, and reaches or recovered wholeness by relaxing ego boundaries. That makes a female-centered *bildungsroman,* novel of formation, radically different. In the classical male version, the hero reaches a full, adult self-awareness after testing his inner sense of

self against reality in a series of worldly adventures. He is then reinte-
grated into society, his wounds healed. During the odyssey of initiation,
he may have *looked* foolish, but he kept his integrity; as a brave individual, he was unquestionably superior to society at large.

The female pattern, says Abel, is circular instead of spiral. Women traditionally remained home until marriage, and were initiated into adulthood as they learned the rituals of human relationships. Abel traces two
basic patterns of development: The first is the chronological apprenticeship Winnie practiced in *The Kitchen God's Wife*, learning what she needed, then steadily applying it, moving from failures to successes. The second pattern is the awakening, either as a single upsurge of consciousness
or a series of brief internal epiphanies that usually occur after marriage,
as a woman begins to question, and sometimes violate, its constraints. We
saw that pattern with varying degrees of completion and maturity in *The
Longings of Women*: Becky reached the stage of discontent but resolved it
by murder instead of growth; Mary had the change forced on her, and
only experienced faint partial epiphanies during her life on the street;
Leila had a dramatic epiphany when she broke her loyalty to Nick and
began—in the language of pop psychology—to recognize her patterns of
behavior and own her decisions.

For women initiated into adulthood through home-based relationships and either an apprenticeship or a need for one, domesticity plays a
powerfully central role in self-definition. As they move from one home to
another, the tasks they perform and the responsibilities they fulfill within those boundaries measure their worth, lovability and stability. Only if
they tie the knots securely and let the roots grow deep into the earth will
their work bear fruit. If they ignore the work of homemaking—but continue to believe in its power to define the feminine—they remain rootless,
unattached, infertile in the broadest sense of the word.

The Sensual Art of Housework

It is possible to see the acts of housework lyrically, as Rabuzzi does when
she describes the connectedness of a woman mopping: "The floor enables
her symbolically to stretch herself along its surface so that she fills its
entire space, extending out from the center of herself to become, in poet
Wallace Stevens's terms, 'a self that touches all edges'" (110). In more prosaic terms, however, the progression of housework over the past century
has drawn us *away* from sensation, as electrical appliances interceded in
direct hands-on work. We have learned to launder and clean using anti-
septic anti-bacterial mildew-resistant acids and scrubbing compounds,
thus obliterating natural odor, texture and patina. We cook with

processed, store-bought foods, untwisting oily plastic and wire wrappers instead of smelling fresh-baked bread. Some house-proud, aesthetically unschooled families actually keep their furniture covered, their lamp shades cellophaned, their carpets pristine under huge loopy throw rugs.

"Tiled, streamlined, relentlessly white with accents of chrome, the typical bathroom in 1930 suggested a public facility or a surgical scrub room rather than a sybaritic Roman bath," notes Jane Davison (88). Minimalism made the ideal for the whole house seamless, uncluttered, with pure solid colors and stark straight lines. The clean modern aesthetic abandoned the sensuousness of an array of interesting objects, plushy draped brocaded furniture, vivid prints and patterns conversing excitedly, intimate niches and nooks and crannies. Similarly, machine-driven, hygiene-obsessed, impersonally performed or purchased housework has killed its own natural connection to world and spirit.

In *Care of the Soul: A Guide for Cultivating Depth and Sacredness in Everyday Life,* Thomas Moore cites Jean Lall, a Baltimore astrologer and therapist who considers housework a path of contemplation. Lall says that, "if we denigrate the work that is to be done around the house every day, from cooking to doing laundry, we lose our attachment to our immediate world." There is a close relationship, she adds, between these chores and our sense of responsibility to nature (179).

In each of the novels in this study, housekeeping shows a sensuous immediacy, merging the outside world with the inside of a home as well as the inside of a woman's psyche. "I would be admiring the web a spider had woven on a bush, perfectly formed and sparkling with pearls of dew," recalled Winnie in *The Kitchen God's Wife.*

> I was wondering if I could later knit a sweater in the same design, using only this memory as a pattern.
>
> But then the birds would suddenly call to one another, and they sounded just like a woman crying. Or the spider would feel my breath and clench its small body tight before scurrying away. And I would be thinking about my fears, the questions I already had in my marriage. (206–207)

In *The Longings of Women,* housework again linked an insect's state of being with a woman's inner turmoil. Becky saw a fly on the inside of the door and wondered defensively, "What harm was it doing? Just trying to escape. Why should she turn it into a mess on the screen? Instead she released the screen and waved it out with a dish towel" (200). Earlier, Becky had borrowed her friend Sylvie's machine to hem bedroom curtains that "looked cheerful," bringing the outside in with a happy print of sailboats sliding along the waves (196).

When Nick brought Leila flowers as a ploy so he could rejoin his lover, she called him on his motives: "If you want to go back to New York early, you don't have to bury me under forty dollars' worth of flowers" (142). Immediately, though, she felt a pang of guilt, "not toward him, but toward the flowers. They must go into water." After dividing the flowers into two vases and placing them in two separate rooms (an interesting, albeit subconscious, choice) she conceded, 'They do look inviting" (143). Nick may have broken the marital connection, but Leila's response to nature was intact.

In *The Other Side*, the nexus of sensuous connections was the kitchen, which Dan considered "a meaningless room without Ellen's governance. Her objects, untouched by her, seem ghostly, artificial. The smell of her spices has disappeared: marjoram, he thinks it must have been, nutmeg and cloves, bay leaves in soups, vanilla, sage." Frowning at the ratty state of the shelf paper, Dan "wishes he'd noticed it himself before this. And then he realizes that, in all the time Vincent's been gone, he hasn't once gone into the kitchen" (32). That was Ellen's place, filled with the redolent leaves and seeds that tied her daily activities to the outside world.

In *Beloved*, even the minor character of Miss Amy Denver, the white girl who helped Sethe deliver, craved sensuous fulfillment: "All she talked about was getting hold of some velvet" (77). Carmine velvet, to be precise. Sethe herself only began touching again when Paul D arrived, but it took her baby daughter's reappearance to reawaken the rest of her senses. Until then, "she could not remember remembering a molly apple or a yellow squash. Every dawn she saw the dawn, but never acknowledged or remarked its color" (39). Finally, reunited with her baby, she could talk about the last color she remembered: the coldly beautiful pink granite of the dead baby's headstone. "Now I'll be on the lookout," she told herself jubilantly.

> Think what spring will be for us! I'll plant carrots just so she can see them. And turnips. Have you ever seen one, baby? A prettier thing God never made. White and purple with a tender tail and a hard head. Feels good when you hold it in your hand and smells like the creek when it floods, bitter but happy. We'll smell them together, Beloved. (201)

Spring did indeed prove wonderful: Beloved "filled basket after basket with the first things warmer weather let loose in the ground—dandelions, violets, forsythia—presenting them to Sethe, who arranged them, stuck them, wound them all over the house." The reunited mother and daughter made "men and women cookies" and tacked scraps of cloth to Baby Suggs' quilt, and their connection was so playful that jealous Denver sometimes couldn't tell which one was the mother (241).

Sexual Connection

One does not normally think of dishpan hands and the fumes of boiling brussels sprouts as alluring. But, properly orchestrated, cleanliness and good food are bodily pleasures with wide doorways to eros. In *Atlas Shrugged,* Ayn Rand muses on the modern divorce of the two realms:

> There is reason, she thought, why a woman would wish to cook for a man...oh, not as a duty, not as a chronic career, only as a rare and special rite in symbol of...but what have they made of it, the preachers of woman's duty?... The work of dealing with grease, steam and slimy peelings in a reeking kitchen was held to be a spiritual matter, an act of compliance with her moral duty—while the meeting of two bodies in a bedroom was held to be a physical indulgence, an act of surrender to an animal instinct, with no glory, meaning or pride of spirit to be claimed by the animals involved. (720)

The characters in *Tracks* suffered no such separation. The trappings of domesticity were easily eroticized; indeed, they carried sexual power. Remember how, after Fleur and Eli's passionate encounter, Nanapush wondered "if Fleur had wound her private hairs around the buttons of Eli's shirt, if she had stirred smoky powders or crushed snakeroot into his tea. Perhaps she had bitten his nails in sleep, swallowed the ends, snipped threads from his clothing and made a doll to wear between her legs" (48–49). The Ojibwa knew the forces of nature, of intimacy, of personal objects and mutual care and magic.

The Other Side offers an Irish-Catholic version of the same kind of connection. One of the grandchildren remembered coming upon Vincent "kneeling on the floor in front of Ellen, who was in a chair. He was holding her bare foot in his hand. He was cutting her toenails. On the kitchen floor there was a blue enamel basin filled with soapy water." Marilyn stood frozen, frightened to reveal her presence, sure she should leave but not sure why. All she could decide was that "she was looking on her first intimate act" (329).

Personal bodily connections may be a more blatantly sexual form of domesticity, but food, too, carries an erotic message. When Nanapush wanted Margaret to live with him, she "refused to unseal the trapdoor in her kitchen, or remove her canning from the underground shelves where those jars belonged. I told her she was trying to starve me from my place, that if she wanted what I gave her every night, she better stay" (125). He was talking about basic survival, individual versus joint; but he was also recognizing the symbolic force of what my grandmother called "setting up housekeeping together."

In *The Other Side*, when Ellen met Vincent at her friends' house, she flirted with him in the boldest way she knew, first meeting his eyes deliberately, then rising and walking into the kitchen. "She'd got up, gone to the shelf for more sugar, though she hadn't the need of it, so he could see her figure and her walk" (138). Marriage soon followed.

Ellen's granddaughter Cam had a painful sexual history, both emotionally and literally. First, endometriosis had made her sterile and caused painful intercourse. Then, even after surgery had corrected the condition, her husband could not bear the burden of having sex with a woman who had once rejected him, and possibly causing her pain again. When Cam finally met Ira, she was reticent and awkward; he wooed her with stories, and "before or after they made love, he cooked for her." Poor Cam found herself feeling awkward: she didn't like to be naked while he cooked (this was a woman who shied away from domesticity, intimacy and vulnerability, and that act would have combined all three). On the other hand, Cam did not want to be fully clothed, either. So she bought a transparent nightgown.

The first time Cam wore the nightgown, she walked into the kitchen and Ira, busily cooking, took in the sight and "put his spoon down. He forgot his cooking; he walked her to the bed; he asked her to keep her nightgown on when they made love." Apparently the nightgown had brought back childhood memories of summers in the country, where the aunts, grandmothers and moms sat at night in the kitchen in their nightgowns playing cards. Sensuous Ira told Cam that "the cloth of those nightgowns was fresh and beautiful. It had a beautiful fresh smell. And the grass smelt wonderful. It wasn't sex, but all your senses were alive and at the same time calm. Well fed" (58).

Ira was doing his best to bring Cam to the same state. Later in the book, she guessed that he had spent the minutes since they talked laying out food in anticipation of their intimacy. "He likes to feed her," she mused. "Nothing nourishing. Starches and salty foods, Boursin, halvah, peanut M&M's, Pepperidge Farm Goldfish, Entenmann's Sour Cream Cake. It always surprises her," practical woman that she's become, "the decorative small dishes in which he presents these foods. An odd set of possessions, she thinks, for a man who doesn't own a colander" (326).

And from Ira's point of view: "He likes to give her all this food; he wants to make her happy..... Many nights in his bed, mornings alone eating a solitary breakfast, he yearns for her with a racking pain" (328). Before they make love, he sets cold glasses of water on the shelf above his bed, and brings "little dishes of salty foods. Today there are cashew nuts and Japanese crackers in the shapes of other foods. Vegetables, fish, peas green as jewels." These treats are festive, imaginative, playful. But the subtext has more to do with caretaking, reparenting and a delicate exchange of power. "He gives her water, he holds her head to drink as if she were an invalid. He hands her the small pieces of food, piece by piece." By the time the dishes are empty, "she has already left him. He does this for her, lets her leave him first. It's his house, she has all that life she must go back to" (373). Ira had taken the passive, receptive, self-sac-rificing route, first mothering her and then magnanimously allowing her to be the one to end the encounter.

Slowly, Ira's plan began to work, relaxing Cam into sensuousness. One day she found "a little wavelet of his shaving soap, delicious as whipped cream. She scooped it with her second finger as if she were stealing frosting from a cake. Then she rubbed the cream between her breasts. It disappeared; she was pleased at this absorption" (235).

Even in the heavier times of grieving, the preparation of food can set the stage for intimacy. Remember, in *Beloved*, when Sethe first began to confide her traumatic past to Paul D, blurting over and over that the white men had taken her milk. She kept busy as she talked:

> The fat white circles of dough lined the pan in rows. Once more Sethe touched a wet forefinger to the stove. She opened the oven door and slid the pan of biscuits in. As she raised up from the heat she felt Paul D behind her and his hands under her breasts. She straightened up and knew, but could not feel, that his cheek was pressing into the branches of her chokecherry tree. (17)

Soon after that first tender, sensuous exchange, they had intercourse, springing open doors of memory and ending years of loneliness. Later, she planned the supper she wanted to fix him:

> Something difficult to do, something she would do just so—to launch her newer, stronger life with a tender man. Those littly bitty potatoes browned on all sides, heavy on the pepper; snap beans seasoned with rind; yellow squash sprinkled with vinegar and sugar. Maybe corn cut from the cob and fried with green onions and butter. Raised bread, even. (99–100)

When Paul D asked, "What you gonna cook?" Sethe fed him possible menu items one by one, and he responded with groans of pleasure, "Oh, yeah." The energy in the exchange, and the love she was beginning to feel for this man, gave her an Earth-mother sense of amplitude and capabili-ty, a new happiness in the haunted house she referred to only by its street number: "There was no question but that she could do it. Just like the day she arrived at 124—sure enough, she had milk enough for all" (100).

In *The Longings of Women*, Leila just as deliberately brought Nick a slice of honey cake, "warm, on a beautiful Imari plate he had given her." She arranged the presentation like a chef, bordering the cake with steaming coffee and a careless pink chrysanthemum. And the food had the desired effect: "She watched him lick his fingers, glance at the clock and then at her body. They would make love" (11). Weeks after the blowup over Nick's affair, Mary cleaned Leila's house and noticed that "Mrs. L. was sprucing the place up. She was cooking again. She was doing that trick of making a meal, eating it once and freezing the rest." Mary reached a long-conditioned conclusion: "The master must be about to put in an appearance" (86–87).

In *A Thousand Acres,* Ginny felt the age-old connection between the erotic and the everyday whenever Jess entered her house, electrifying the everyday by giving it a new purpose, magnifying her actions, suggesting that intimate partnership was possible. "The house seemed to float on him, on his being there," she mused. "To work at a daily task and sense this was a goading, a prickling pleasure for me, invested significance in the plates I was rinsing and the leftovers I was scraping into the garbage can"(160).

Food is the most obviously sexual domestic element, but the erotic dimension goes well beyond the kitchen, taking shape in the very configuration of a home's rooms. In *The Other Side,* Cam spoke metaphorically with Ira about the lost ways of male-female relationship: "We keep bumping into furniture, things we have no more use for, names we hardly know and never say. Armoires. Credenzas" (29). As she continued, the metaphor grew more dangerous and more intimate: "We keep walking in the dark, bumping into these things with sharp corners, falling onto overstuffed things that could swallow us up.... [Seeing] mattresses on the floor with stains from God knows what" (30). Later, after their relationship had deepened, Cam tried to decide whether she could live with Ira, and she again used furniture as her test, walking into what would be their bedroom and imagining how wonderful it would be to wake up beside him in the morning (377).

Cam's mother, Magdalene, had obsessed about interior design and antiques with her gay friend Kevin, and Cam had figured out "that the decorating scheme had everything to do with sex." What she was too young to realize was that "Magdalene and Kevin worshipped the accoutrements that were supposed to lead to sex, but found the act itself abhorrent" (170).

In *The Longings of Women,* when Becky had sex with her teacher, she paid more attention to her physical surroundings than the orgasm. "It felt pleasant to lie kissing in his king-sized bed with lovely plaid sheets," she recalled dreamily. "Everything was clean and sweet-smelling, including him" (57). She gave the same sort of aesthetic compliment 100 pages later, after she met Terry and decided she wanted to make a home with him: "He did not smell of sweat or beer or tobacco, but discreetly of lemony aftershave. He wore tassel loafers shiny enough to slide on or good sneakers. His hands were always clean," the better to keep their future furniture free of smudges (140).

Family Values

Being a "housewife" means tying yourself—as willingly as Sethe, with bright silk ribbons—to your home, to nature's cyclical rhythms, to your husband's needs as well as your own. And it is from those bonds that domestic rituals take their power.

Sethe had never even seen a wedding, but she knew enough about the ceremonial elements to replicate them for herself and Halle. Forbidden a special meal with their friends, she resolved to at least stitch herself a special dress, and she found the fabric scraps in her daily work. "The top was from two pillow cases in her mending basket. The front of the skirt was a dresser scarf a candle fell on and burnt a hole in, and one of her old sashes we used to test the flatiron on." She could not find something quickly for the back of the dress, something she knew she would be able to restore intact when she took the dress apart and replaced all the stolen fabric. Halle honored her need for ritual by waiting patiently: "Finally," she recalled, "I took the mosquito netting from a nail out the barn. We used it to strain jelly through. I washed it and soaked it best I could and tacked it on for the back of the skirt" (59). Thus, they were married.

Sethe felt the same kind of love for Halle that Winnie felt for Jimmy Louie: "It was a true love, not just the devotion that comes from feeding a husband and raising his children" (77). The word devotion is a domestic sort of word, and Tan uses it to connote wifely loyalty. The same word, however, can cross genders and slide up the scale of intensity as fast as a good trombonist. In *The Other Side*, Ellen's granddaughter, Marilyn, saw the intimacy between her grandparents, realized Vincent's adoration of Ellen, and thought immediately of devotion. She defined it as "a wholeness of attention. Fixed regard. The body's posture: bending towards. Here I stand, bending towards you. There is nothing you cannot ask" (331).

That definition summarizes the quality of domesticity at its finest, when it incorporates a glad, healthy willingness to give to one's partner or other family members. But it also conjures the intensity of passion. When Marilyn saw Vincent on his knees cutting Ellen's toenail, she thought of "food, dirt, animals, children, childbirth, menstrual blood, flu-

ids of sickness, sex." It was easier for her to think of her grandparents as
lovers than her own parents, since her mother shied away from anything
earthy. "All the delicious foods, the warm sweet puddings, heavy breads,
carrots spilling their moisture into meat and taking in that juice," were
forbidden by Marilyn's mother, Theresa, who wanted to rear her children
"safe from her mother's filth" (331).

Theresa's domesticity proved laughable compared to Ellen's, which
was easy with nature, rich with sensory stimuli and anchored in intense
erotic devotion. It is in precisely such an emotional climate that domestic
ritual thrives, its repetitions connecting the family to deeper meanings
and reminding them of their unity, strength and wholeness.

When Ellen recalled her early childhood in Ireland, for example, a
handful of images, each almost an icon, summarized her faith in family.
She saw welcoming, thatched-roof cottages and instantly imagined
"cheerful life. A woman bending at the fire, and at least the possibility: a
steaming kettle, laundry whitening on the hedge" (87). Ellen and her
mother had their own earthy, accepting rituals, extending all the way to
the nearby graveyard:

> They had a morsel of a garden where her mother set the washtub in fine
> weather; she would sing then as she washed and when they finished,
> she and Ellen would take a piece of bread and butter in a napkin and
> walk among the dead Protestants. (89)

Life unafraid in the midst of death; faith strong in the midst of the hea-
then; joy simple and pure in the midst of drudgery.

If Ellen's mother had been an African-American slave, however, such
a cozy home and family would have been virtually impossible. Paul D's
nervousness about settling down with Sethe was understandable—even
without a resentful Denver and a troublesome baby ghost. Still, when Paul
D started making himself at home, singing as he mended broken objects
and reset table legs, it was clear which way he was headed (40). Just as
Nanapush, in *Tracks*, knew that when Eli showed up with a stash of flour,
lard and sugar, it meant he wanted to stay with him (96).

During Paul D's trial period, domestic harmony first broke apart, as
emotional powerlines shifted, then reassembled itself in a stronger configuration. When Denver asked Paul D how long he was going to be
around, "the phrase hurt him so much he missed the table. The coffee cup
hit the floor and rolled down the sloping boards." He redeemed himself
by swiping at the spilled coffee with his blue handkerchief, an act both
tender and tough. "I'll get that," Sethe called, jumping up in classic
female fashion (43). "In silence she wiped the floor and retrieved the cup.
Then she poured him another cupful, and set it carefully before him. Paul

D touched its rim but didn't say anything," carefully negotiating these new family dynamics (44).

Later, when Paul D had Beloved's seductive spells to contend with, he grew even more nervous. By then he knew not to blame it on Sethe, "whom he loved a little bit more every day: her hands among vegetables, her mouth when she licked a thread end before guiding it through a needle or bit it in two when the seam was done, the blood in her eye when she defended her girls" (115). Paul D had three images of Sethe, the first two plainly domestic, the third familial.

Throughout *Beloved*, meals or preparation times often triggered family conflict or revelation. One evening, "Sethe cut a rutabaga into four pieces and left them stewing. She gave Denver a half peck of peas to sort and soak overnight." Then Sethe sat down to rest, and as she dozed she felt Beloved touch her, looking into her eyes longingly. That opened a conversation in which Sethe, for the first time, enjoyed her own past by telling it to her daughter (57–58). On another evening, Sethe was dishing up bread pudding when Paul D noticed the adoring look in Beloved's eyes and started to interrogate her about her origins. The conversation made Sethe recall the days when the house was a way station, "where bits of news soaked like dried beans in spring water—until they were soft enough to digest" (65). Paul D was suspicious of Beloved: The moment he thought of a way to get her out of the house, she "strangled on one of the raisins she had picked out of the bread pudding" (67).

Morrison used a domestic vocabulary to establish conflict and then its three-stage resolution: sisterly harmony, a true mother-daughter reunion, and finally, fraught with conflict, a widening of that embrace to include Paul D. Since the sisters' emotional histories and needs were less complicated, they bonded first, and their relationship took root as Denver taught Beloved about household chores. In one simple, lyrical scene, Beloved held still while Denver took frozen underwear and towels from the clothesline and laid them in her arms (120). The clothes would "thaw slowly to a dampness perfect for the pressing iron, which will make them smell like hot rain. Dancing around the room with Sethe's apron, Beloved wants to know if there are flowers in the dark." Beloved twirled and spun like any playful, loving little girl, "her waist in the apron strings' embrace," needy of her mother's protection and approval (121).

Once the sisters were inseparable and Sethe had embraced both daughters, she would be able to return to her own romantic life. But at this point in the novel, too much emotional work remained undone. When Paul D met Sethe after work, she was delighted, but once they were home, her priorities shifted to her girls. "They were a family somehow and he was not the head of it." Plain as this was to him, he still begged the questions. "Can you stitch this up for me, baby?" Sethe told him she had to finish Beloved's petticoat first. "Any pie left?" Sethe replied serenely, "I think Denver got the last of it" (132). The tasks' priorities made her own emotional hierarchy crystal clear.

In *The Longings of Women*, Terry did not try to integrate himself into an existing home and family; rather, he found himself an apartment to defy his parents, realized he needed domestic assistance to survive there, and promptly proposed to Becky. The apartment, after all, was "absolutely bare except for the refrigerator, stove and sink and the bathroom fixtures," and that bareness struck fear in his spoiled, waited-on heart. The apartment, like his future, was "empty, a box to fill with some as-yet untried, unlived life" (182).

The kind of single, separated loneliness Terry was trying to ward off hit Leila like a ton of bricks. After interviewing people connected with his murder, she was "so depressed she sank into a kitchen chair and sat for half an hour, unmoving." Kitchens were the hearth, the place for solace and replenishment. "She was not hungry, because of the brownies she had eaten at the Souzas and the Sara Lee pound cake at Helen Coreggio's, but she felt a strong desire for real food, a sit-down dinner face to face with family, companionship. Something warm." In the sort of everyday ritual Leila craved, the spiritual blended with the physical so smoothly that food could quell emotional hunger. "It was Saturday night, and where was her life?" she asked herself (66). Her next act answered the question: "She opened a can of sardines and threw together a salad from what was left in the crisper," her carelessness speaking volumes (67).

The antithesis of Leila's solitude was Nana, Becky's grandmother, who lived in the eye of the family storm.

> Nana held the house together. If Becky's mother was swamped, she cooked. She cleaned up what got missed in the confusion. She did the extra laundry. She wiped up what the baby spilled while Gracie was putting him to bed. She made up brews of herbs and weeds for ailments and heartaches. She made a piece of beef or fish go further. She could cook soup out of anything.

After her death, the family, uncentered, fell apart. They lived on fish, leathery chicken and backyard rabbits, and "Nana's garden was choked in weeds" (88).

While Nana had relied on organic methods to care for her family, the next two generations of women have mainly used machines. Becky went to school eager to "find a job, get off their backs and give a little in return. Then she would buy a dishwasher for Mama" (51). The appliance represented an ease her mother had never known, an entrance into the affluence of modern life.

For Ginny in *A Thousand Acres*, the acquisition of a high-tech appliance marked a tangible break with familial domesticity: "I had reduced my links to the old life even more by investing in a microwave oven," she noted. "For six months, I had microwaved every meal I didn't eat at the restaurant" (348). Her plastic microwave plates would have shocked her mother, in whose cupboards they found "glassware and stainless and old cake plates and coffee makers and cut-glass dessert plates and clear cups and saucers." Most of these objects, Ginny had not seen in 30 years: she "felt a small, chilled inner blossom of surprise" when she remembered how "Mommy would have the Lutheran ladies over for coffee and cake on a Sunday afternoon" (358).

Ginny and Caroline continued rooting through the cabinets, finding well-used, absurd, familiar and specific objects accumulated over years of domesticity. The litany took on an odd power:

> There were three vases with dried-up flower cubes crumbling in their bottoms, a soup tureen shaped like a lemon, a Tupperware cake holder and two Tupperware pie holders, a ten-inch pie plate, a nine-inch pie plate, and four cupcake tins that I knew well, but also a china cream and sugar set with roses painted around the rim that I hadn't seen in thirty years. There were eight glass jars with lids, old olive jars and pickle jars and peanut butter jars.

When Caroline asked which things belonged to Rose and which to their mother, Ginny replied that, practically speaking, they all belonged to Rose now anyway. But Caroline stuck stubbornly to the sense of personality that soaked the objects, pointing out that the napkins were "more like Mommy than Rose" (359).

Just as domestic objects entwine with their user, domestic acts convey that person's love as well as her physical service. In *Beloved*, when Sethe was put in jail, Baby Suggs took food: "She handed me the food from a basket; things wrapped small enough to get through the bars, whispering news" (183). Both the news and the food, so considerately packaged, were forms of communication.

In *The Kitchen God's Wife*, Winnie, too, had to go to jail after Wen Fu framed her as a bigamist. She and the other women traded domestic kindnesses, one girl spontaneously doing her laundry for her:

> I asked Auntie Du to bring me a piece of wood so we could cover up our toilet smells. I found ways to keep our room clean, no bugs in the bed. When two girls asked me to teach them how to read and write, I asked Auntie Du to bring me old newspapers.... When we were done with our lessons, we tore the sheets into strips to use for toilet paper. (481)

More than simply covering odors or softening daily hygiene, those every-day acts were signs of hope, self-respect and dignity.

In *The Other Side*, Ira's deliberate linking of cooking, stable love and sexual pleasure worked because Cam had good family memories of food as emotional nurturance, beginning with the grandmother who rescued her from her alcoholic mother. Even when Cam was an adult undergoing hysterectomy—ending her own version of imprisonment—her grand-mother smuggled food into the hospital.

Cam's mother didn't even bother to visit. Quite a contrast to Sethe, stirring cane syrup and vanilla into warmed milk after the ice-skating expedition, then wrapping her daughters in quilts and blankets before the cooking stove. It was at that moment that Sethe heard Beloved hum-ming an old made-up lullaby, and all the pieces clicked into place. Strangely calm, Sethe did not fall apart, fly out of the room or pull down a mental curtain; rather, she "wiped the white satin coat from the inside of the pan, brought pillows from the keeping room for the girls' heads" (176).

Instead of escaping from pain by breaking with the everyday, women have traditionally used their domestic tasks to carry grief and tenderness. In *Tracks,* Margaret mourned her son Nector's alienation from the tribe (he'd lost them their land) by picking quart after quart of his favorite juneberry and filling the house with the "rich sweet steam of preserves and jellies," sweetening his treachery (219). In *The Other Side*, before Vincent left Ireland, he let his mother "arrange walks for them that he knew led her to say to herself, 'This he'll not forget.' And smooth it down in her mind, one task done, a piece of linen mended, or a blanket put down in the chest for winter" (241).

In *The Kitchen God's Wife*, Pearl and her mother took turns worrying about each other. One scene was almost comic: Pearl kept urging her mother to see a doctor, and Winnie answered, "Eat some noodle soup first. See what I made? Same kind when you were a little girl, lots of pick-led turnip, a little pork just for taste. On cold days, you were so happy to eat it!" Pearl obediently took a spoonful, asking as she ate, "But what did it feel like, the pain?" Instead of answering, her mother asked worriedly, "Too hot?" Pearl said no. "Not hot enough?" Pearl said, "It's good, real-ly." Only then, with the connection established and the necessary reas-surance given, could Winnie tell Pearl the story that was causing her such pain (101–102).

But just as domestic acts can bind mothers to their children, they can also wedge siblings apart. Ellen cared for her friend Delia's son Tommy, but her children "grudged him every spoonful, every drop of medicine, every stitch of clothes" (108). In *The Longings of Women*, Leila's son was older, but nearly as prickly, when he found out his mother's dead friend's daughter was coming to Thanksgiving dinner, and might move in with Leila. "Don't you think Melanie would have tried to do for you?" Leila asked him reprovingly. "She certainly would have made Thanksgiving dinner for you." David was appalled. "Mother! Gross! Have you arranged for someone to sew the buttons back on my shirts should you be run over by a large truck?" (111).

That Thanksgiving was the turning point for Leila. She was convinced that "she must create a warm holiday that would reconfirm the three of them as a family unit. It was her job to rebuild and conserve.... forget her disappointments and her moodiness and make it work" (114). She bought the makings of a feast: fresh organic turkey, two fat buff butternut squashes, pumpkin, leeks, cranberries, pumpernickel, hard rolls (Nick's favorites) and an expensive bouquet of radicchio. When David started unpacking a suitcase stuffed with dirty laundry, she busied herself making "her" maple Bavarian cream, clearly a special treat over which her labors had given her proprietary rights.

> He lay on the couch with Vronsky on his chest telling her his adventures at school while she trotted in circles straightening, fluffing pillows, waiting for the cream to set enough to add Madeira. She put the cranberries on to cook in kosher wine, threw in a handful of orange peel, rushed back to David. (112)

Trotted? Rushed back to David? The passage turns Leila into a domesticated animal, making her actions a frenetic sort of busywork that, while skilled and charming, seemed more prescribed and fearful than glad. Leila was trying too hard, but she won what she needed when she offered her son rugalach, and he said, with an adolescent's sweet new nostalgia, "Rugalach always reminds me how when I was little, you used to make pies. Apple, rhubarb, blueberry. And you'd make extra dough and roll it out and bake it sprinkled with cinnamon and sugar for me" (113).

That kind of pleasurable, motherly caretaking is hard to relinquish; thus, even when the world mocks them, domestic skills can anchor a sense of worthy usefulness. When Leila sent Mary out to California to care for wayward Debbie's family, the usually self-effacing Mary said staunchly, "I've never been afraid of hard work. I know how to take care of babies and big kids too. I raised two kids. I can cook, I can shop, I can do anything that nurse did" (389–390).

And she was, indeed, a blazing success, scorning Debbie's low-fat margarine for real butter, cooking delicious chicken and gravy, winning the kids' hearts through that time-honored digestive path. "They liked her cooking. No more tofu hot dogs and sprouts. Abel, who had been stuffing himself on Big Macs before coming home after school, arrived on time and called first thing, 'What's for supper?'" Mary was what "he had always wanted his mother to be, asexual, a good cook, available, solid" (422–23).

Domesticity and Community

Although most of a house's activities are private and internal, front doors and back yards open domesticity to the neighborhood and surrounding community. Or, they block the connection.

African-American culture and female culture are both known for their cooperative ethos, but in *Beloved*, Sethe's crime cut her off from the community. She even stole a little from her employer so she would not be forced to stand in line at the window of the general store with all the other blacks; she "didn't want to jostle them or be jostled by them. Feel their judgment or their pity" (191).

Virtually everything important that happened in the novel happened either inside Sethe's house or in her past, but all the turning points—Paul D's arrival, Beloved's return, the family's healing—were ways of reconciling Sethe and moving young Denver back out into the world. By the book's end, she had broken the family's isolation, knocking at Lady Jones' door so timidly the woman assumed her visitor was a child bringing raisins. The vocabulary of domesticity served a larger purpose: Lady Jones was expecting raisins so she could make "her own special creation," as well staked-out as Leila's maple Bavarian cream, for the church supper. Her idle monologue, debating the rewards of heating her bake oven for the task, soothes us through from the excitement of Denver's broken silence, preparing us for the extraordinary by distracting us into the ordinary.

Sethe's house was not the first to be quarantined by a woman's shame or self-containment. In *The Other Side*, Vincent wondered why his wife had let so few people into their house over the years. Just a few of the kids' friends, and the union people for a while. "I always wanted someplace where people could just come in," he thought to himself. "Someplace to sit down, be themselves, and feel that they were happy" (307).

In one sense, domestic bliss is not real until it is shared with those outside its circle. Historically, the purpose of a home and family has been woven into political theories about democracies, republics, communitarianism, responsible property ownership and citizenry. Consequences of internal harmony, sociable values or alienation ripple from the home outward. Standards of neighborliness become indices of social change, thermometers for conflict.

Back in the 1920s, just a few houses lined Ellen and Vincent's street, and everybody helped each other. They kept a certain formal distance, of course: "Always, they called each other Mr., Mrs., through the years of nursing, burying, the marriages and christenings, the food passed back and forth. They didn't visit each other in their houses; they talked on the sidewalk and the porch" (80). Then, the neighborhood grew crowded, Ellen built a chicken fence, and the chickens ostracized her from her neighbors, who loathed them.

When Dan grew up, he had no such problems dealing with people. His clients confided in him, fell in love with him, gave him presents. Cam's clients gave her presents, too, but they tended to be

> cakes that are large, heavy, oversweet, or cookies made with honey, spongy breads, their hard crusts shiny with brushed egg. The cakes Dan's clients bake are miracles of invention and new industry: Julia Child's three-chocolate bombe, the Pinwheel Fruit Tart from *The Silver Palate Cookbook*. In his closet, Dan has seven framed needlepoint renderings of scales of justice. Cam has, in a secret bureau drawer, a papier-mâché object, three inches high, brought back by one of her clients from her home in Guadalajara. (28)

The needlepoint done so painstakingly for Dan reeked of domesticity; the papier-mâché figure—a woman in white with a cavity in her chest—begged for wholeness and love. Objects reveal a great deal about their givers, recipients and owners, as Mary Burke knew well in *The Longings of Women*. She would clean her clients' homes "in a frenzy," then select one room to investigate, drain of secrets, scrutinize for clues. She wanted "to learn where everything was kept and to read whatever was legible of their lives." Not because she was nosy, but because she needed this surreptitious intimacy to survive: "It was important for her to keep track of their habits so that she could fit herself into the interstices of their lives" (17).

How different the mood was when Mary and her homeless friends shared scrounged meals: their preparation, long anticipated, was half the pleasure. One day Mary had leftover bread—"nice Italian bakery bread"—as well as a couple of apples, a few biscotti, and some walnuts and carrots pilfered from one of her "ladies." "Houdini could not chew the walnuts or the carrots, since he didn't have enough teeth left, but he soaked the biscotti in water. She had stopped and bought hot dogs, which they boiled in the battered pan. It took forever over the Sterno, but the smell was great" (346).

Similarly, in *The Kitchen God's Wife*, Winnie forged a domestic camaraderie with strangers to soothe herself during the bomb scares of the war. "We chatted with the same people we saw every few days," she recalled, "exchanging advice on where to find the best noodles, the best yarn, the best tonic for a cough" (371). Without such freely shared advice and assistance, neighborliness would be moot, and each home would break off from its community, brittle as dead wood. Domestic rituals, patterns and habits are principles of coherence; even when they are carried out in solitude, they relate back to a community, reinforce its commonality, keep open the chance of mutual help.

EIGHT

POWERS OF LIFE
AND DEATH

Learning to use a knife

is the single most important

step you can take toward

having authority in the kitchen.

from "Knives," by Carroll Stoner

It is one of life's great ironies: tasks considered drudgery often tap into profound sources of power, while executive acts boil down to abstract paper shuffling. We think of dirt as a lowly nuisance or harbinger of disease, yet both anthropologists and literary critics claim it as an organizing principle in culture. Palmer, for example, notes that "the concept of 'dirty,' like other emotionally significant abstractions with which it is connected—sex, birth, nourishment, death—has a history inextricably linked with changes in family life, in cultural representations of bodies and regulation of sex, and in organization of work" (139). Whoever shoulders the mantle of dirt removal is confronting one of life's most powerful forces.

Food, too, is a powerful social construct. It helps create and maintain family relationships by healing, strengthening, expressing care and showing responsibility. Each member takes a different role *vis à vis* the shared food: paying for it, preparing it, chopping ingredients or setting the table, cheerfully eating a disproportionate share, refusing to eat at all, as a message of autonomy or depression. The messages sent by food reveal degrees of power and status, inclusion or rejection, boundaries and their dissolutions.

At the center of all this subtle information is, most often, a woman (especially if she is a mother), note the authors of *The Sociology of Food.* The "woman of the house" becomes a clearinghouse for reciprocal exchange: not only does the food encode and reveal relationships, but those relationships determine the choice and allocation of food. "Portions of meat especially are distributed unequally between family members, among whom men have a privileged position, while children and women occupy second and third places" (Mennell et al. 91). The person who decides which plate goes to whom—and who gets the icing roses—wields a power it behooves us not to underestimate.

Domestic Manipulations

Is it an accident that the Latin word *destine* means "that which is woven," and in most cultures, women have done life's weaving? Romines uses the distaff, age-old symbol of women's work, to reveal the link between housekeeping and power: the distaff is a rod used in spinning thread, and "it is also an emblem of the Fates, who control human destiny by spinning, measuring and cutting the thread of life" (5). Domestic work cannot be as trivial as it seems today, if we use its vocabulary to fashion cosmology.

Women first acquired social power through domestic roles, and they have bent those roles to political purposes for centuries. Where did this manipulative aspect first take hold? At a mother's knee. "It seems to be a fact of life," writes Baym, "that we all—women and men alike—experience social conventions and responsibilities and obligations first in the persons of women." Usually at mid-adolescence, an American male begins to be more overtly socialized by other males, she continues, "but at about this time—if he is heterosexual—his lovers and spouses become the agents of a permanent socialization and domestication.... the only kind of women who exist are entrappers and domesticators." Baym uses this observation to explain how, in American myth, the woman becomes the temptress, antagonist, or obstacle to self-discovery (12).

Oakley gets more specific about domesticity, "an area in which the undoubted social power of women has not been considered at all." Sociologists usually examine power by doing a "male-oriented stratification analysis," she adds, "presupposing that's the only kind of power and diverting attention from informal, unarticulated power exercised in the private sphere." At home, authority is less visible, less legitimate in official public terms, and less open to sociological study (*Sociology of Housework* 14). Yet high voltages of power flow through that sphere.

In their 1976 text, *Dependence and Exploitation in Work and Marriage*, Diana Leonard Barker and Sheila Allen hint at the same omission, remarking that "the domestic idyll ideology denies the reality of calculative relationships between family members" (2). In the vine-covered cottage scenario, deferential relationships occur with children, who have more limited access to the outside world and depend heavily on their parents, but they also occur between a traditional housewife and a husband who works outside the home, gaining broader experience and validation. "By inhibiting the development of consciousness of subordination and the possibilities of action to change it, deferential relationships are unusually stable," the authors add (11).

In the work of postmodern thinkers such as Michel Foucault (see *Power/Knowledge: Selected Interviews and Other Writings*), domestic power assumes a wider political context. The body is the place where tiny, local social practices link themselves with the large-scale organization of power. The body is the place where, as organizers of the second-wave women's movement would say, the personal is political. Taking the body as a starting point, then, we can easily see how hunger, satiety, dirt, cleanliness, discomfort and ease are politicized, and become indices of social and economic status. Homeless Mary Burke, furtively changing her rubber-banded clothes in the lavatory stall, was in a far different sociopolitical position than anyone "comfortably well off," as we so accurately put it. The "unwashed masses" were not named by accident, nor were "starving artists" and "fat-cat politicians," and the "filthy rich" simply pushed the domestic/economic correlation to extremes so far apart they met.

Catherine Bell emphasizes Foucault's definition of ritualization as a political technology of the body and a central pathway for power. Our rituals turn our bodies into social and political tools, in other words, creating and revealing a particular balance of power. This definition holds as true for domestic ritualization as it does for a *Zieg heil:* the shifting network of power relations between husband and wife is expressed by the rituals within their marriage, and those rituals become not only a forum for individual strategies, but a source for a political ruler's power. (Family values have become a political catchphrase for good reason.)

The process of ritualization defines, empowers and constrains, Bell notes, because it is constructing and enacting relationships of domination, consent and resistance (204, 221). Ritual—even, and perhaps especially, domestic ritual—proves more Machiavellian than it seems, enabling us "to deploy schemes that can manipulate the social order on some level and appropriate its categories for a semicoherent vision of personal identity and action" (216).

If you doubt that the household's cook wields manipulative power, recall the effects of young Dan's lunchbox in *The Other Side.*

> The other children brought to school bologna sandwiches in lunchboxes with blazoned pictures of Roy Rogers, the Lone Ranger, Mickey Mouse. But he carried, in a workman's black, serious lunchbox, leftovers his grandmother had put aside or re-invented for his taste: meat pastries, ham salad made from Sunday's meat, a chicken wing, a thermos full of pea soup or beef stew. Each lunchtime was a mortification to him,

though he knew his food tasted better than the other children's. He
hated the smell of their flat sandwiches, even as he craved them. (79)

Dan's ordeal was about far more than bologna; he was cursed with a
"mother" of another time, and her immigrant seriousness cut him off
from the overprocessed mainstream of American life. For a sensitive
child, food can be a ticket to popularity or a shameful proof of difference,
causing a kind of pain Ellen never understood. Simply by not paying
attention, she exerted power over his sense of alienation at school, and
that alienation no doubt became part of his formation.

Cam's lover, Ira, also had a sensitive, conflicted childhood: playing
ball in the streets, something he was good at, "he'd hear his mother's
voice, calling him to come in, to do something that minute for her, it
couldn't wait, take some soup up the block to his grandmother, go down
to the drugstore." Those simple domestic requests were enough to make
him feel "like he was drowning. He felt she didn't want him to live."
When he turned down desserts, she made four a day to coax him. The
only time they both enjoyed the domination was when he was sick: "He
liked sitting on a chair when she put fresh sheets on his bed. The cool
sheets when you got back in them they were like heaven" (377). And she
knew it.

What effect did Ira's close rearing have? "He is terrified of the impe-
rialistic life of women in a house." His wife continually tried to converse
with him about redoing the bathroom or picking the upholstery fabric,
and because these were issues in which he had zero interest, he perceived
her approaches as manipulative and overbearing, wanting more from
him than he could comfortably give. By the time he began the affair with
Cam, he was sick of household matters, "grateful that he needn't think of
her out shopping for the prettifying and domesticating object.... Her
hunger is to change the world, not the house." Ira called his wife's compulsive interest "domestic hunger," bitterly remembering "the time he
bought a child's paintbrush and spent a week painting antique molding
a quarter-inch at a time." The fact that it was a child's paintbrush creates
a significant context for the question he blurted to himself: "Why do I fail
to be a normal man inhabiting a house?" (328).

The preceding examples involved manipulations of domestic ritual,
some deliberate, others unconscious. Another salient instance was Rose's
seduction of Jess, in A Thousand Acres. "I remembered that Jess used to
like his mom's Swiss steak," she said innocently, "so that's what I
brought" (11). By invoking the maternal, the creaturely comforts of home
and the flattery of memory, she set in motion forces of attraction powerful enough to lure even a man who'd since become a vegetarian!
Meanwhile, she was using similar maneuvers to keep her husband's vio-

lence in check; on one occasion, she calmed him with a simple, homely promise: "Pete, why don't you go outside and have a smoke? I'm going to make some decaf" (141).

But ritual can be manipulated as well as manipulative. If societal changes split a ritual's deeper meanings from its physical process, Driver reminds us, "the ritual becomes a fetish" that is dangled and exploited by those who hold societal power (162). We've seen such a shift over the last several decades, in advertisers' invocation of domestic guilt; manufacturers' high-tech appliances, designed to make women feel they were still "doing" something; American popular culture's continued equation of domesticity with femininity and virtue. Remember: the manipulation of images and associations reached a peak in the 1950s, after a war that had taken women *out* of their houses into the public sphere, severing the connection between domestic rituals and the female role. Those ties had to be restored.

Healing Touch

The most benevolent aspect of domestic power is the ability to heal, which was once taught alongside cooking and cleaning because women were expected to do much of their families' medical care. Interestingly enough, there are more instances of healing in *Tracks* than in any of the five novels—unlike other domestic categories, in which the Ojibwa novel, quantitatively at least, comes in last.

Writing about the historic period in which *Tracks* took place, Neithammer reminds us that "medicine women spent much time wandering around the wild areas surrounding their villages seeking out the elusive herbs and lichens, gathering leaves and bark, and grubbing for days in search of particularly efficacious roots." The Ojibwa had an extensive pharmacy of their own making, according to Ruth Landes' eyewitness accounts; it even included animal products, such as bear gall and skunk secretions (147). Men were usually the shamans, the *mide*, gifted with special healing powers. But if a woman found a way to learn and use medicinal skills, she was accorded the same honor.

In issues of power and ego, then, Ojibwa healers paralleled the stereotypical Western European pattern. The differences were in their world view and perceived purpose. The Ojibwa believed that the rhythms of nature were both sacred and powerful, and their methods of healing came straight from the natural world. Rather than hook up some tubes and artificial life support, the shaman often encouraged a dead soul to join its ancestors.

Pauline was not a shaman, but she sat the death watch many a night

(54). She helped the mourners in practical ways, looking after children or cooking for the funeral festivities, but she also eased the dead into the next world. Nanapush, however, was the best nurse of the living, first bringing Fleur back from the plague, and later, carefully tending Fleur's daughter, Lulu: "I bathed those feet in water and pickling salt," he recalled proudly, "fanned them with purifying smoke" (169). In another, more mischievous episode, Nanapush "nursed" Pauline out of an obsessive, masochistic twist of self-denial that sent her to the privy only once a day. "It was a hard yoke that I accepted, but I hadn't yet failed," she recalled. "However, I was seduced by Nanapush's false kindness, for he had brewed a special pot of strong sassafras and mixed sugar into it." Then he started talking about water, describing it 100 different ways until she wet her pants (148).

Earlier in the novel, Nanapush's generous hospitality had effected his own cure. After he saved Fleur, she stayed with him and they grieved for the spirits of the dead. "The invisible sickness" of depression sank them into a heavy stupor, and they stopped eating, and "the names of the dead anchored their tongues" (6). Then Father Damien, the new young priest, showed up at their door, and hospitality galvanized them into health again. "We could hardly utter a greeting, but we were saved by one thought: a guest must eat," recalled Nanapush. "Fleur gave Father Damien her chair and put wood on the gray coals. She found flour for gaulette. I went to fetch snow to boil for tea water." Then, "oiled by strong tea, lard and bread," Nanapush started talking in both languages, and the sound of his own voice convinced him he was alive (7).

Tracks' most frequent healing episodes concerned childbirth, with the women serving as each other's midwives—and psychologists. When Pauline became pregnant out of wedlock, she admitted that "only Bernadette's constant and assessing looks, only the spoonfuls of lumpy soup she forced down me, only the bed she made from then on at the foot of her own, kept my promise" not to abort the baby (132–33).

Margaret used alder to slow Fleur's delivery, and after she gave birth, nursed her back to life. She "packed wormwood and moss between her legs, wrapped her in blankets heated with stones, then kneaded Fleur's stomach and forced her to drink cup after cup of boiled raspberry leaf until at last Fleur groaned, drew the baby against her breast, and lived" (60). Years later, Margaret tended that child again, after she nearly froze to death. "Margaret warmed blankets on the stove to heat you," Nanapush told the grown Lulu, "tore off your clothing, wrapped you naked in three hot layers of flannel" (165).

That same kind of steady, resolute nursing took place in *The Other Side*. First, Vincent held the basin for his seasick wife, washed her vomit down the sink, helped her change clothes (266). Then, when they arrived in Ireland, Ellen took on Vincent's gentleness to tend her sick mother. He "saw his wife become a thing he'd never thought she'd be: devoted... holding the old lady's hands grown swollen and fattish from her idleness, the square nails as tough as any man's. He saw her make the special foods for her mother and stay by her" (267).

Nursing did not come naturally to Ellen; Irishwomen are better known for rosaries than magical healing. African-American women, by contrast, share the Ojibwa legacy of skill with natural remedies. Jones reminds us that, as spiritual counselors and healers, black women exerted informal authority over their communities (7). Grandmothers brewed medicines, "gave cloves and whiskey to ease the pain of childbirth, and prescribed potions for the lovesick." Kids were dewormed with "Stinkin' Jacob tea," a concoction of turpentine, castor oil and Jerusalem oak (30).

Even the white girl, Amy Denver, knew something of folk healing, for she strung Sethe's flayed "juicy back" with spiderwebs (80). And when Sethe arrived, ill and exhausted, at Baby Suggs' house, the kindly old woman led her to "the keeping room," fittingly enough, and "by the light of a spirit lamp"—and a strong faith—bathed her in sections. "While waiting for another pan of heated water, she sat next to her and stitched gray cotton," her hands busy in the timeless, soothing way of traditional domesticity. After each bathing, Baby covered Sethe with a quilt and put another pan of water on the stove. "Tearing sheets, stitching the gray cotton, she supervised the woman in the bonnet who tended the baby and cried into her cooking," all emotions mixing. Baby "cleaned between Sethe's legs with two separate pans of hot water and then tied her stomach and vagina with sheets. Finally she attacked the unrecognizable feet." All her movements were slow, gentle, steady. "She helped Sethe to a rocker," a symbol of maternal soothing, "and lowered her feet into a bucket of salt water and juniper." As Sethe soaked her feet, Baby softened the crust from her nipples with lard, then washed it away. When Denver woke at dawn, she was able to take her mother's milk (93).

Juniper, saltwater and lard might have traded places with other substances in China, and more emphasis might have been placed on food, but the focus on patient healing would have been the same. Chang explains how, in traditional Chinese culture, "food management is critical to all harmony—in one's own body, in one's social life, and in one's interaction with the world" (366). Herbs and dietary medicine, self-administered or prescribed by an herbalist for sacred curing, are used to strengthen and build ch'i, life energy. Ginseng and ginger are general stimulants; chicken broth is as valuable as it is to the stereotypical Jewish mother; and feasting serves specific purposes (367). Foods are believed to have properties of hot and cold, yin and yang, which must be delicately balanced.

When Winnie brought Pearl "some Chinese medicine," for example, she instructed her to "put this pad on your arms and legs, the herbs sink into your skin. And every day you should drink hot water three or four times a day. Your energy is too cold.... Are you listening?" (531). At Bao-bao's wedding, Pearl poured herself a cup of chrystanthemum tea, and her mother and Helen started telling her about the wonderful tea in Hangchow, made from a rare flower, costly for just a thimbleful. "That's all you needed," added Auntie Helen. "You swallowed that little amount. It went down inside you, changing everything—your stomach, your heart, your mind. Everything sweet" (526).

On the day Pearl's father died, one of his wives had tried to feed him rice porridge. "Every day I had to fight to open his mouth and pour something down his throat," San Ma recalled. "Really, he was more trouble than a baby, wouldn't eat, always soiling his bed." She had grown exasperated, and shouted, "Goddess of Mercy, open his mouth!" And he had stared at her with clear eyes. She urged him to eat, and he said, "Then give me something proper to eat" (484). The entire household trooped upstairs, carrying dumplings, buns, bowls of noodles (485). And thus, ceremonially honored, he died.

The Dark Side of Domesticity

Wherever we find the power to heal, we also find the power to withhold healing. Oakley finds "the incidence and patterning of illness among members of a family is interlocked with the emotional interior of the family: thus another logical corollary of women's pivotal position in this unit is their capacity to affect not only health, but ill-health" (*Sociology* 14). The more Western medicine learns about mind-body unity and, more prosaically, prevention and family medicine, the more obvious that becomes. Those who keep a house and care for a family also wield the power to admit chaos and toxins, to neglect a living thing, to let it die.

In *The Longings of Women*, Nana's inability to continue her tending gave Becky the perfect image for her own bitter emotions: "Her marriage was like Nana's garden when she lay dying, little pale lettuce plants choked by jungles of rampant weeds" (235). In *The Other Side*, Cam thought just as bitterly of her mother, Magdalene, whose land had become the barren remains of an emotional battlefield: "You hated gardens, because your mother was good at them," Cam mused. "Nothing grew beside our house" (314). Magdalene's profound inability to nurture created a cold distance she would regret in later life, when her daughter was "trying to cover her mother and yet not have a moment's contact with her flesh" (320).

Cam's reluctance came from a long-buried emotional history. So did Pauline's in *Tracks* when she found Fleur in labor and near death. Fleur gave her careful directions to "fetch moss to stem the blood, fetch rags, scrape the root upwards, into the water, find a small leather packet and some other leaves." But even calm Fleur was panicky: "'This is too fast,' she said, her voice rising a pitch." Pauline's first reaction was to physically distance herself:

> I moved away from her, fumbled in the woodbox, down in corners, tipped the water over, scalding my own leg, and had to boil it again. I do not know why the Lord overtook my limbs and made them clumsy, but it must have been His terrible will. I never was like this during sickness before, not since Bernadette taught me. (157)

After a visit to the world beyond life, Fleur managed to return and survive, thanks to Margaret's help. The incident revealed an instructive difference between Pauline's inability to love, nurture or heal and Fleur's active ability to either heal or destroy. Earlier in the book, when Fleur was dragged out of the lake and George Many Women bent to look at her, she hissed at him, "You take my place." He eventually drowned in his own bathtub (11). Thus even the small domestic world became lethal under Fleur's curse.

The whole tribe knew Fleur was capable of doing just the opposite of her shamanistic healing. After her rape, when the boy Lazarre could speak nothing but nonsense, people "imagined that Fleur had caught Lazarre watching and tied him up, cut his tongue out, then sewn it in reversed," inverting the natural order to mend his ways (49). In a later encounter, Fleur used her knife to cut a few of Lazarre's eyelashes, sweeping them into a white square of floursacking that she then carefully folded into her blouse, putting it close to her heart as a signal of her power over him (120).

It is easier to understand the dark side of domestic power if we explore the double-edged sword of all ritual practice: "If rituals play, part of their playing is with fire," notes Driver, "and their mode of renewing life requires them to be more than slightly in touch with death" (99). It is precisely that connection Dilys Laing alludes to in her 1954 poem "Springclean," in which housewives "mounted their next-to-Godly brooms/and scurried to the scrubbing of the Spring." They went on to sprinkle the earth with the "scouring powder" of their discontent, and to chop the heart as fine as chives. In the end, these "good women in cahoots/with tidy death rub April clean as bone" (373).

The women's deeds may be well-intended or perverse; all we know is that they carry ritualistic power. As Driver reminds us, ritualistic performance has a sinister side (99). One of its functions is "to release and direct aggressive impulses in such a way that aggressive hostility is kept under control" (155). The witch in Hansel and Gretel reverses the sacrificial mother who breast-feeds and bakes cookies, notes Rabuzzi. The witch is instead a poisoning, devouring woman so obsessed with her children she could "eat them up" quite literally, appropriating their essence. "In such demonic reversals of what *caretaking* ordinarily suggests, the words *I'll take care of you* assume a deeply menacing quality" (130).

Cleaning, too, can have both dark and sacred power: "In its demonic form housekeeping is extremely distasteful, sometimes even frightening, as the myth of Sisyphus, with its endless, meaningless repetitions, appropriately suggests," notes Rabuzzi. Yet in its sacred form, the same work can elicit a sense of flow or unity. Then, "performer and performance are virtually indistinguishable," as are the prayer and the prayed, the dancer and the danced in mystical tradition (98). The sacred dimension depends on balance, however; when housekeeping is "divinized" in an unhealthy way, becoming a woman's sphere so exclusively it takes on a disproportionate, consuming role, it is "demonized" in equal measure for the rest of the household, impeding their shared life.

In *Tracks*, Margaret was not obsessed by domesticity, but she knew how to use its power for her own ends. When Eli set a trapline around the lake, she set a trapline "just as carefully laid out, around the kitchen table. She placed dishes, cups, coffee and new gaulette, grease and dried berries, bait for whoever might come." Pauline took the bait, and she was so in need of nurturing that her defenses were soon stripped by Margaret's hospitality. "It was as if she took the first drink, and from then on the drinks took her.... She stuffed bread down and babbled through the crumbs" (52). Her mouth, open wide, had become the locus for two forms of social communication, and Margaret was plying her with one to elicit the other. Thus Margaret learned all she needed to know about the relationship between her son and Fleur.

Language and domesticity often intersected in *Tracks*. In a noteworthy exchange, Nanapush called Margaret a jealous hen who liked to squawk, then quickly downed the thick berry pudding she had served him before she snatched the bowl from his hands. "Some men just come over here to stuff themselves," she snapped, and he retaliated in a flash. Rising to go, he said, "I'm leaving you empty bowls" (53). And in that quick insult, layers of possible significance overlapped: the preparation and serving of food; the infertile uterus of midlife; the supposed receptivity of the female; the hollowness of shrewishness; the inability to fill a need.

Nanapush may have been eloquent, but he was too kindly to do real damage. The truly dark domestic passage was Pauline's sabotage of Fleur and Eli's love. It began with her urgent desire for Eli and bitter envy of Sophie, Bernadette's nubile, carefree daughter. Pauline thought about what it would be like "to be inside Sophie's form, not hunched in mine, not blending into the walls, but careless and fledgling, throwing the starved glances of men off like the surface of a pond." A few days later, she bought blue material from the trader, paying for it "with coins that had shut a dead woman's eyes."

Pauline "stitched the dress right on the girl," and the image was duly vicious. "She slouched, her hair a tangle, dirt blotching her thighs and elbows, a smell coming off her like duck feathers, oiled and sly," sufficiently raw, earthy and animal to make Pauline's spirit-mad psyche snap. There was something inescapably erotic in her malice, however: "She was pleased at the color of the flowered calico, at the pull of it across her chest and hips because I sewed it so close there you could see her nipples when they tightened" (78). In archetypal symbolism, clothing represents persona, the way others perceive us, the outward sign—whether accurate or deceitful—of the inner self. Thus, by making the dress pull in a sexually suggestive manner, Pauline was using her ability as a seamstress to present Sophie as a harlot—use her to entrap Eli—and steal Eli from Fleur.

Pauline traded candles and ribbons, pleasantly feminine, romantic objects, for a "dreamcatcher," a sack of medicine powder to snare Eli. This "dust" was the supreme domestic weapon, "crushed fine of certain roots, crane's bill, something else, and slivers of Sophie's fingernails." With all the anticipation of a bride learning to cook, Pauline planned how she would bake it into Eli's lunch. Sophie unwittingly aided the project with "natural ability," bringing Eli ginger water or specially made lemonade. Pauline, meanwhile, was adding pinches of charm dust to Eli's food, "to lay the seeds of wanting. Then, under my encouragement, Sophie put the rest of the food together with her own hands, the bread cut too thick, the meat tough and greasy, the sweet cake flattened by her clumsy knife" (81–82). Pauline's scorn was palpable.

Eros flooded the next domestic scene, as Pauline slid Eli's "twice-risen bread" into the oven, envisioning

> his worn blue shirt and sash, his workpants rubbed smooth across his knees and back end...It took the baking time of one batch for him to work his way over to the slough.... I tipped the baked bread from the pan. The crust was barely hardened before Sophie filled the water jug, took a block of butter, tucked the loaf into the crook of her arm. (82)

Time itself was measured by a domestic clock—the baking time of one batch. Across that framework, Pauline's potion worked its harm, and her malice seemed to increase: "I scalded the water for the girl's bath that night, and added it to cold. I peeled off her clothes, showed Bernadette where she had bled." Later, she sat quietly, her domestic chores reflecting the state of her soul: "I stayed in my chair and cleaned ripe gooseberries until my fingers and then my hands grew dark and stained" (85).

In *Beloved*, domestic power took an entirely different shape. In describing *The Heroine in Western Literature*, Meredith A. Powers wrote about an alternative view of consciousness: instead of the linear, cerebral, Appollonian, discriminating intellect, there is the chthonic dimension whose archaic depths are embodied, ecstatic, transformative. This undifferentiated, irrational realm admits rage and grief ; spurns goals and civilizing rules; attends instead to the seasonal rhythms of life and death, and a pre-ethical natural law. When women "descend" into this realm, they gain strength and self-knowledge, and reach a wholeness unfathomable to Western logic because it transcends the clash of opposites. Sethe, in this view, is the archetypal goddess, motivated by profound love and absolute outrage. Powers compares her murderous attempt to protect and escape with the strategies of Paul D and Baby Suggs, who are so gentle and so wounded they "love small" and stay safe. Sethe resists that fragmentation, and grounds herself instead in the mother-child bond. But "like other chthonic heroines she becomes an aberrational figure among her own people," and must suffer her way back to harmony (188).

Like darker powers, the chthonic, mythic forces often surface in the domestic realm. Denver regarded their haunted house "as a person rather than a structure," and approached it shivering (29). When the nameless soulless "schoolteacher" hunted Sethe down and she killed Beloved rather than see her enslaved, she "made a low sound in her throat as though she'd made a mistake, left the salt out of the bread or something" (151). Years later, when Sethe finally told Paul D what happened in the woodshed, all domestic order vanished and "she was spinning. Round and round the room. Past the jelly cupboard," prosaic sign of daily care; "past the window, past the front door" (161). She kept circling the room and the subject, chattering about a piece of calico Mrs. Garner had given her, a remnant of domestic stability.

> Stripes it had with little flowers in between. 'Bout a yard—not enough for more 'n a head tie. But I been wanting to make a shift for my girl with it. Had the prettiest colors.... and do you know like a fool I left it behind? No more than a yard, and I kept putting it off because I was tired or didn't have the time. So when I got here, even before they let me get out of bed, I stitched her a little something from a piece of cloth Baby Suggs had. Well, all I'm saying is that's a selfish pleasure I never had before. I couldn't let all that go back to where it was. (163)

What for other women was "drudgery," was for Sethe a sign of selfhood so intense, so precious that it symbolized, first her deepest love for her baby girl, and then a freedom she would kill rather than lose. The domestic imagery returned with a bitter reference to "whole towns wiped clean of Negroes.... human blood cooked in a lynch fire" (180).

The domestic darkness in *The Rest of Life* had no such drama; it worked itself out mainly in small jealousies and hatreds. Theresa, for example, had hated her niece Cam ever since she came to live with Ellen, and this hatred "unrolls and throws itself out like a bolt of cloth" (205). We think of Hera, interpreted by Thomas Moore as "a fitful, outrageously infuriated, betrayed, and violated wife" (106). Hera's rage is deepseated, and Moore can justify its motivation:

> While [Zeus's] desire goes out to the world, Hera's rage speaks for the home, for family and marriage. Their tension is the yin and yang of home and world, of 'us' and 'other.' He is the extrovert, she the introvert. Erotic creativity is the making of a world, jealousy is the preservation of the hearth and interiority. If we did not become jealous, too many events would take place, too much life would be lived, too many connections made without deepening. Jealousy serves the soul by pressing for limits and reflection. (107)

Theresa's malice may have come from a misguided impulse to guard the family's, just as Cam's hatred of Magdalene was a plea for the proper order of home life.

In *The Longings of Women*, even gentle Mary Burke admitted that, "toward the raw end" of her marriage, she had derived a certain "relief from contemplating a dash of rat poison in the soup" (43). But it was Becky who followed through. Her murderous impulse had its root in her desperate efforts to create a home. Once again, danger expressed itself in a domestic vocabulary. Watching her daughter's fiancé, Becky's mother said bluntly, "I see how he looks around the house. Like he doesn't want to touch it, dirt and trouble might come off on his fingers" (165). Watching her mother, Becky concluded disparagingly, "Mama simply could not see past the great walls of the rut where she labored daily, trying to hold her family together" (162).

Becky took the first step toward the chasm when she ate dinner with Terry's parents. She studied the living room, "all white and blue, everything perfect, everything placed carefully. There wasn't a broken or spoiled or soiled object." The chthonic realm was walled out; artifice ruled "every cushion that was artfully placed in a scene of domestic beauty intentionally created. She had seen such rooms in magazines, but never in life" (165).

Mrs. Burgess claimed the room proudly, boasting that she had not turned to an interior decorator for help, but had picked everything out herself—probably in the same spirit that Winnie chose her trousseau, determined to insure her future happiness. Becky, meanwhile, was imagining her mother in the room, carefully seating her on the white sofa so she could put her feet up on the white leather hassock, in stark contrast to her usual daily grind. Becky envisioned her mother's

> skirt spread out around her the way she did sometimes when she was dressed up and able to sit for a moment, so that Becky would catch a quick glimpse in Mama's lined face of a young girl waiting in barely suppressed joy for something that surely would happen. Something nice for once. (167)

Becky was fantasizing a *Bewitched*-style release from domestic obligation, restoring a carefree, hopeful youth. But by the novel's end, she was acting out the dutiful-wife scenario herself, with different motivation. "I'll use the time next weekend to give the house a good cleaning, catch up on ironing," she told Terry when he left for a golf vacation, adding cheerfully (for credibility's sake), "You know how I hate to iron!" As Terry left, Becky thought smugly to herself, "she really was a good wife.... She would make the condo perfect" (281).

In a masterful stroke of irony, Piercy had her finish the thought by stating her plans to get Sam up into the bedroom that weekend (281). Apparently, Becky saw no contrast between good wifeliness, infidelity and murder. That Sunday, she quickly "put Sam to work" changing the bed linens and helping her clean, as her husband would never have done. The break in traditional roles even extended to transportation; it was Becky who drove Sam to her house and took him home again. Once back in the condo, "she immediately ran to do the laundry. In a wild frenzy, she had the place looking unused and smart by three," hiding many layers of guilt beneath a domestic excellence that, culturally, had long bespoken virtue (313).

On the morning Terry was to be murdered, he did nothing to change Becky's mind; instead, she saw with even harsher clarity his finicky habits, "objecting to the milk, claiming it was turning, as if he wasn't home all day and couldn't just go and buy some." At that point, Becky smiled. "It was marvelously bracing to her patience to think of bashing his head in" (340).

Before he died, however, he did acknowledge—as petulantly as usual—domestic guilt, immediately turning it against Becky with the implication that she was one of those obsessed, neurotic housewives society both expects and dreads:

Becky, I feel as if everything I do here just messes up the condo for you.
If I put the sports section down, you pick it up and throw it in the trash.
I take off a jacket and you carry it away. You're always cleaning up
behind me like I'm an old dog, don't you see? You look at my things as
if they're covered with dog shit.

This admission/accusation surprised Becky, because she thought she had
disguised her instinctive revulsion. She retaliated in time-honored fashion, cutting straight to the unconscious: "I'm just trying to keep our home
neat—like your mother" (358). It was a reasonably subtle reminder of
Terry's own domestic formation and expectations, and his disloyal
breach of the implicit marital contract.

Even the murder itself carried domestic overtones: "Blood was all
over the good blue spread and the beige carpeting" (378). Like the berry
stains that marked Pauline's hands after she played her trick on poor
Sophie, those bloodstains bothered Becky far more than any stain on her
own character. While Sam "unlocked the door from the outside," occu-
pying the traditional male realm of securing and opening the passageway
to the outside world, Becky carefully cleared away the bowl of drugged
soup, placing it in the dishwasher she had so yearned to buy her mother.
"Lazy Terry hadn't even turned on the dishwasher loaded with the morning and noon's dishes" (378).

When the case came before the court, the assistant district attorney
told the judge how brutal Becky's deed had been—"As if she hadn't tried
to keep things simple and clean," she thought indignantly (428). By now
her thinking was so distorted that domestic performance had conflated
with morality.

After all, housework is a family's common work, and family dramas
invariably get worked out in the domestic realm. In A Thousand Acres,
Ginny and Rose each had their father over for dinner once a week, and
reported the ritual to each other. "I've fed Daddy," Rose told Ginny defi-
antly one evening, explaining that he had refused to eat at a later, more
convenient time, and thus forfeited his invitation to a family dinner.
Ginny was appalled by such defiance, but Rose was beginning to realize
the insanity of catering to their father's rigid schedules and demands
(96).

The dark power of such family gatherings became apparent at the
annual Father's Day dinner: "Daddy was sitting at the head of the table,
and he was not having a good time," Ginny noted to herself. Even the
food reflected the emotional tension: the crown pork she had special-
ordered "sat heavily on the white tablecloth," waiting the results of a
quibbling debate over how to carve. Everyone coped with the tension in
their own fashion: "Linda and Pammy were poking each other angrily

under the table, and Pete was in the kitchen getting another beer." Ty just snuck in a patronizing insult: after Ginny told her niece the little sticks on the potatoes were rosemary, he sighed, "Ginny's been reading the paper again." In her defense, domestic tradition was invoked: Rose remembered fondly that "Mommy put rosemary in potatoes." In the end, Ginny gave a succinct summary of the dinner's psychological effects: "It was exhausting just to hold ourselves at the table, magnets with our northern poles pointing into the center of the circle. You felt a palpable sense of relief when you gave up and let yourself fall away from the table" (101).

In yet another telling incident, Ginny was late arriving at her father's house to fix him breakfast. He met her at the back door and "his tone was accusing. It meant, I'm hungry, you've made me wait, and also, you're behind, late, slow." Ginny's utter insecurity in the face of her father's judgment welled up instantly. She first tried to defend herself, adult fashion, by explaining that she'd been tidying her own house, but her father mocked the explanation with a "Hmp." Then she apologized and donned an apron, only to hear him charge her guilty again: "Nobody shopped over the weekend. There's no eggs." This brought Ginny to a crisis: did she return home to get eggs and make her father wait, or continue with his breakfast and deprive him? The power was in her hands, but she did not perceive it there—and perception is nine-tenths of reality. She considered pushing past him to prepare "a breakfast without a center of gravity," casting her cooking in cosmic terms. Then she caved in and rushed home to fetch the eggs.

As Ginny ran home, she was painfully aware of her own body, "graceless and hurrying, unfit, panting, ridiculous in its very femininity." The self-hatred in that comment was swiftly linked with the still-unremembered incest of her childhood: "It seemed like my father could just look out of his big front window and see me naked, chest heaving, breasts, thighs, and buttocks jiggling, dignity irretrievable" (114–115). For Ginny, silence and resigned, tractable obedience somehow equated with domesticity; by the time she was frying the bacon and eggs, her temper had cooled into passivity. "I served up his food silently.... My job remained what it had always been—to give him what he asked of me." Emotional prison was safer than any alternative; as Ginny stood by the stove, patiently waiting to pour her father more coffee, it "seemed like a simple and almost pleasant task" (115).

When Ginny had her first flashback of incest, both the setting and the stimulus were again domestic. She returned to the homestead and settled her lover, Jess, into her old bedroom, perhaps enjoying the intimacy of him lying between the yellow flowered sheets she had slept in for years. "In the linen closet was where I found the past," Ginny recalled, "and the reason was that Rose and I always washed the sheets on Daddy's bed and put them back on, and we always washed the towels and washclothes in the bathroom hamper and hung them back up." She'd paid for this housekeeping shortcut in lost knowledge, since no one looked in the linen closet—or visited its buried memories—more than once a year. Behind the stack of towels, hidden entirely from sight, was a half-full box of Kotex pads and an old belt, a remaindered sign of Ginny's adolescent femininity. She made up the bed and lay down, staring up at the ceiling. Suddenly, undeniably, the truth flashed. "I knew that he had been in there to me, that my father had lain with me on that bed, that I had looked at the top of his head, at his balding spot in the brown grizzled hair, while feeling him suck my breasts" (228).

Later, all manner of physical clues triggered that memory again. When Ginny and Rose discussed their father's fuss over a brown velveteen coat he swore had belonged to Caroline, Rose explained that actually, it was hers, but their mother cut it up for polishing rags after Rose threw up on it and she couldn't get the stain out. Domestic failure, domestic thrift, ricocheting years later in unrelated emotional strife. When Ginny described their father's tone of voice as he insisted the coat was Caroline's, she said she almost fainted—and Rose realized she knew (274).

When Ginny was dealt her next blow, the news that Rose and Jess were in love, she kept "seeking perfect order and cleanliness" to ward off the pain (308). But the sight or sound of the lovers pushed even domestic distraction away, and Ginny realized she had to free herself. Her plot to poison Rose had the sound of an elaborate recipe, with the "deliberate savoring of each step, the assembly of each element, the contemplation of how death would be created." Deciding on liver sausages and kraut, a dish that, after years of sisterly intimacy, she knew only Rose liked, she began scouting "wet areas" for hemlock. She picked two heavy round cabbages from Rose's garden, thawed pork loins, their name inescapably sexual, and took out sausage casings—"all operations as familiar as my own kitchen." After rinsing away the hemlock, she tied off the sausages "about as thick as a man's thumb." The intimacy of her malice "was not unlike the feeling you get when you are baking a birthday cake for someone. That person inhabits your mind. So I thought continuously of Rose."

Ginny took great, ironic pride in her work: "The perfection of my plan was the way Rose's own appetite would select her death." And Ginny was as sociopathically free of any guilt or remorse as Becky in *The Longings of Women*. "The orderly progress of cooking something put me in the usual serene mood," she commented. "I was finished and cleaned up by two" (313). She continued cleaning rhythmically: "finished the dishes, swept the floor, wiped the counter, cleaned the seams in the counter with a toothpick, scoured the drip pans and burner grates, applied the toothpick to the assorted corners of the stove, and cleaned the oven door with Windex." As before, the chores "coalesced into a kind of waking dream," almost an altered consciousness. Even thinking of Jess did not deter her; she simply mused for a second, "then bent down and began to scrape dirt out of the little round feet that supported the front of the stove" (316–317). The sense of evil in her blitheness brought to mind the archetypal fairy tale, in which the witch so casually shoves the children into the homey kitchen stove.

By the end of the book, Ginny was free of her obsessive domesticity, free of her marriage and her daughterly obligations, aware of the unconscious memories that had controlled her. A great distance had come between her murderous past and her mature self, and she finally had some insight about "the canning jar of poisoned sausage and the ability it confers, of remembering what you can't imagine." She could not forgive her father, but she could sense how the unthinkable urges must have goaded him. And that insight was her sole treasure, a "gleaming obsidian shard" she held close to her heart (370–371).

In *The Kitchen God's Wife*, too, the dark power of domesticity sank into *thanatos* as the novel progressed. First, the pom-pom fish swam backward into Winnie's memory, reminding her of the special fish she bought her beloved husband Jimmy, a fish so freshly caught "it was still angry." She told the butcher to wrap the fish live, in clean white paper instead of newspaper, and proudly—absurdly in retrospect—carried it home on the bus, feeling it thrash about, imagining how it would please her husband. But first she had to fight nature:

> Before I killed it, it puffed its gills out, spouted bubbles from its mouth to make me think it was poisonous. And even after I gutted it, it jumped up and down in the pan and threw itself on the floor, flopping all around as I chased it with a hammer. And after I cooked it, it still found a way to fight me. Jimmy ate only one bite before a little bone swam down his throat and got stuck, so that each time he swallowed he thought that fish was biting him from the inside out, all night long. (69–70)

Jimmy needed surgery to remove the fishbone, and Winnie almost forgot the O. Henryish good news she had bought the fish to celebrate: She had found a job making noodles. So at least they would be able to pay the hospital bill.

Other brief, almost surreal domestic memories concerned Winnie's mother, who abandoned her when she was ten. Once, looking at her mother's portrait, the child "saw a little spot of mold growing on her pale painted cheek. I took a soft cloth and dipped it in water, washed her face. But her cheek grew darker. I washed harder and harder. And soon I saw

what I had done: rubbed half her face off completely!" She sobbed, thinking she had killed her mother—a vivid representation of any child's
deepest fear when abandoned by a parent (103).

Winnie continued her reminiscence, focusing on the particularly
wonderful day that turned out to be their last together. Her mother had
taken her out, showing her things, delighting and instructing her. That
day ended with a simple, intimate meal in their room. "Afterward, my
mother showed me how to do an embroidery stitch, one she said she had
invented herself," a domestic legacy handed down quite literally. "I
copied her very badly, but she did not criticize me, not once," added
Winnie. "She praised what I had done" (113).

The next day, her mother was gone. A servant brought Winnie soy-
milk soup, but she let it cool, waiting for her mother. "A lump grew in my
throat, and I waited for my mother to return so I could release it, cry and
tell her how long I had waited. I decided that when she did return I
would point to my cold bowl. I would demand some English biscuits, at
least three to make me happy again." It was domestic manipulation in
reverse, Winnie counting on her mother's caretaking for emotional black-
mail. Then she escalated to rebellion: "I tipped over my bowl and made
a big mess," the chaos signaling inner turmoil. "I stood on a chair and
brought down the biscuit tin myself," angrily self-reliant (115).

Hurt, alone, Winnie grew up with the sense that invisible powers surrounded her, and the desire to find her own power in the domestic realm.
When she was older, mending clothes for rebellious cousins who "fell
down on purpose," docile Winnie was appalled by the damage: "Big
holes at the knees and elbows! So many stains! I decided most of those
clothes were too bad to fix.... And then I smiled, remembering how I had
secretly left a little hole in one of Old Aunt's jacket pockets. Maybe some
of her powers would drain away" (141). Secretly sabotaging her oppres-
sor, Winnie drew on a voodoo-like cosmology.

That world-view grew sinister when Winnie was pregnant, busily
sewing baby blankets and tiny sweaters: The baby kicked her, and she
dropped her scissors on the floor. "They landed with their points stuck on
the floor, just like a little soldier, waiting to take orders. At first I laughed,
but then—eh!—I felt something very strange. The baby stopped moving
inside me" (304). Old Aunt had told Winnie it was bad luck to drop scissors. "I called my servant right away and told her to throw those scissors
into the lake," she explained (305). The next day, the baby girl was stillborn.

Winnie waited more than 100 days before using scissors again, but
she missed sewing and knitting, so she decided to replace them.
Troublesome Helen recommended a certain kind and gave Winnie tricky
directions to the shop; she got lost, saw starving children, an old man

coughing and choking, kids fighting over a few lucky coins. Finally, quite by accident, she found a young woman with scissors on her table. "Wouldn't that also make you feel someone was playing a big joke on you?" she asked the reader. "Wouldn't that make you feel you only got things in life you didn't want?" (308).

The scissors were arranged in neat rows, one style elaborately wrought into the shape of a crane. "The blades were thin and tapered to look like a long beak," Winnie recalled. "Where the blades connected with a metal pin, that was the eye. And the two holes for putting your fingers through, those were the wings.... It looked as if the crane were talking and flying at the same time" (309). She was charmed by the scissors, admired their "bite" of the cloth, and liked the fact that they'd been crafted with a skill handed down through the woman's family. Then she learned they were made of American steel culled from "a foreigner ghost truck" that crashed (310). She was appalled—but not too stunned to bargain the price down. Alas, her purse slipped, the end of the table toppled, and 40 pairs of scissors fell to the ground. She "stared at them, all their bird mouths flung open, all that bad luck pouring out," then ran away empty-handed, believing she had "made a bad deal, like a deal with the devil" (311). When she reached home and heard that Wen Fu's army jeep had turned over, she decided it was her fault (312).

Actually, no one would have blamed her. When she had her baby, the obnoxiously insensitive Wen Fu came into the hospital kitchen demanding food for himself. "He had pushed the cooks out of the room," just as he eventually pushed Winnie out of her domestic devotion. Then "he had picked up a big cleaver, the kind you use to chop a large bone in half. And—pah!—he chopped up the table, the walls, the chairs. He knocked over jars and dishes. He smelled each pot, cursed its contents, and dumped out all the food they were cooking" (324–325). Later, when he moved into her father's house, she woke to more domestic chaos: "Wen Fu shouting at the top of his voice and then the sound of something breaking on the floor." She went downstairs and found breakfast dishes scattered, noodles flung across chairs (438). Wen Fu's violent intrusions made mockery of gentle domesticity.

> By this point in their marriage, Winnie was astute enough to blame his mother!—for having given birth to him, for tending to all his desires as if she were his servant, for always feeding husband and son first, for allowing me to eat only after I had picked off bits of food stuck to my father-in-law's beard, for letting the meanness in her son grow like a strange appetite, so that he would always feel hungry to feed his own power. (325)

In that kind of domineering domesticity lies the root of dark power, generating destructiveness in those it tends.

One of the novel's final domestic images went full circle, returning to the house of Winnie's father. During the war, a Japanese officer had admired the furniture, praising its antiquity and value, then promising that if he cooperated in Shanghai, his furnishings could remain intact. In response, Winnie's father threw a cup of tea—gentle, healing, ritualistic beverage—against a 200-year-old scroll painting, ruining it. Later, news came out that he had betrayed his people to cooperate with the Japanese. His servants left him and, emotionally and domestically destabilized, he collapsed with a stroke.

Now, Wen Fu was in the house, convinced there was treasure, tearing up walls and floors in his rough, greedy way. The ironic joke was the futility of his efforts. "Now your father is ordering Wen Fu around," San Ma told Winnie. "Now Wen Fu is chasing your father's dreams. Now that house is falling down on top of him" (487). Once again, a violent, chaotic power was destroying domestic harmony.

And using domestic weapons to do so.

NINE

THE SACRED
IN THE MUNDANE

*"When thinking, speaking, and
doing are one, this is magic time.
God time."*

from "Fall from Grace" by Noelle Oxenhandler

We have explored some of the many subtle, complex, social, historical and psychological ways that domestic traditions and practices shape women's consciousness. The final uncharted realm is the spiritual one— which sounds a bit highflown for such an earthbound, concrete set of acts and values. Yet it is precisely the physicality of domestic acts and objects that leads us toward pure spirit. In *The Origins of Religions*, Julien Ries traces the word "sacred" to the root *sak* and branches over to its Latin verb form, *sancire*, meaning "to confer validity, reality, to make something become real." What is deemed sacred determines what is considered real—thus the only way to explain the sacred is by means of real experience (119). By sustaining everyday life and restoring simple order, a housekeeper builds a bridge between experience and its sacred meaning. As cook, cleaner, hostess and healer, she plays roles of mythic, even cosmic import—whether she knows it or not.

Thomas Moore indicates this intersection of spirituality and domesticity with a poetic depth psychology that honors the "gods of the house." "To them," he writes, "a scrub brush is a sacramental object, and when we use this implement with care we are giving something to the soul" (179). Already, in one brief quote, we can distinguish a sense of general sacredness ruling the home; a particular sacred object; an attitude of reverence as we use it to perform daily chores.

It is dangerous—and paradoxical—to try to analyze the irreducible or label the intangible. Before we artificially separate sacred objects from actions and simple actions from rituals, then, we must at least note the impossibility of the task. Domestic objects become sacred through association with domestic rituals, beliefs or experiences—and the next ritual then draws some of its sacred power from these objects. The sacred realm, in other words, is a fluid, interpenetrating whole whose various aspects constantly inform and inspire each other.

A Catholic priest once explained to me that when we put archetypal elements (universally powerful elements such as earth, water, fire and air) in the context of a myth (some narrative expression of deeper, otherwise inexplicable meaning), we arrive at a particular gesture. Bread in the context of the Exodus gives us Passover; bread in the context of Christ's death and resurrection gives us Eucharist. In the same way, objects which represent the values of home, shelter, nurture, care, fidelity, cleansing, intimacy and communion can connect us to the spiritual realm. When we honor those objects' deeper significance by treating them with a certain reverence—not necessarily bowing to a scrubbie, but valuing its role in our life—we tacitly acknowledge that spiritual realm. And when we use those objects in repetitive, performative ways, guided by an underlying myth about home or relationship or society, we are engaging in domestic ritual.

Sacred Objects

James Joyce once said that "any object, intensely regarded, may be a gate of access to the incorruptible eon of the gods" (Lawlor 12). In *Ordinarily Sacred*, Lynda Sexson makes this sentiment specific, suggesting that everyday household objects and acts can be hierophanies, windows to the sacred (9). We can readily see her premise in an extreme example: the cauldron, chalice, wand and *athame* used in the magical arts of witchcraft (Wicca) traditionally have been simple household utensils: a blackened soup kettle, a cup, a broomstick and a knife. Not only were these utensils easy to whisk back to normal duty if a ceremony was interrupted, but they honored nature, everyday reality and traditional women's work, all of which lay at the core of Wicca's mythic structure.

What if you're not a witch? "Usually we limit our perception of symbols to a narrow range of forms—the flag, the cross, the dollar sign—but every object can be infused with symbolic content," notes architect Anthony Lawlor. "An old baseball glove can become a symbol of a child's freedom and innocence; a sweater knitted by a friend can represent loving companionship" (10). The big white ceramic bowl you inherited from your grandmother can represent the tenderness and generosity of spirit with which she kneaded bread for her family. And Andy Warhol's collection of Fiestaware can represent his creative whimsy, commanding a high price at posthumous auction.

The objects that took on symbolic resonance in the novels were, with what almost seemed disproportionate frequency, domestic objects. The more we know about the hidden powers of the domestic realm, the better we understand that frequency. In *The Longings of Women*, Leila focused on the Imari plate as a symbol of marital love—and shattered it when infidelity was proven. In *A Thousand Acres*, Ginny reverently approached the contents of the linen closet, the green beans and relishes of dinnertime. In *Beloved*, Sethe's sacred objects were bread and fire, ribbons and flowers. And for the characters in *Tracks*, whose world-view already accepted objects as imbued with spirit, anything from the doll sewn by Nanapush's wife to tea, berries, an ice bucket or a knife could carry sacred power.

Occasionally, objects sacred to one person will carry an import others see as dark, false or negative. In *The Kitchen God's Wife*, those objects included the evil bird scissors that carried the power of death, as well as the benignly symbolic sewing machine Winnie left to sustain her friend, and the ambiguous silver chopsticks that represented her futile dreams of a happy marriage. In *The Other Side*, Ellen's granddaughter, Marilyn, mused about the precious carpet of her childhood home, which was treated as though it covered an altar to Zeus: "The fierce saving for it: pennies stolen from the family pleasure. And the pride, the interdictions: Don't walk on it with your shoes on. No food on the broadloom.... The yearned-for, unapproached God" (338). That sacred object was static and untouchable, representing something to be desired and cherished, revered and fiercely protected—but never with familiarity, lest the mother offend what she idolized and jinx her contingent security.

From Objects to Action

Some sacred objects simply sit on a shelf, collecting dust and adoration. Others we use, putting their power into motion. The motion need not be choreographed into a ritual; it may instead be a mindless chore, a gesture that triggers certain thoughts or feelings, or a mechanical routine, empty of deeper meaning. But even those simple, nonritual activities have a spiritual dimension: as Sexson notes, everyday chores—like more formal, recognizable sacred rites—"realign us with the known and keep us safe from the chaos of new perception" (86).

In the symbolic actions that propelled their plots forward, the six novelists often uncovered correspondences between the mundane and the sacred, naming them so briefly or casually that a reader could easily miss their deeper significance. In *Beloved*, for example, kindly Stamp Paid brought his harvest of freshly picked berries—a reminder of creation's abundant goodness—to the community, then stayed to watch them, corporately, with gratitude and reverence, "sampling one at a time the berries that tasted like church" (136). The gift was a simple act; it used an object that carried a certain symbolism, but in a one-time mimesis of formal ritual.

In *A Thousand Acres*, Ginny and her husband, ready to separate, felt the weight of unspoken words in the familiar steam of supper preparations. Suddenly Ginny remembered the broiler, and although she and Ty remained silent, "the contained roar of the gas and then, a minute later, the first sizzling of meat juices, took on the volume and weight of oracular mutterings, almost intelligible." It was as though the objects already knew her innermost state, already knew the inevitability of her next act. After listening to them speak for her soul, Ginny gathered enough courage to ask for $1000 and leave (330). Not a ritual act, just an act alive to symbolic meaning.

From Act to Ritual

When the action using symbolic objects is regularly repeated, in a prescribed way, to achieve a certain effect whose meaning is based in a mythic understanding of reality, that action enters the realm of ritual. Here, objects and gestures unite in the context of a shared explanatory narrative. Symbols become props and prompters, knowable, sensible representations of what is invisible. They lend power by allowing our consciousness to ally itself with forces bigger than itself.

In ancient civilization, rituals used symbolic objects to create, as concretely as possible, a perfect correspondence with the archetype, whether it be the life-giving earth mother, the mystical higher self or the omniscient wise father. Similarly, in *The Other Side*, when unhappily married Cam wished her friend Silvia would perform a magic ritual with tea leaves or the "entrails of chicken still warm from the slaughter," those natural objects symbolized—and made real in Cam's mind, if only for a moment—a power to know what was hidden, and to influence the cosmic pattern (28).

We have mentioned the object—what about the subject? Because the powers, principles or values brought to life by a domestic ritual are invisible, they must be performed symbolically for a witness—even if the witness is only "an ideal spectator who is not visible, God, perhaps, or a dead mother" (Driver 81). Observation mediates the ritual act, connecting the physical event with its spiritual significance across the bridge of symbolism.

Thus observed, symbolic objects, already meaningful, come to dynamic, efficacious life when a ritual puts them into play. Action is vital:

rituals "are more like washing machines than books," quips Driver, emphasizing the active process of ritualization instead of treating ritual as a static repository for wisdom (93). In emphasizing the importance of "display"—the showing of a doing—Driver stresses the ritual's verbs rather than its nouns. Although display "moves the enactment toward a certain objectivity," giving it a tangible reality outside the self, it still places emphasis on the process. "The commitment of the body remains crucial" (88).

From this emphasis on action, it is only a short step to the actor. Rabuzzi notes that, in domestic rituals, "enactment relates both to a way of performing tasks and, in the case of housework, to a mode of relationship the housewife establishes between herself and her home" (98). Driver reminds us that the ultimate purpose of any ritual is not the achievement of its immediate goal, or the incidental achievement of social solidarity. "The ultimate purpose of ritualization...is nothing other than the production of ritualized agents, persons who have an instinctive knowledge of these schemes embedded in their bodies, in their sense of reality, and in their understanding of how to act" (221).

You are what you eat, my grandmother used to say; here we could add, you are how you clean and cook. Which means a woman doing housework can assume the position of a shaman, who transforms reality independent of any institution, rather than serving a particular religious body as a priest would. The difference leaves the woman or the shaman closer to the elements, simpler, as we can infer from Morrison's contrast of "a white preacher who prayed for their souls while Sethe peeled potatoes and Grandma Baby sucked air" (120).

Identifying Domestic Rituals

For those of us accustomed to ritual as a stiffly ceremonial event at which one sits, stands and kneels with docility, it may be difficult even to recognize the domestic version. Sacred domestic objects are not draped in purple or elevated in gold, but can be as simple as an egg; sacred domestic language is not Hebrew, Latin or Sanskrit, but the wordless language of familiar bodily movements; sacred domestic enactments are not imbued with authority, but hidden away in a humble home. Yet domestic rituals, too, are about performance, power, the bringing about of a certain effect. Ritual "invokes the presence and actions of powers which, without the ritual, would not be present or active at that time and place" or in that way (Driver 97).

Clarissa Pinkola Estés tells the story of Baba Yaga, the Wild Mother, who "instructs the ordering of the house of the soul." Vasalisa's first task is a domestic ritual: she must launder her clothes, which in the old country requires descending to the river and performing specific ablutions. By renewing the cloth, Vasalisa cleanses her psyche. Washing "not only means to purify, it also means—like baptism from the Latin *baptiza*—to drench, to permeate with a spiritual numen and mystery" (95). Vasalisa's next task is to sweep, and Estes notes the organic nature of this task: "In Eastern European fairy tales, brooms are often made of sticks from trees and bushes, and sometimes the roots of wiry plants." Vasalisa is using nature itself in a ritual that clears away debris and restores order, just as "a wise woman keeps her psychic environ uncluttered" (96).

After reading examples such as these, any household chore might seem like a sacramental ritual. But circumstances radically alter the chore's spiritual content. In *The Longings of Women*, Becky looked around at the Burgess's blue and white living room and gloried in the *absence* of domestic work: "Mama would love the room. It would feel better than church, clean and uplifting and nothing to do in it, nothing to straighten or scrub or dust" (167). "Church" for Mama meant serenity: a moment of peace and contemplation that freed her from mundane obligations to a flawed disorderly reality. Her mundane obligations may have been repetitive, but they were far too wearying and oppressive to be ritual.

In happier circumstances, however, domestic rituals can *celebrate* spiritual connections to our embodied, sensuous, everyday lives. Poet Anne Sexton finds joy "in the chapel of eggs I cook/each morning,/in the outcry from the kettle" (Sewell 200). Ecofeminist philosopher Carol Bigwood notes that "sometimes, in the midst of the familiar and the most humble circumstances, a most strange giving occurs: in the kitchen, for example, with a freshly cut cabbage" (289).

When domestic acts are not oppressive, they can act as windows to the sacred, breaking light into the dull solid brick of daily life. The private, unofficial domestic rituals that grow out of regular shared acts of cooking, eating, cleansing and mending are rooted in our physical, instinctive life, but that does not exclude them from performing as vehicles for the sacred. Quite the contrary: these acts take their shape from our most basic biological needs, yet they can communicate complex ideas and carry us into the highest realms of intuition, creativity, empathy and reverence.

How do we know when that's happening? Ritual has become such a ubiquitous way of perceiving and analyzing human experience that it is hard to identify with any specificity. Bell says there is no explicit consensus about what's intrinsic to ritual, but lists three consistently cited characteristics: formality, fixity and repetition (92). When a domestic act is formalized and performed a certain way, by a certain person, at a certain time and after a given interval, we may be looking at a domestic ritual.

Its supernatural endpoint or message could be any of hundreds; the arena is as large as human experience itself.

We can begin to classify domestic rituals by considering the three basic rites of passage described by anthropologist Victor Turner: rites of separation (washings, cleansings and other purifications) that remove us from a certain status or condition; rites of incorporation (the sharing of food) which allow us to reenter society on a new basis (Driver 157); and rites of the threshhold (ceremonies at certain points in the life cycle, liminal states, transformations). All three categories yield ready domestic parallels, reminding us how closely the physical realm of housework connects with the spiritual realm of ritual.

Purification Rites

To understand domestic "purification rites," we first have to understand why dirt would be considered impure (a concept with which many teenagers struggle). In *Purity and Danger,* Douglas explores the "pollution" concept, linking it to the human fear of ambiguity. She says that by walling out certain conditions and setting criteria for purity, we protect cherished principles and categories from contradiction and therefore from corruption. What is unclean represents what is unclear; "dirt is essentially disorder." By ridding ourselves of dirt's chaos, then, we make a positive effort to organize our environment. "There is no such thing as absolute dirt," Douglas adds quickly; "it exists in the eye of the beholder" (2). Furthermore, while disorder may spoil our pattern, it also represents the ground, the materials, the infinite potential for pattern making; thus carries both danger and power.

We can easily note the subjectivity of dirt, the varying attitudes toward disorder and the idiosyncratic standards of cleanliness as we sweep through the novels, moving from Ellen's rough old-fashioned housekeeping to Fleur's natural ease and Winnie's nervous frenzy; from Becky's worshipful tidying to Leila's sloppy order, her sister's chaotic order, her housekeeper's obsessive order. Sethe kept the house functioning but didn't worry about outside eyes, except Paul D's when he first arrived. But Ginny, even before the lawyer's advice, cleaned for the world to see.

All these characters had their own rituals of purity and impurity; each took shape according to the degree of unity and conformity the woman demanded from experience, as well as the extent of her need to work out symbolic patterns and display them publicly. In *The Longings of Women,* Becky was drawn toward absolute newness, cleanliness and order as a way to free herself from the chaos of childhood poverty. When she and Terry moved to a new condominium, she "drifted through the rooms, touching the new objects, the lamp she had just learned she was not to leave in its cellophane wrappings." Becky made it obvious that she would have preferred the pristine cellophane, with its implicit guarantee of security from dirt or damage. Every day, "she touched the newly bare lamp shade, she touched lightly the clean ivory wall, she stroked the Formica counter," sensuously aroused by the material orderliness and beauty of these objects. Her actions might seem empty, merely ritualistic, but to Becky, their ground was existential: after all, "she thought this was paradise," holding out its promise of life after the deathly rot and ugliness of her past (197).

As Douglas explains, "pollution ideas work in the life of society at two levels, one largely instrumental, one expressive." At the instrumental level, people try to influence each other's behavior. We find jointly held beliefs about danger, contagion, the laws of nature and the moral code, as people try to force each other into good citizenship (or women intimidate each other into virtuous domesticity). At the expressive level, pollution ideas are used as analogies for the social order (3). In *The Kitchen God's Wife,* instead of Winnie trying to teach her daughter the importance of proper housekeeping (instrumental), we see the filth of their resting places as they flee the chaos of war, or the decay of Winnie's father's house after he consorts with the enemy. "Paint was peeling everywhere, tiles on the floor were cracked, so that dirt underneath showed," and the greenhouse, nurturing repository of new life, had grown black with mold (429).

Floors surface again in *A Thousand Acres,* where Ginny seemed always to be vacuuming, scrubbing or waxing one, her method so regular and so transcendent it does indeed qualify as domestic ritual. That is not surprising, if we consider Lawlor's architectural analysis:

> The floor beneath your feet embodies the desire to find stable ground in a world of constant flux. Level and firm, it externalizes the consciousness of support and uplift, acting as a spreading field of information that gives walls and pillars a place to stand. The floor is a stage, the unmoving, eternal base upon which the diverse play of life is enacted. When we make a floor, we engage in the primal act of marking the boundaries of our personal territory. Drawing lines on the spreading earth establishes our home in the world. (80)

Ginny had grown up in a world where careful lines plotted valuable farmland, the source of security, the root of being. Now those boundaries were being contested, and their supposed security was beginning to seem oppressive. So she redrew the boundaries of her own, smaller world within a world, purifying the foundation to make it safe and her life worthwhile.

The purifying, baptizing, sacralizing dimension of washing revealed itself most clearly in *Tracks*, when Pauline—ostensibly so holy—mortified her flesh (and presumably stifled her libido) by refusing to clean herself or her clothing. Finally, exasperated, Fleur forced her to bathe.

"She ripped off my homemade underwear, threw my shift and knickers in a steaming iron cauldron," recalled Pauline, almost with relish. "She also had a smaller kettle boiling, and a couple large tin kerosene cans of water that she poured into the washtub along with the snow." Pauline paid reverent attention to the details—the receptacles, the procedure—of the impromptu ceremony. "I stepped into the warmth," she recalled, her resistance quite literally stripped away (153–54). After the bath, she let Fleur take her clothes out to the yard "to air over a smudge fire of slow-burning sage and sweetgrass" (154).

When Pauline was clean and dry, she visited the outhouse, an interesting passage to another form of cleansing, and a linkage of bodily purity with vulnerability. "Fleur had thrown my nest of underclothes"—an almost wild image—"out in the woods once they boiled apart. She gave me floursacks to wear, luxuriously smooth." After the ceremony, Pauline recalled, "the habit was warm against my newly opened skin and the cold air rushed in through the pores of my hands and face. The wind was like an elixir that put me mindless and at peace. I felt no jealousy or zeal. I purified myself and then, very quietly, returned" (155). She had been exorcised of her demons, forced into a sensory awareness of her body, reordered into harmony and integrity. The pollution of her distorted sense of self had been cleansed away, barriers of social acceptability firmly reestablished.

In *The Kitchen God's Wife*, Winnie's ritual self-cleansing was a desperate attempt to purify her body and soul after Wen Fu's degrading sexual invasions. "When he was done satisfying himself, he would get up and go to his room, not one word spoken between us," she recalled.

> I would get up too. I always kept a basin of water in my room for just this reason. I would wet a rough cloth, then wash myself, rubbing hard wherever he had touched my skin, over and over again. And when I was done, I would throw this dirty water out the window. Pwah! (422)

The intersections of intimacy with purification are not always cleansing or cathartic, however. In *The Other Side*, Dan's daughter Staci hated staying at her great-grandparents' house; she was frightened of her cousin John, but determined not to give him any power over her. Sweaty, she took a shower, hating the disgusting old linoleum and feeling that John was outside on a ladder watching her. As intense as Sartre writing about the objectifying power of the gaze, confused young Staci "can smell the dust in the water; even the water doesn't seem clean. The shampoo on the side of the tub must have been there for a million years." She applied it anyway, wishing in vicious detail that John would fall off the ladder and break his neck. "She takes the towel off the rack and begins to dry herself. She makes sure she does it the way she always would, no special way for him," keeping to her own ritual of bodily cleanliness despite the break in routine that has forced her into a new awareness of her body (204). Then she stands at the window, staring at him so he knows she knows.

Meanwhile, as Ellen lay dying, the chthonic chaos she battled over a lifetime of housekeeping flooded her bedroom. Too ill for performance, she contented herself with a sort of anti-sacred language, speaking "curses. Maledictions. Dreadful wishes. Also simple filth." Her brain reached "down to the sea's bottom, back, down, to the bog's soaked floor, to mud, then to the oozing beds of ancient ill will, prehistoric rage, vengeance, punishment in blood." The bars of her hospital bed shook with rage, and even the drugs could not "stop her telling what she has seen. It is dirty; there is nothing; we should suffer, all of us, for it is all that we deserve" (6). Ellen was overcome by filth at several levels: sexual, earthly, primordial, and finally, as the teleological destination of all those lesser filths, the cosmic dirtiness of a world without grace or purpose, a world impossible to purify.

An interesting parallel occurred in *Beloved*, where Sethe used the word "dirt" to describe the results of race hatred. "Anybody white could take your whole self for anything that came to mind," she explained, aching to make her baby see the truth. "Not just work, kill, or maim you, but dirty you. Dirty you so bad you couldn't like yourself anymore. Dirty you so bad you forgot who you were" (251).

Rites of Incorporation

With the possible exception of "fast food," most meals are sufficiently symbolic to become a sacred part of ritual. Because it is primary, crucial to human survival, food takes on deep universal meaning in every culture. In *The Sociology of Food*, Mennell and his coauthors describe eating as "the physical act that mediates between self and not-self, native essence and foreign matter, the inside and the outside." They emphasize the importance of this mediation by reminding us that, "until eaten and absorbed into one's bodily system, food is no more than a substance 'out there.'" In our daily munchings and slurpings, we forget what a profound and powerful transaction we are experiencing. But, the authors point out, "when the demands of survival necessitate an inventive stretching of one's definition of food," we find our very sense of self tested.

> Psychological survival hinges on the wresting of meaning from arbitrary infliction of humiliation and pain; survival of family and the ethnic group not only presupposes individually successful eating but may demand unusually difficult 'swallowing' to ensure a continued supply of nourishment for the next generation. (26)

In *The Longings of Women*, we learned a great deal about Becky—whose values had more to do with materialism than sex—when she wandered happily through the new condominium, noting "three rooms for just the two of them, everything so clean and sweet she could have popped the refrigerator and the vanity chair into her mouth" (197). That exaggerated impulse—not yet a ritual, but certainly illustrative of incorporation—told us she wanted to take these objects, and the success, wealth and safety they represented, into her very self.

In *Beloved*, too, the meaning of food surpassed social ceremony and took on existential import. When Denver was crying because she had no self, panicking because she could not figure out where her own body started and stopped, crashing through a cold house to find Beloved, she thought in a flash, "Death is a skipped meal compared to this." At precisely that moment, memories started to flood back, and Denver remembered "sitting at the table eating turnips and saving the liquor for her grandmother"—an act of lively relationship that doubled the shock of learning Baby Suggs was dead (123).

Finally, consider the incident in *Tracks* where Margaret "shared out some dried meat from the pocket of her dress, tore at it like a young snapping turtle" (50). Nanapush envied her strong sharp teeth, and his gaze and sucking triggered raw sexual innuendo. Again, the act was too casual to qualify as ritual, but it showed us incorporation soaked with the vital energy of the life force.

Later in *Tracks*, Nanapush returned from a life-denying state of depression after Margaret forced "last summer's berries" into his mouth (127). And toward the novel's end, he presided over a very formal ritual of incorporation: First, he built a blazing fire, hot enough to drive away Pauline's "scavenger" eyes. Then, he recalled, "the water on the fire boiled, steam rose before me, and Moses began to sing. That is when I put my hands through the stirring cloud, into the swirl, and brought up a bit of choice meat. Fleur ate this very quietly, chewing slowly" (189). The description harked back to the cauldron of skulls Fleur once stirred, but it also lent a magical dimension to this healing incorporation; the meat was choice, life-giving flesh, and Fleur took it into her body reverently, "taking strength" (189).

In another ritual meal, Margaret offered her starving family a thin soup of "shredded meat, marrow, and some cattail roots, boiled." The food signaled the difficulty of survival, yet "it scented the room, called to the body with its fragrance." Margaret served carefully, starting with her man, Nanapush. "She dished the next plate to Eli, then one to Fleur, who halved hers with Lulu." Fleur was gaunt from pregnancy, and Lulu ate with "ravenous attention." Pauline got the little that was leftover, and had drunk it before she realized Margaret had taken none for herself. "Nanapush handed his nearly full plate back to Margaret, who took a spoonful and passed the dish to Fleur, whose bowl was already cleaned by Lulu." Margaret explained away her self-sacrifice, lying that she had eaten while she cooked, and adding, "We old ones don't need much, because our stomachs are too bitter" (145).

Toward the end of *Tracks*, Father Damien came to show Nanapush, Margaret and the others the foreclosure notices that showed their land would be seized. As offering, he brought with him "a slab of bacon, a can of lard, a sack of flour, and a twist of baking powder. Margaret had rice and a pound of green coffee beans. Unbelievably, her pockets bulged with turnips," which looked to Nanapush "like treasures" (172). The hard-to-get foodstuffs were enough for a ritual meal: "The bread," whose ingredients had been brought by a Catholic priest, "was passed around," and the participants ached "to lose control, to wolf each crumb into ourselves with snarls, to cry out at the goodness of it." Their response, driven by bodily hunger, was as intensely reverent as any priest could wish: "Everyone concentrated on each slow bite, and there was no sound but chewing" (173).

In *A Thousand Acres*, family meals felt less like a ceremonial sharing and more like a tense drama, but they were ritualistic in their predictability, and did prove capable of gluing together a fragmented group of people. After the initial upheaval over the farm, Ginny mused:

> It did occur to me that we wouldn't want the problem with Caroline to affect our usual routine, so when it was my turn to have Daddy over for supper, the Tuesday night after the property transfer, I cooked what I always did for him—pork chops baked with tomatoes (my third-to-last quart from the year before), fried potatoes, a salad, and two or three different kinds of pickles. (47)

The mood of that dinner was entirely different from the ceremonial anniversary dinner the sisters and their husbands had six years earlier at the Starlight Supper Club. "They had three kinds of herring on the salad bar and some kind of garlic toasts that had been fried slowly in butter until they were as hard as canning jar lids, except that they fragmented and vanished as soon as you put them on your tongue," recalled Rose, blissful at the near-eucharistic recollection (58).

A communal rite of incorporation also occurred in Beloved at the impromptu feast hosted by "Baby Suggs, holy." She was inspired when wise old Stamp Paid brought blackberries and fed some to baby Denver, whose "thrilled eyes and smacking lips" instantly reminded everyone around her of the goodness of creation. "Finally Baby Suggs slapped the boys' hands away from the bucket and sent Stamp around to the pump to rinse himself. She had decided to do something with the fruit worthy of the man's labor and his love." First, she made pastry dough and decided to share the pies with her neighbors, then Sethe suggested bolstering the gift with a couple of chickens. Like loaves and fishes, "it grew to a feast for ninety people" (136).

Alas, Baby Suggs' holiness and largesse, her unconcerned public display of abundance, turned her invited guests against her, just as a prophet's good works often win bitter envy and reprisal. Baby's house, "rocking with laughter, goodwill and food for ninety, made them angry. Too much, they thought. Where does she get it all, Baby Suggs, holy?" They ate her food, but they resented her wisdom, her faith, her tireless "loving, cooking, cooking, loving, preaching." They resented the ritual power "to take two buckets of blackberries and make ten, maybe twelve, pies; to have turkey enough for the whole town pretty near, new peas in September, fresh cream but no cow, ice *and* sugar, batter bread, bread pudding, raised bread, shortbread." So much bread, so much sustenance, how *dare* she? The community's self-hatred turned to venom: "Loaves and fishes were His powers—they did not belong to an ex-slave" (137).

Leila's Thanksgiving feast had an entirely different purpose and tone, but it uncovered the same archetypes of fruitful harvest and the good earth mother. (It also served the same unnerving function of unleashing deepseated familial and communal tensions—as though people could not partake in such a ritual meal without their emotional truths surfacing.) Like Baby, "Leila liked the ritual feel of preparing a feast." She lovingly included "old favorites David would have been furious if she forgot, like the two desserts, the cold maple Bavarian cream and the hot rum pumpkin pie." Her acts were not entirely self-sacrificing, however: the feast was "her folly, partly designed to please her family but partly designed to please herself." It proved more folly than she realized, revealing her husband's adulterous paternity and the futility of her own good-faith, good-wife efforts. In preparing her ritual feast, she had "aimed to impress some archaic deity, a goddess who would reward her for being a good woman by allowing her to keep what she had" (117). Instead, she was forced to see the truth of the archetype that had held her captive for so long.

There were feasts in *The Kitchen God's Wife*, too: huge feasts prepared by Winnie with her dowry money for Wen Fu's friends; feasts at weddings and after funerals; special intimate meals with parents; special homecoming meals after journeys and separations. K. C. Chang acknowledges the importance of feasting in traditional Chinese culture:

> Where Western hosts would devote their attention to silverware, tablecloths, candles, and centerpieces to underline the formality or importance of a dinner, the Chinese would escalate the quantity and variety and quality of the contents in the plates and bowls for the same purpose. (315–316)

The degree of formality increases with the importance of the occasion and the class of the participants, effectively separating the feast from the mundane. "There is little of the Indian attitude that all food transactions are sacred and even the humblest meal is like a divine sacrifice," notes Chang. "The Chinese belief is the other way round: a sacrifice to the gods is a projection or type of a meal, a subset of ordinary meals in which gods and spirits, rather than visible, tangible humans, are the fellow diners" (367).

The cosmic dimension of feasting makes extra sense of Winnie's carefully chosen trousseau of chopsticks, dishes and other domestic accoutrements, symbolic as well as practical objects. The importance of the Chinese New Year, a major holiday in which fancy foodstuffs and alcohol are offered to ancestral spirits, sheds light on Winnie's remarks about offerings to the Kitchen God. And the Chinese thinking about yin and yang qualities in foods, with harmony and balance as the overall goal for both nutrition and life, explains Winnie's pickiness about certain foods and her steady trust in tea as a cure. It also explains her aunt's vehement letter, urging her to "drink lots of hot things if the sickness runs cold, cold things if the sickness runs hot" (426).

Tea, to the Chinese, is far more than a thirst-quenching beverage. In her wartime travels, Winnie was warned about a Lady White Ghost: "She likes to pull people off the road, make them stay longer and drink ten thousand rounds of tea with her. The tea of immortality, we call it. You drink one sip, you never want to leave her cloudy house" (291). Parallel to the Christian eucharist, this was a rite of incorporation that spirited one *away* from everyday life, opening the door to eternity.

Crossing the Threshhold

The final rite of passage is the rite of the threshhold—in other words, passage between two places or states. Often the locus of the ritual's power is the liminal state between the two—*limen* being Latin for threshhold. The state's been described (with reference to a marriage ceremony, just before vows are taken) as the moment a trapeze artist lets go of one swing, as she whirls in midair to take hold of the other.

Because such existentially charged passages often transform us, transformative rituals slide easily into this category, beginning with simpler instances when the transformation is something the person brings about, rather than undergoes. Baking bread, for example, is a strong, fundamental domestic act, and if we look closely we recognize it as a creative process, a rite of transformation common to so many times and places it is almost universal. In "The Acolyte," Denise Levertov writes about a woman baking bread, noting that it's not "the baked and cooled and cut/ bread she's thinking of," but rather the way "the dough rises and has a life of its own" (Sewell 187). In the act of transformation lies the ritual's meaning.

In *The Other Side*, even the barely domesticated Magdalene knew this when she set out to redecorate her house, staving off cancer in the process. It was the hunting of the antiques and the draping of the purple curtains that promised her life. Just as, in Beloved, it was the kneading of the bread that kept away painful memories.

Most domestic ritual can be considered, in the loosest sense, transformative, because it alters the conditions of one's life. When Ginny was cleaning house at triple speed, wearing her nice cotton dresses to trim the lawn and keeping everything ship-shape, she was actually creating a blameless life in her neighbors' minds, using the public display of her housework to enact ideals of virtue and social responsibility. Pauline did the same with her ministrations to the dead; Leila with her Thanksgiving feast. Winnie selected her trousseau as a way to signal her wifeliness to the world. Mary, the perfect homemaker, quite literally enacted her way into a home again. All these women were making domestic processes public, and thereby using them to create or transform part of reality.

There are more specific kinds of transformation, however, that occur as we cross life's various threshholds. A healing ritual, for example, carries someone over the threshhold that divides illness from health. When Nanapush saved Fleur a second time, he did so with supernatural help, dreaming the method of mixing and crushing certain ingredients to cure her illness. "The person who visited my dream told me what plants to spread," he told Lulu, "so that I could plunge my arms into a boiling stew kettle, pull meat from the bottom, or reach into the body itself and remove...the name that burned, the sickness" (188). He did indeed plunge his own flesh into the mysterious boiling cauldron and restore Fleur's strength.

His contact with the supernatural was far more healing than Pauline's sadomasochistic devotion. Hoping to lose herself in God's tasks at the convent, she scraped her hand raw shattering ice on the kitchen buckets. "I continued to smash my fist into the water until the water told the story, turned faintly bloody," she recalled, at which point another nun "appeared at my side and held my fingers still in hers. She led me from the stove, dabbed my hand clean, wrapped it in a cloth." The other nun's careful, loving actions were not ritualistic in themselves, but they had a blessing quality, and when she sent Pauline back to sleep, gently admonishing her that "even a Saint must rest," Pauline went obediently (164).

In *Longings of Women*, one of the more prosaic liminal states was the threshhold between waking and sleep. "Most people had going-to-bed rituals," observed Mary, detailing the observable clues—which ranged from sheets redolent with sex to a TV set for David Letterman to the warm milk and nutmeg she had preferred when she had a home. Now, she never slept soundly, because she could not trust her surroundings (150).

In *Tracks*, Fleur led us into liminal states whenever she ventured into the spirit world. But she first took on mythic proportions when we saw her boiling heads:

> Her green dress, drenched, wrapped her like a transparent sheet. A skin of lakeweed. Black snarls of veining clung to her arms. Her braids were loose, half unraveled, tied behind her neck in a thick loop. She stood in steam, turning skulls through a vat with a wooden paddle. When scraps boiled to the surface, she bent with a round tin sieve and scooped them out. She'd filled two dishpans. (22)

The passage made it easy to perceive Fleur as the bride of the lake monster, closely identified with nature, wildness and power, unafraid, victorious over death, extracting its remains for her own purposes. We had already heard Nanapush echo her liminal, between-worlds role when he followed the dream spirit's instructions and boiled a cauldron of meat to heal her: "The water on the fire boiled, steam rose before me, and Moses began to sing. That is when I put my hands through the stirring cloud, into the swirl, and brought up a bit of choice meat" (189).

Pauline would have been incapable of recreating that scenario; at the threshhold between life and death, her only ability was to push people toward death. She had "the merciful scavenger's heart." When a girl her age died in her presence, the dark intimacy of that moment loosed something in her. From Bernadette, who gathered up her torn cloth and knitting when she went to a deathbed (66), Pauline learned to make death welcome with domestic chores, scrubbing and waxing and polishing, chopping wood, kneading and baking bread for the living in the house of death. She also learned the ritual of arranging the body, "the washing and combing and stopping of its passages, the careful dressing, the final weave of a rosary around the knuckles" (69). She could not weave the strands of life together, but she could release a corpse's soul into the next world.

In *Beloved*, ritual significances flowed like bloodied water when the women of Sethe's community undertook an "exorcism." Denver had sought their help, explaining the murdered child's presence. "Shall we pray?" the women asked the fiercest of their number. "First," she answered. "Then we got to get down to business." They accumulated slowly outside Sethe's house, and "some brought what they could and what they believed would work. Stuffed in apron pockets, strung around their necks, lying in the space between their breasts" (257). When they arrived, "catfish was popping grease in the pan and they saw themselves scoop German potato salad onto the plate," their imaginations turning instantly to communal celebrations of bygone days (258). They prayed and hollered. Then the white man Edward Bodwin drove up, and Sethe saw him, and all the past's hell broke loose. She went after him with an icepick. And the women stopped her.

The liminal, threshhold state Sethe fell into afterwards, when Beloved had gone for the second and final time, offered a stark contrast. Paul D returned to the house and found an earthy pairing of life and death that had its own natural dignity, nothing dirty about it. First, he saw a "riot of late-summer flowers where vegetables should be growing," a replacement of duty and practicality with carefree beauty. The ethereal was paired with the earthly; next he noticed "the odd placement of cans jammed with the rotting stems of things, the blossoms shriveled like sores. Dead ivy," twining in its organic state, accepting the morbid as necessity. "He walks to the front door and opens it. It is stone quiet," again a reminder of death. "In the place where once a shaft of sad red light had bathed him, locking him where he stood, is nothing"; the ghost has departed. "He glances quickly at the lightning-white stairs," reminiscent of heaven, and just as celebratory: "The entire railing is wound with ribbons, bows, bouquets" (270).

Paul D went into Sethe's room, but she was not there; the small bed had been stripped, and the room was hot, its air sealed in like a tomb. He finally found Sethe in Baby Suggs' room, "lying under a quilt of merry colors. Her hair, like the dark delicate roots of good plants, spreads and curves on the pillow" (271). As bound up in nature as Fleur, Sethe had been through an experience of the supernatural, and was hanging in the balance between life and death. The quilt of merry colors that had held Baby Suggs together was protecting her, and with Paul D's love she would now return to human life healthy and whole.

It took the symbols of both life (ribbon, flowers, color) and death (the rotting shriveling plants) to clear a path for Sethe's passage from one world to the other, and to offer hope for the future of her entire people. As Driver reminds us, "Rational political methods alone cannot bring about transformation of society from a less to a more just condition, because they cannot fuse the visionary with the actual (the absent with the present) as rituals do, thus profoundly affecting the moral life. Nor can ideas alone do this.... Ritualization is required" (184). That was true for Sethe; it was true for Winnie, who worked through her own past with the story of the Kitchen God's wife; it was true for Fleur, who protected her tribal home with a ritualistic trick, sawing down trees she loved in order to cheat the oppressors of their stolen treasure. Fleur's act was indeed liminal: it symbolized the killing of her people's culture, and the transcendent hope offered by spiritual resistance.

Transcending Time and Space

Rituals that evoke liminal states take away the limits of personal identity, suspending the particulars of geography and temporality without erasing consciousness. Indeed, we are aware of our own awareness in a heightened way, and the performance of the ritual unites the doing with the observing (Driver 157, 83). The rituals and symbols build an imaginative bridge between the visible and the invisible, shattering the boundaries of space and time to link us with both the unconscious and the transcendent.

A ritual takes place in a sacred space, a place consecrated to its purpose and delineated in a way that focuses the mind on deeper significance. In that place, the ordinary becomes significant and sacred "simply by being there" (Driver 48). Thus the ordained place of every spatula and strainer in a woman's kitchen; thus the freighted meanings found in *The Dining Room*, the A.J. Gurney play about a room whose ritual role in American family life has rapidly been hollowed by everything from TV to fragmented overbusy schedules.

Rabuzzi writes about consecration, "the ritual by which any space is formally sacralized," as a symbolic act that transforms an ordinary house into a home. Consecration does not require water any holier than tap water, however; we consecrate whenever we claim spiritual power in order to give physical reality meaning. "The qualities that make home sacred are the same ones that most people find so commonplace," she notes. "Yet ordinariness is not necessarily the same as neutrality" (58). Any space that functions as a home will carry, within its ordinariness, a promise of safety to ease our human fears; it will convey a sense of centeredness, remind us of our origins, link us to each other.

In *Beloved*, however, the home was haunted, and the safe sacred space was the clearing where Baby Suggs preached. Sethe thought of that place when the guilt, sorrow and rage of past hurts overwhelmed her, and she missed Baby's gentle ministrations, her faith-filled advice to lay down sword and shield, let the violence go. Missing Baby and her husband, Sethe decided that what had happened to Halle deserved ritual acknowledgment, "an arch built or a robe sewn. Some fixing ceremony" (86). So she went to the clearing with her daughters, all three shawled.

Smiley showed us the spiritual difference of different places at the end of her novel, when Ginny remembered the restaurant where she had found sanctuary from domestic emptiness:

> each cheerfully lit table bright with menus and paper place mats. On the other side of the black windows of Rose's kitchen, though, there was only outer space, a lightless, soundless vacuum that on this thousand acres came right down to the ground. (348)

The farmland Ginny had once cherished for its familiarity and security had metamorphosed into an existential landscape that was alien, transcendent yet full of dread.

Time is the other category broken by the liminal state. Ritual happens in other kinds of time than chronological, discretely measured clock time. Instead, we may feel Bergson's emotionally intuited duration, or the cyclical, biologically based time of the seasons, sex and reproduction, life and death. Then, as the ritual opens us into kairos, sacred time, we may approach the timelessness of the mystical state. Such descriptions of time sound a bit philosophical for a discussion of housekeeping, but there is a lost-in-time quality, an absorption in the present that happens when someone performs the tasks ritualistically, without hurry or self-consciousness or resentment. The physical boundaries of time and space collapse, and the limits of materiality and ego dissolve. There is also a cyclical quality to a task that "typically links its performer back in time to the company of female ancestors," notes Rabuzzi:

> To do a task precisely as you observed or were taught by your mother or grandmother is to experience a portion of what they each once did. Two kinds of knowledge are thus imparted: knowledge of what it is to be a housewife and knowledge of what it was to have been Grandma X. (102)

In "Women's Time," Julia Kristeva links both cyclical time and "monumental," all-encompassing, infinite time to female subjectivity, which she says emphasizes repetition and eternity. "On the one hand," she writes, "there are cycles, gestation, the eternal recurrence of a biological rhythm which conforms to that of nature." These cycles unite us with "extrasubjective," cosmic time and deep unnameable joy. And on the other hand, there is "the massive presence of a monumental temporality, without cleavage or escape," nonlinear (16).

We see both kinds of time in the novels. In *The Other Side*, Dan reminisced about his grandparents' steady domestic life, anchored in Ellen's homemaking and Vincent's loyalty. He realized suddenly that they had been "keeping the thread you were born holding between your fingers," just like the primitive societies he studied in college (346). Earlier in the novel, we saw the same kind of realization hit Ellen: she imagined her mother "young and running, singing, lifting the towel on the bread dough as she checked its rising."

The ritually-induced memory could not change physical reality, could not erase "the real truth of her mother, silent or gibbering, an animal, no woman now" (112). Still, the memory was both transcendent and transformative, hence Ellen's terror that if she, the only one who remembered, let go, the memory would be lost forever. By keeping her knowledge and love alive, she was honoring the best of "the young mother singing, her bare arms covered in soapsuds to the elbows, singing as she scrubs her husband's shirts. The clever fingers making shapes out of the dough: birds, animals, a pointed flower." Ellen's memory was sustaining her mother spiritually in much the same way the mother had sustained her family physically and emotionally, by making a home for them. "If I forget," Ellen thought, "she will become nothing, will disappear, will be homeless in the universe" (113).

In *Beloved's* even more circular narrative pattern, several historical incidents—especially the baby's murder—served as points of repeated return. Most were occasioned by a domestic ritual that opened the way for intimacy; then memory sent the characters spiraling forward again, but never toward closure. Chronological time did not confine the characters or regulate their movements, but memory served as a constant reminder of the importance of the past, and the interpenetration of past, present and future.

Memory and domestic ritual blended in *Tracks*, too: after suffering the masculine humiliation of being tied up, Nanapush got depressed, and it took Margaret's concerned nurturing to revive him. "She forced into my mouth a spoon of last summer's berries, and with that taste the sweetness of those days came back," he explained, adding that he "had not been certain those times would come again" (127). In other words, the act of feeding reawakened his body's will, and because the berries had significance in the cycle of nature's seasons, they evoked memories of the past and thus created hope for the future.

In *The Kitchen God's Wife,* Winnie had the same kind of synesthetic experience, with certain memories linked to her senses yet vanished from her intellect. "My tongue doesn't taste things the same way anymore," she complained. "Like celery, I can't eat celery anymore. All my life I loved celery. Now, as soon as I smell it, I tell myself no. And I don't even remember what made me not like it anymore." Winnie was baffled, not only by her loss of sensation, but by what she perceived as her mind's betrayal: "Why do some memories live only on your tongue or in your nose?" she asked plaintively (296). Like Sethe in *Beloved,* Winnie had felt too much pain and gone quite literally numb, her senses dulled by emotional truama. If Sethe could no longer see life's vivid colors, Winnie could not taste its savor.

Beneath ritual lies a foundation of myth, the cosmic narrative we use to explain and transform reality. Myth is meaning-making. Nanapush was acknowledging myth's significance when he talked about Fleur foolishly leaving the shelter of his house: "She was too young and had no stories or depth of life to rely upon. All she had was raw power, and the names of the dead that filled her" (7). Nanapush, by contrast, was nearing the end of his life, and he "had to squeeze so many stories into the corners of my brain. They're all attached, and once I start there is no end to telling because they're hooked from one side to the other, mouth to tail." In other words, they were living creatures. Nanapush went on to say he had saved himself during the year of sickness by starting a story: "Death could not get a word in edgewise, grew discouraged, and traveled on" (46).

The Ojibwa were especially open to the mythic realm because they did not distinguish between animate and inanimate; instead, they saw all of creation as animate, and space itself as filled with consciousness. Ceremonies of food, cleansing and story were frequent. And Erdrich's tales about Misshepeshu, the voracious water monster, or Fleur, shapeshifting into a bear or visiting the spirit world, explain life's horrors without reducing them to the physical, thus heal the listener and restore a transcendent sense of hope.

Tan's legend of the Kitchen God was the narrative that allowed Winnie to reevaluate her painful marriage and rediscover her identity. Similarly, in *Beloved,* Denver told her new sister the family stories, "giving blood to the scraps her mother and grandmother had told her—and a heartbeat. The monologue became, in fact, a duet as they lay down together" (78).

Both Chinese-American immigrant culture and post-slavery African-

American culture forged strong bonds between women. Community was their very source of survival, and connections to nature and the body were vital. In rituals of rootworking, herbal medicine, conjure or ghost talk and midwifery, comprehensive folk cultures emerged, and in animistic stories and myths about the supernatural, we see their particular symbols, structure, language and cosmology.

In *Beloved*, the natural and the supernatural were held in creative tension, neither dominating the other, and the result was a shrewdly practical, down-to-earth approach that accepted superstition and magic without batting an eye. Hence Baby could heal others in the clearing and her own psyche with a rainbow of colors, while a ghost banged pots and pans and a mother cooked and cleaned her way through sacrifice, resurrection and redemption.

(Note which novels anchored domestic rituals in relatively explicit mythologies: *Beloved*, *Tracks* and *The Kitchen God's Wife*, the three novels distanced by race and oppression from the white American mainstream. These novels were full of experiences that dehumanized and enslaved people because of their membership in a particular group, stripping away their traditions, meaning, purpose, security, relationship, dignity and identity. In the context of such deprivation, rituals and the myths that infused them restored hope and existential courage, linking and sustaining those who suffered.)

It's easy to speak of threshholds in an individual woman's life: menarche, the passage from the family home to the married home, childbirth, menopause. But the female body itself is often associated, especially in patriarchal cultures, with liminal states: it is perceived as the locus of a new life's coming-to-being and entrance into the world; as a representation of earth, irrationality, our lack of control, death; as a receptacle in which two separate bodies merge; as a fey repository for the irrational, a negotiation between this world and the next.

In *Reading Woman: Essays in Feminist Criticism*, Mary Jacobus describes patriarchy's creation of "woman as silent bearer of ideology.... a reserve of purity and silence" necessary in the din of the material world (28). This kind of ideology has given us "the angel in the house," woman as guardian of the domestic sanctuary, keeper of the home fire. Similarly, classical Greece gave us women as the muses, the sirens, the fates—and Navajo culture echoed those links with the Navajo Spider Woman offering the gift of weaving, the thread of destiny, the fabric of life and death.

All those powers of protection, nurturing, maintenance, inspiration, preservation have been—are—enacted every day, in the intimacy of the home, by women and, more and more often, by men, inheritors of domesticity's complex history, rich vocabulary, and deep significances.

TEN

MAKING HOME

everybody is drunk

and dancing in the kitchen

from "good times" by Lucille Clifton

I'd like to be able to report that a deepened intellectual understanding of domestic ritual has swept me up in a transcendent cloud of happy home-making. But scrubbing skin scales and grit off the bottom of the tub still feels like drudgery, and with my husband's affinity for '50s-style salty overprocessed casseroles, cooking is rapidly losing its charm.

Still, there are moments. Quick flashes of insight, like a wink from the Kitchen God's wife, when I do something domestic in order to soothe, celebrate, make safe or bring comfort. Now I *know* why homemade soup cures you, why fresh sheets refresh a tired mind, why making the same Thanksgiving dinner every year reminds a family they're a family. I also know the trace of my own mallet—why PMS turns the refusal of a second helping into a sure signal of unworthiness; why I bake to cajole and clean to feel virtuous. Comfort comes with the sure knowledge that I am not alone, that each act and response meshes into a vast set of domestic traditions stretching around the globe and back to prehistory.

As the novels suggest, those traditions are not stuffed with trivia. They are powerful, biologically based, socially constructed ways of sustaining a shared civilized life. They make subtle and varied statements about individuals, families, communities. And because domestic traditions are assigned in large part to females, they encode information about perceived feminine attributes and responsibilities. Passed down most often from mother to daughter, reshaped by everything from economic structure to technology to political rebellion, domestic traditions serve as norms each individual can either follow or reject. Either way, they have their influence.

What struck me first about the six very different stories in the novels was how intense emotion could drench even the tiniest household tasks, influencing their outcome. In short, attitude was all. When tasks were done with a pure, heartfelt purpose, either as an acknowledgment of feminine duty to the tribe or as a sign of fidelity to husband or children, they were done with calm, sweet contentment or joy, and they made a positive difference in the lives of household members. When tasks were done for a hated or unfaithful spouse— or done in the context of a life that had lost all hope of meaning and fulfillment— they were done obsessively, compulsively, grimly, resentfully, angrily, manipulatively, even murderously. The tasks themselves had not changed, and the characters had elsewhere proven themselves capable of a completely opposite response. It was the emotional context that altered and distorted the tasks' consequences. In other words, the character's attitude toward the rest of her life, and toward her life partner or family, could make or break her attitude toward domesticity.

Of the many intersections between attitudes and domesticity, we need only a few images from *The Kitchen God's Wife* to make the point. First, visualize Winnie, pregnant by the evil Wen Fu, sewing herself a dress, carefully cutting loose threads and drawing it over her head, with disastrous results. "I put only one arm in before I realized: I was stuck." She made the connection in the next paragraph, "Stuck in my dress, stuck in my marriage, stuck with Hulan as my friend" (242).

Next, visualize Winnie's cousin Peanut, escaped from a "mock" marriage to a homosexual, now living in a community of embittered runaway wives, where she passes out revolutionary leaflets instead of cooking family meals (448). Finally, visualize Winnie happily showing her daughter "a funny picture" of herself in an apron, acting like she was cooking while her beloved second husband Jimmy took her picture. "Actually, in this picture I am not really cooking anything, only pretending," she said. "Your father liked to take natural pictures" (469). And what could be more natural, than his wife doing the cooking she'd long wanted to do for a man she loved?

The most frequent reason for such sharp contrasts in domestic attitude seems to be motivation: whether a woman feels she has desired and chosen her life's circumstances, or been trapped into them. Pauline felt betrayed by fate itself, which had left her plain, mixed-blood, unloving and unwanted. Becky and Winnie felt betrayed by cruelly demanding husbands; Cam by a lazy, selfish mother and a hasty, soon sexless marriage. Ginny felt betrayed by her father, her sister, her kind but dense husband, the farmland itself, and her inability to conceive a child. But those women who were still in love with something—Margaret, with her children and Nanapush; Sethe, with Paul D and her daughters; Leila, with her son and now Zak; even Mary, who had never stopped loving, only stopped being loved—continued to participate willingly in domestic rituals that soothed, healed, made the world beautiful.

Toni Morrison's Sethe, for example, had enough love in her heart—first for Denver, then for Paul D and Beloved too—that her cooking and mending and cleaning stayed glad. Except, of course, when she was at the restaurant, cooking for a man she decidedly did *not* love. "You better get them pies made," Sawyer told her, and in an almost sullen obedience, "Sethe touched the fruit and picked up the paring knife." The only happy note of her day was taking provisions home to her family when the clock's hands closed in prayer: carefully, "she got a metal-top jar, filled it with stew and wrapped the gingerbread in butcher paper" (189).

I think also of Margaret's generous sharing of the scarce broth; Mary's transformation of Debbie's harum-scarum household; the many instances of gracious domestic hospitality in the novels, from Baby Suggs' feast to Ginny's steady provision of country meals, pots of coffee, even hot pepper jelly for a guest with odd tastes. I think of the healing done by domestic means, from Nanapush's exorcising cauldron of meat to Leila's urging that Melanie's daughter make herself a cup of tea and sit down, "by the time you drink it, I'll be with you" (12). I remember, with greater understanding, how domestic images were linked to sex at some point in every novel, intersecting the powers of connection and relationship; paralleling the physicality of bodily needs and desires. Beyond eros lay the domestic coziness of family, a sense of belonging so strong that when Ellen became ill, Vincent wondered where he would take his meals. Finally, there was the domestic hospitality of neighborliness and friendship that temporarily extended home's safe welcome to those outside the family.

It's a simple truth, that a set of activities can be either inhibiting or anchoring, depending on why you do it and under what circumstances. Too often, I think, we assume some women are born with scouring pads in their hands, while others simply cannot be "domesticated." Scientists have not located a housework gene that dictates pleasure or pain while all other variables hold constant; instead, as the novelists in this study show us, it is those other variables that determine our approach to domesticity.

Having said that, do I tolerate repetitive chores any better? Not a bit. By temperament I crave novelty, and infinitely prefer cooking with a new recipe, cleaning with a new wonder-product or tackling a one-time project. That part is temperament. But today there are so many ways of making home that, if we divide the monolithic "happy housewife" stereotype into small pieces and tinker with each, we can all find a way to achieve domestic order, harmony and spiritual connection. We will fall short of the standards set in the obsessive-compulsive '50s, we will continue to hate Martha Stewart. Some of us will have dinner catered or buy cleaning services, some will abandon their mothers' standards and reinvent traditions that make sense for them. Ritual is powerful, but it is also surprisingly flexible—especially when it's shaped by willingness and love.

The Complexity of Domesticity

The second revelation about domesticity was how multivalent even the simplest chore can be. I did not choose the six novelists because they had any particular notions about housework, or treated it specially, or insisted on tapping its most complex possibilities. Yet in their casual or instrumental inclusions of household chores and rituals, I found an array of roles, significances and associations so wide it surprised me. In relationships, housework served as a conduit for intimacy, love and legacy—but also as a means of manipulation, oppression and even murder. Simple tasks of cooking, sewing, laundering and scrubbing tamed irrational or frightening impulses, soothed the mind into a contemplative state, blunted painful memories, instilled humility, allowed catharsis and connection. The very same tasks, done with different motives, were used to dominate, reject, coerce, exploit, placate or thwart intimacy.

Throughout the novels, domestic acts brought order from chaos, paradoxically creating a sense of the sacred and the transcendent by immersing their performer in—and then releasing her from—the dirt and decay of finite human life. Symbolically, domesticity represented—to the characters as well as the reader—womanhood, creativity, nature, mythic realities and cyclical time—but also irrational forces, social oppression, emptiness, endless drudgery and earthbound heaviness. Overall, domestic roles gave a sense of identity, purpose, accomplishment, tradition, security, intimacy, sensuality and healing—but they also functioned as reminders of oppression, alienation, meaninglessness, emptiness and disappointment.

The complexity of domesticity's function in these novels dissolves any doubt about the need to understand its realm. First, if we do not study the "everyday" core of our lives, where intellect meets more basic forces of family, nurturance, comfort and survival, we cannot hope to understand "higher" concepts and social patterns in proper context. Even the most abstract and brilliant thinkers are shaped by the exigencies of domestic life and the degree of comfort, safety and love communicated in their domestic surroundings. Many a political election has turned on homely concerns (*how* many chickens in that pot?) and the ways people relate to each other in the public sphere and workplace often take their cues from roles at home.

Second, if we do not stop trivializing and ignoring tasks traditionally associated with women, we cannot hope to re-value and integrate our foremothers' legacies. In an age of "letting it go" or using quickie appliances, older ways of performing domestic tasks are fast becoming obsolete; yet by knowing, understanding and remembering them, we gain great insight into the women, families and social structures of other times. History is no longer dead heroes and wars; with a recovery of domestic ways, we can broaden our understanding of everyday rhythms and needs, making our insights more grounded and more personal. In the words of architect Lawlor, "Wholeness is restored not by escaping the boundaries of everyday living but by embracing them" (208).

Finally, if we do not rewrite our notions of creativity, sacredness and power to make them compatible with mundane acts and responsibilities, we will continue to alienate the artist, priest and leader from the healing stability of everyday life. And we will miss what is artistic, sacred and powerful in ordinary human lives.

Elemental Wisdom

The third revelation about domesticity was how cosmic its realm could be, how full of significances, the signings of spirit. In *The Temple in the House*, Lawlor maintains that the five ancient elements—earth, water, fire, air, and space—are not chemical elements but "qualities of consciousness or patterns of intelligence that portray the characteristics of physical form." Every architectural form and every part of the body can be described as a combination of these elements, he notes. Our perception, in other words, confirms the elemental connection between the self and its surroundings.

> A curved staircase, for instance, displays earth in the support of each tread, water in the fluid shape of its handrail, fire in its color and shades of light and shadow, air in its rise above gravity, and space in the gaps between the balusters and treads. The form and function of your hand expresses earth in its firmness, water in the folds of the kin, fire in its warmth, air in its dexterity, and space between the fingers. (103)

When I looked at patterns of domestic significance in the novels, I found the same elements. The ordering of chthonic chaos dealt necessarily with earth, and the hollow emptiness of the domestic role was rushed with air. The many connections and relationships expressed by domestic acts diffused boundaries and filled needs as fluidly as water. The power of healing or malevolence had all the energy and danger of fire; the capacity for transcendence through symbol, ritual and myth broke open space itself.

Was I just reaching? I don't think so. If the correspondence seems a romantic imposition, it is only because the domestic realm has been trivialized for so long, it's hard to remember how essential it is, how deep and primal and powerful. Also, because domestic rituals have taken place by definition in the home, their highly personal, private nature has shielded them from extensive rational analysis. Domestic norms have existed like the societal "keywords" described by Fraser and Gordon, which "typically carry unspoken assumptions and connotations that can powerfully influence the discourses they permeate—in part by constituting a body of *doxa*, or taken-for-granted commonsense belief that escapes critical scrutiny" (310).

Philosopher Carol Bigwood notes that, "because the notion of 'home' is so saturated with patriarchal domesticity, and because, moreover, the concept of home has been taken up by the rhetoric of the New Right," many feminist theorists would like to continue ignoring its realm. But in her opinion, "there is no other place to go than the most immediate here that we inhabit and where our habits are nestled" (291). Rather than cave in to old definitions, she writes of "home" as "a nomadic place, an unfinished place of variable historical and geographical boundaries, but a belonging-place nonetheless." By revisioning "home" as a moral sphere, a strategy of survival, a point of intersection between self and other, a locus of shifting identities, and "a crossroads of difference," Bigwood positions it as central to any contemporary exploration of self and world (292).

One of the oldest and most frequent metaphors for the body, after all, is "temple of the spirit," and that sense of sheltering and care repeats in the relation between the body and its literal, brick or straw or wood-framed home. Lawlor reminds us that

> diverse cultures have related the body's form and function to environmental shapes and processes. The belly or womb was represented by a room, the intestines by a labyrinth, breathing by weaving, the veins and arteries by the sun and moon, the backbone by the central pillar, the heart or navel by the center of the world.

In Lawlor's view, a home is neither separate from us, stolidly inanimate and alien, or impersonally functional. Rather, it is a completion of the needs of mind and body. "It provides shelter from the elements, a place to cook and eat, a setting to bathe and sleep. By physically supporting the renewal of the spirit, architecture can become a means of healing" (100).

Native American attitudes toward home keep that relationship clear. As editors Evers and Zepeda note in *Home Places*, Native peoples have created civilizations inseparable from the land. For them, the earth itself is home, "a place to live within ever-widening webs of community that spin out to include not just humans but all the living things of the natural world" (vii). The discrepancies between Erdrich's *Tracks* and the other novels make more sense when you realize how cosmically "home" is defined in the former, how societally in the latter. As Elizabeth Woody writes later in *Home Places*, "My bed is inside the River" (45). As Joy Harjo notes four pages later, "My house is the red earth" (49).

A narrow, disconnected form of the same quest for home pushed Becky toward the beautiful condo. With a quick twist, the same dynamic made Mary profoundly happy and purposeful, not just physically relieved and comfortable, when she moved into Debbie's house. Inverted, this dynamic made Sethe's haunted house frightening and restrictive for young Denver. That house was not physically supporting the renewal of the spirit, as Lawlor's designs are intended to do, and as the Earth itself does for Native peoples. Instead, this house was reminding its occupants of a *troubled* spirit. After the murder of Beloved, "124" had changed from "a cheerful, buzzing house where Baby Suggs, holy, loved, cautioned, fed, chastised and soothed" to a building closed down, veiled over and shut away, "the plaything of spirits and the home of the chafed" (86–87).

When my husband and I were house-hunting, we walked away from one perfectly logical possibility and exclaimed, simultaneously, "I *loved* it!" (him) and "I *hated* it!" (me). Incredulous, he asked me what was wrong with that perfectly nice house, and all I could think to blurt was, "My spirit wasn't happy there." It's become a standing joke ("Is your spirit happy here, dear?") but I, at least, knew precisely what I meant. Now, I would simply cite Lawlor's book, which explains *how* a building "instead of being a mere tool of form and function, can play a key role in renewing the human spirit. Through the precise language of form, color, and texture, buildings ground the elusive qualities of consciousness in the physical world," for better or for worse (x). Thus clients and students come to Lawlor asking for design methods that reflect consciousness itself:

> They want to know how the stages of transformation through which the psyche journeys—the pain of separation, the search for meaning, the trials of the path, and the resolution of unity—are reflected in the environments that shelter and sustain them. (xi)

He makes his own replies, couched in the language of physical form— geometry, structural integrity and interconnection, color, texture, density, size, emptiness, purity, naturalness, artifice, simplicity, complexity, detailing, scale, lightness, darkness, historical reference, abstraction, and relationship to surroundings. But if we switch to the language of literary symbolism, we find the novels of this study making similar reflections. "It was clear why Baby Suggs was so starved for color," Morrison informed her readers early in *Beloved*.

> There wasn't any except for two orange squares in a quilt that made the absence shout. The walls of the room were slate-colored, the floor earth-brown, the wooden dresser the color of itself, curtains white, and the dominating feature, the quilt over an iron cot, was made up of scraps of blue serge, black, brown and gray wool—the full range of the dark and the muted that thrift and modesty allowed. (38)

What Becky noticed in her succession of condos was not color, it was newness, freshness, cleanliness, and above all, the presence of modern amenities, such as a washing machine in the basement (208). What Fleur cared about was the land itself, the herbs and trees. What Ginny dwelt on was the farmhouses' isolation, their emphasis on appearances and their battle against the elements. Each woman was tapping into a different correspondence between herself and the world; a different view of the cosmic powers and meanings operating in their relationship to their home.

Ritual Possibilities

My next realization was that many of the elements which gave domesticity its power—regular repetition, dynamism, an intimate physicality, a correspondence with life processes, a performative aspect, an aesthetic aspect, a normative aspect—were precisely those elements that carried it into the realm of ritual. The family meals in the novels, the weekly cleaning chores, the searches for special scissors, fabrics, teas, foodstuffs and flowers—none of these incidents can be stripped of that added layer, reduced to basic acquisition, hygienic shelter and the fueling of the body. It is easier, now, for me to see domestic ritual as a form of communication overlaid with deeper meanings and a sense of magical efficacy.

Initially, I worried about discussing every dishwashing as ritual, calling every soapsud sacred. They are not. But Sexson reminds us that, since the human mind perceives nature, spirit, and every other category through metaphor, we cannot formally separate art from life; the sacred from the mundane; or the transcendent from the domestic (2). The possibilities of ritual, symbol and myth are always present; by the same token, "there are no inherently sacred objects, events, or thoughts; they are made sacred by a special context" (3). In the novels, it was the way the characters *thought* about what they were doing that placed their acts at a particular point along the continuum from pointless mundane habit to sacred ritual. That way of thinking could have changed from one moment to the next, just as a meal of bread and wine can be a sacrament, a seduction, or a solitary, hurriedly gulped snack to hush a growling stomach. It is dangerous to cast either the secular or the sacred in stone; when we act in ordinary life, we seldom stop to categorize our behaviors as either ritualistic or pragmatic. If we did, we would no doubt find a confused jumble of the two.

In *The Magic of Ritual,* Driver points out that "the processes through which ritual regulates the life of a society...are mostly hidden from consciousness" (147). We get a vague sense of something's necessity and we ritualize it, making it sacred in the most basic sense of the word, and weaving it into life's regular rhythm. Americans have done that with everything from Saturday morning cleaning to Sunday family dinners, holiday celebrations, spring cleaning, summertime barbecuing, even morning coffee. Each of these rituals loops a biological need into a social one, giving it the context of family and community, and the power to signify deeper feelings and less tangible needs. We fasten down some of the trimmings (morning coffee in our favorite mug, a special striped apron when Dad barbecues) and underscore the time element, so the ritual carries its own alarm clock, and enters our space-time matrix in a reliable way.

Nowadays, though, it is harder and harder to find any domestic rituals whose integrity we can defend. How can I scold the dog for muddying a floor I never scrub, or my husband for arriving late to a microwaved dinner? Second-wave feminism renewed the rebellion against domestic obligations, and the absolutes duly crumbled. From the rubble came a conservative outcry for family values, for social stability, for the comforts of old certainties. Both phases were no doubt inevitable; rebellion breached social customs and forced us to face the inadequacy of our established ways. We tried to resolve the crisis in many different ways: by suggesting all housework be communal or paid; by demanding an equal split of household chores between men and women; by mocking our mothers' emphases on sparkle and shine and three squares a day. Now many of us are living without norms or consensus; each carving out her or his own relationship to domesticity. Unfortunately, what has often been lost en route is the meaning, value and symbolism of those once-prescribed tasks.

Driver says that, in times of moral crisis, human beings go in search of new ritual forms, shifting the magic circles and redefining the sacred, so that these new or altered ritualizations can help us navigate new moral obligations (50). But everyone I know is too busy, overwhelmed and resistant to tackle the infusion of new forms and meanings into their daily routine. We take the approach of Pearl in *The Kitchen God's Wife*, waiting until everything piles up and then dropping the kids off at their grandparents' or sacrificing a three-day weekend, somehow finding a way to periodically dig ourselves out, get at least the big stuff done. Or we try Cam's approach, diving headlong into career and seeing things domestic as potential traps. And so we continue, most of us doing without special holiday rituals, soft clean linens, top-to-bottom spring cleanings, and healthy, carefully prepared meals eaten at leisure and graced with good conversation.

The Loss of Comfort

The next pattern revealed the tremendous changes mechanization and computerization have wrought in domestic acts and rituals—what tasks are automated, how and for whom. I remembered Ginny spinning her mind into a frenzy with the carpet-cleaning machine; Leila hiring someone else to come in and clean her house; Becky ordering in pizza and coveting more things; Magdalene entertaining a gay friend with frozen entrées in front of the television set. It was easy to see a contrast with the traditional, hand-wrought domesticity of Ellen, Margaret, Winnie, Ginny's mother. The older women were not necessarily happier or holier, but the way they did their domestic work was slower, steadier and more personal.

One way to look at domesticity's shift is in terms of its ritual dimension. "Ritual belongs to what the ancient Greeks would have called *techne*, the root of our words technical, technique, and technology," Driver tells us. "Ritual is a sort of technology because it is a method (a time-honored one) for accomplishing something in the real world," but instead of manipulating physical objects by mechanical or computerized means, ritual acts in "a divine, human, animal, and vegetative cosmos of mores, moralities, and mutual relationships." You'd never know it, to look at the way domestic rituals have been altered in the twentieth century. And that is precisely Driver's point: "When the techniques of ritual are cast off in favor of the apparently more rational technologies of genes, machines, atoms, and particles, humane values are jeopardized.... We enter then upon a time of ritual misapprehension and ritual boredom, which cannot but be a time of dehumanization" (47).

Another way to see the domestic shift is by differentiating between bodily and machine-driven rhythms. Writing on *The Human Condition*, philosopher Hannah Arendt differentiates between labor and work, linking labor's necessity to the biological process of the human body, its growth, metabolism and decay. Work, on the other hand, corresponds to the unnaturalness of human existence; it is not embedded in the life cycle, but "provides an 'artificial' world of things" (7). In classical antiquity, both women and slaves were subordinated and hidden away, she writes later, not because they were property, but because their life was "'laborious,' devoted to bodily functions" that included household work (72). Modernity has freed us from any sense of shame about bodily functions, but it has also done much to turn labor into work. Today, "tools and instruments ease pain and effort and thereby change the modes in which the urgent necessity inherent in labor once was manifest to all," Arendt writes. "They do not change the necessity itself; they only serve to hide it from our senses," forcing us into an accelerated, machine-driven rhythm designed to distract us from the still-repetitive nature of the tasks (125).

Take washing machines, for example: they have made it possible to do laundry at any hour of any day, removing the urgent importance of wash day and trivializing the chore—even though it remains imperative, as becomes obvious when a member of the household lacks a clean shirt. The machine has its own rhythm, and we match our pace to its pace, answering the buzzer quickly so the permanent-press items do not wrinkle. There is no longer the rhythm or the physicality of scrubbing and wringing and hanging clothes out on a line, a fact for which most of us are profoundly grateful, but one that takes us another step away from the real nature of the process.

As architect Christopher Day writes in *Places of the Soul*, "In the days of hand-power it was easier to go round a tree-root or a boulder or follow a contour than go straight through. The lines that resulted...(were)...in conversation with the landscape. Powerful machinery finds it easier to disregard the irregularities of the surroundings" (13). Inside homes, the same truth holds: machines do the work for us, eliminating close contact with each substance and element. Sethe untwisting a bread wrapper would have not had the same sensuous appeal as Sethe kneading, or dropping soft white rounds of dough onto a baking sheet. Ginny's murderous sausage canning would have felt quite different, had she simply wangled arsenic from a pharmacy and dropped it in a storebought jar. And Ellen's mothering of her shaken grandchildren would have communicated different, more consumption-based values if she had followed the next generation's norms. As Arendt concludes, "the ideals of *homo faber,* the fabricator of the world, which are permanence, stability, and durability, have been sacrificed to abundance" (125).

Yet another way to get at the shift is by following Rybczynski's analysis of the ideals of domestic comfort—intimacy, beauty, humanity, privacy, ease and real convenience—which were lost in the modern machine age. (By real convenience I mean space to work, places to put things, an organization of space oriented to human needs—not fast foods and fancy appliances.) Studying Dutch interiors of the Bourgeois Age, Rybczynski notes that, as the house became more intimate, it became more feminine and more family oriented, and began to conform to set standards of cleanliness and domesticity. "Homely domesticity depended on the development of a rich interior awareness," he writes, immediately linking that awareness to women's role in the home (75). By my reading, this was not because women were any more introspective than men, but because their presence as full-time housewives linked the home with the creation of family, and family made a secure nesting-place more crucial.

Next, however, came the development of labor-saving appliances, and Le Corbusier's assertion that "a house is a machine for living in." By the time we reached the modern period of design, the very notion of domesticity was suspect. "Coziness had to go, the moralists were clear about that.... The home was being remade in a new image, stripped of its bourgeois traditions and bereft of easeful intimacy and well-established ideas of comfort. The more radical architects were open about it. Extreme measures were required to 'prevent us from falling prey to dullness, to habit, *and to comfort*' (emphasis added)" (200). Rybczynski describes an artless, minimalist modern home: "The precision with which materials are joined is severe; its perfection intimidates and accuses at the same time. No wonder everything must be put away. It is not only clutter that has been removed from this interior but all signs of sloppiness and human frailty" (198).

That development even changed the way we evaluate domesticity; note Marge Piercy's careful notation of Leila's messiness; Becky's love of anything machine-made, mall-bought and pristine; her mother-in-law's painstakingly rigid blue-and-white, dyed-to-match and never-used interior decoration. How different from Sethe's mad ribbons down the banister, Ellen's warm runny custard, Fleur's home in the forest, and the doll hand-sewn by Nanapush's wife.

The Stigma of Dependency

Alongside technology's ascendancy, another huge social shift must be factored into the evolution of domesticity: the shift in the concept of "dependency," which has been closely analyzed by Fraser and Gordon. Before the Industrial Revolution, both men and women were usually dependent on someone else, and only a handful of the wealthy were truly "independent." But as machines separated the home from the workplace and the economy reorganized itself, the categories shuffled into a new configuration. By the turn of the nineteenth century, the definition of economic dependency had divided into two: a "good" household dependency, attributed to children and wives, and a "bad" charity dependency, to be avoided at all costs.

In our own century, the Bureau of the Census and the Internal Revenue Service installed the category of "dependent" as the norm for wives (320). The choice of words was unfortunate: "In the 1950s, social workers influenced by psychiatry began to diagnose dependence as a form of immaturity common among women" (325). With second-wage feminism, the entry of women into the labor force, the increase in divorce, the changing norms for family life and the popular revolt against welfare entitlement, "dependency" became progressively more onerous and stigmatizing for women. "With all legal and political dependency now illegitimate, and with wives' economic dependency now contested, there is no longer any self-evidently good adult dependency in postindustrial society" (324).

What does this mean for the concept of homemaking, which entails no revenue? It suggests that domestic performers are not pulling their own societal weight, and are perhaps emotionally crippled, incapable of self-sufficiency. A choice that, less than a century ago, was the highest virtue to which a woman could aspire, is now seen as irresponsible or deficient. With the family wage clearly nonexistent for most sectors of the economy, and a double income necessary to support children—sometimes just to support two adults—the woman engaged full-time in domesticity is an increasingly rare phenomenon. The independently wealthy woman does not usually muss herself with domesticity's practical chores; the welfare mother must, but she has lost society's approbation for it.

Perhaps it is just as well; as Adrienne Rich warned several years ago, the image of the mother in the home has become

> a dangerous archetype: the Mother, source of angelic love and forgiveness in a world increasingly ruthless and impersonal; the feminine, leavening, emotional element in a society ruled by male logic and male claims to 'objective,' 'rational' judgment; the symbol and residue of moral values and tenderness in a world of wars, brutal competition, and contempt for human weakness. (52)

Rich complained that the split put the physical and psychic weight of responsibility on women, and I agree. But rather than opening domesticity to participation by all members of society and revitalizing its rituals, we have continued to devalue domestic tasks, roles and purposes. The book *Megatrends for Women: From Liberation to Leadership,* revised and updated in 1993, indexes no reference to housework, housekeeping or domesticity (Aburdene and Naisbitt). *The Modern Woman's Guide to Life* begins a chapter on housework: "Drudgery. There's no other word for it" (Chapman et al. 171). As Ruddick notes, "There is still little but contempt and indifference for this kind of work, these efforts. (The phrase 'wages for housework' has the power to shock today that the phrase 'free love' possessed a century ago)" (xvi).

The novels demonstrate how directly a woman's attitude toward her husband or family affects her domestic behavior, but given recent changes in perception and attitude, we must also consider the woman's attitude toward domesticity itself. Put plainly, what is so awful, in contemporary American men's and women's minds, about domesticity? The findings of William R. Beer in *Househusbands* echoed the findings of Ann Oakley in *The Sociology of Housework:* factors that promote a positive attitude toward household chores include the ability to talk to other people while working; being in the right mood; having enough time; having enough money; having the right tools and work environment; having one's work appreciated. The factors that make household chores onerous are social isolation; the wrong mood; not having enough time or money; the wrong environment or tools; monotony and repetitiousness; having to think about work (59).

If we look at that list, then think about the historical shifts in domesticity over the past century—many of which are reflected in the novels, which span precisely that period—we can see what has happened. The frequently communal nature of women's work, whether expressed in quilting bees or friendly gossip across outdoor clotheslines, has vanished, leaving each homemaker isolated in an empty kitchen or basement. The tools and environments have become mechanical, uncomfortable, artificial and often dehumanizing. With fewer people home during the day, that isolation has intensified. Repetition and monotony frustrate us more every year, as we grow used to the accelerated pace and constantly distracting stimuli of a cyberworld.

For those who work, there is never enough time. Fear and scarce resources are tightening purse strings and doubling work loads across the nation. The dream of increased leisure has morphed into a nightmare of hyperstress. Without ample time, sufficient money and a basic sense of security, *no* one, not even Martha Stewart, can be in the right mood to create new and delightful domestic rituals. And without that sense of willingness, leisure and delight, what is left to appreciate?

At first glance, all this looks like middle-class feminist angst, but Oakley found "no social class difference in the frequency with which housewives are satisfied or dissatisfied with their work" (62). Nor did education make a difference. She does say that working-class women seem more apt to respond positively or neutrally to a question about liking housework—even if they later admit to dissatisfaction—because loyalty is expected of them, and a politicized rebellion is not (66–67). Middle-class women, on the other hand, tend "towards a disengagement from the housewife role on a verbal and cognitive level (despite an underlying childhood identification with the mother-housewife): instead of a striving after satisfaction with housework there tends to be a recognition of housework dissatisfaction" (188).

Attitudes toward domesticity are complex and often ambiguous. What is significant is how few people of any class or gender hold out much hope of *resolving* this dissatisfaction, short of hiring or persuading someone else to perform the tasks. Even contracting with a cleaning service—a luxury that's often the only sensible solution for the overworked but amply-paid professional class—reminds us that we're not even capable of cleaning up after ourselves; haven't the time even to remove our own filth.

The Need to Reinvent Domesticity

The strongest message running through any study of contemporary domesticity is the general, urgent need to reinvent its forms. For the sake of our sanity, and our lives together, we all—both genders, all classes and ages—need a way to perform everyday chores attentively, with care and imagination. Moore remarks that, even though we all know daily work affects our character and our lives,

> we usually overlook the way soulfulness can adhere to ordinary house-work and the gifts it can bring to the soul. If we let other people do our ordinary work for us, or if we do it ourselves without care, we might be losing something irreplaceable and eventually experience that missing element as a painful sense of loneliness or homelessness. (180)

I have never been described as fastidious, and my husband, while orderly, can tolerate a good half-inch of dust. But even we notice a difference in our general sense of orderliness, comfort and well-being when we come home to a neatly made bed piled invitingly with pillows and covered with a fluffy comforter. Or wake up to a sparkling clean kitchen instead of a sinkful of crusted dishes. On the other hand, when we first moved into our house, we naively scribbled a tight schedule of chores that, were we to adhere to it, would leave us no time for the precious moments of relaxation, friendship and intellectual stimulation that are equally crucial. A balance had to be struck. And now it has to be maintained, which sometimes seems like fighting against a tide. The only weeks it's easy to tend to domestic needs fully and without rushing are the four-day weeks of national holidays, and those long weekends only feel the way a weekend ought to feel, with tasks stretched out and punctuated by pleasure. We need a week's vacation to feel the jubilant, carefree, indolent joys of a holiday.

Something must be done. I agree with Estes that "too much domestication"—which has so often been women's lot— locks us "into an absolute and repetitive pattern for any and all circumstances," deadening natural instincts and killing creative freedom. "The instinct-injured woman has no choice. She just stays stuck" (232). But if, at the other extreme, we lose all sense of meaningful domestic ritual, we also lose a chance to reintroduce some bodily-oriented, human-paced, sane and predictable common ground into our lives. Complaining of the rush of modern life and our need to reconnect our minds with natural processes, Bigwood writes that "it is no longer a matter of *making* more time but, more vitally and radically, of *letting time be* in its life rhythms of coming and going" (287). And that is precisely what the cycles and seasons of domesticity give us permission to do.

Does reconnecting mean a Martha Stewart Christmas? Not necessarily. Mary Beth Danielson has reinvented "Family Rituals": "As for creativity, I don't need to set the table in fancy ways or cut the children's breakfast toast into cookie-cutter shapes. Rituals are not about artifice but about acceptance" (157). Her motherly insight also hints at the unconscious equivalence between domesticity and unconditional motherlove. (Which may be why we react strongly to anecdotes suggesting that Martha Stewart is really a tough ruthless, businesswoman, not a loving, earthy, ever-present Mom.) In the novels, the ritualistic domestic acts that had efficacy confirm Danielson's point: the bathing of Pauline was a consummate act of acceptance, as were the healing of pregnant women and new mothers; Winnie's ceremonial gifts of sewing machine and fabric; Denver's sisterly tutelage of Beloved as they shared household chores.

The need to reinvent domesticity goes beyond loving expression, however, cutting to the very core of female identity. The longstanding linkage of femaleness with domesticity affects the women who do not meet the standards as well as the women who kill themselves to meet them—not to mention the men trying agreeably to edge their way into a realm long defined as someone else's. In a recent article in *The New York Times* headlined, "Orderly House, Orderly Mind," Dorice Bailer quotes Sandra Felton, a high school teacher who founded Messies Anonymous: "It's a terrible thing, for women especially," Felton insists. "Your house is a reflection of you. When you feel that you are capable, but your house is just the opposite, it affects your personality. It affects your social life." Felton's *The Messies Manual* sold close to half a million copies (6).

The novels showed many different women's craven need to excel in domestic ways, in situations as different as Winnie trying to cook for Wen Fu's friends in China and Leila trying to expend the energy of a failed marriage on her impulsively adopted cat. She broiled a solitary sword-fish, gave the skin to the cat and said proudly, "See, a real meal" (80). The need came even clearer with her Thanksgiving stab at earth-goddess abundance and her relief once the house was emptied of her family; she was finally free of the burden of meeting their needs, paying attention, making nice (157). The same need lay behind Ginny's feverish cleaning and her Whitmanesque cataloguing of the meals she prepared— "sausage, fried eggs, hash brown potatoes, cornflakes, English muffins and toast, coffee and orange juice" (28). Sethe apologized fervently for the state of her house, as did Winnie's father's servant, and Cam's pathetic cousin Sheila spent a great deal of her life arranging fancy cheese shapes.

Perhaps what is most interesting about this pervasive need is the exception: the women in *Tracks*—with the exception of the mixed-blood, alienated Pauline and her desire to make lace in town—showed no anxi-ety whatsoever about meeting preordained standards. Ojibwa culture was different from the other novels' cultures in three salient ways: it respected women's power and intelligence; it gave the family and the tribe priority, rather than a marriage based on property relations; and it divided labor by gender but did not force rigid adherence to that divi-sion. How else could Fleur have been a woman who "messed with evil, laughed at the old women's advice and dressed like a man" (12), and who "kept her gun above the flour cupboard in a rack of antlers," care-lessly combining domesticity with male pursuits (59)? How different Fleur's easy ways with either skillet or shotgun were from the internal battle waged when Ginny returned to Rose's kitchen:

> I thought I was doing quite well. I stood up easily and walked into the kitchen without a hitch. I found the cast iron chicken fryer and a pan for the potatoes. The only trouble was, the kitchen seemed arctic. The blue gas flames of the burner fluttered coldly. The grease in the pan popped chillingly. When it spattered my hand, the burned dots felt frozen. I looked around, then took Rose's old beige sweater off the hook behind the door. I huddled into it, browning chicken and shivering. It seemed an impossible defeat that I was back in this kitchen, cooking. (348)

So many women associate domesticity with times of oppression in their adult lives—or their mothers' lives—that it has become easy to charac-terize the entire realm as drudgery, and difficult to think of it as delight-ful. Yet I recently went back to kindergarten (to research a newspaper story on alternative methods of education) and I found two long-estab-lished methods—Waldorf and Montessori—using everyday domestic tasks to teach small children everything from hand-eye coordination to process and follow-through. "It's soothing, too," added one teacher, watching a boy carefully circling the surface of a plate with his very own cotton towel.

Performance art, like kindergarten, can be trusted to see what the rest of us miss: on January 7, 1996, Janine Antoni debuted her "Loving Care" piece at the Wadsworth Atheneum. First, she dipped her long black hair in a bucket of the dye her mother used to cover the gray. Then, Antoni mopped the floor with her hair, forcing the audience out of the room. "It's really important for me that you look at my work and you know a woman did it," she told *New York Times* writer Kay Larson.

Which reminds me of a native-American woman I met recently. She is a single mother living with AIDS, and has made many close women friends who are in the same predicament. She has less patience with the HIV-positive men she knows; they, she says, have given up, resigned themselves to dying, and in the meantime, all they do is complain. "A lot of women have a real innate strength to carry on, to deal with high levels of stress, to keep the home running," she tells me. "You get the laundry done, you get the kids to school, you make dinner, you keep going. Sometimes it's moment by moment, but you definitely keep going." You have to; you are responsible, and responsive, to other lives. That kind of sustained caretaking lies at the root of any unpaid domestic endeavor. And for all its tedium, it can keep you going.

The Domestic Vocabulary

Whether as individuals or by cultural consensus we manage to reinvent any domestic rituals is not, in the end, my concern. Even if the domestic realm remains fragmented and haphazard, it will continue to wield power—and it is a power that deserves acknowledgment, honor, articulation and analysis.

Domesticity may no longer provide all women with a shared and automatically internalized set of norms, but it has left us a vocabulary rich with imagery, metaphor and significance. In *Beloved*, Denver thought "the flesh between her mother's forefinger and thumb was thin as china silk" (239). In *A Thousand Acres*, when the characters played Monopoly, Rose was a shoe, faithful husband Ty was a dog, dangerous lover Jess was a racecar, and domestic Ginny was the thimble (76). Cathy, Sam's mother in *The Longings of Women*, "was a chatty woman and her seams were loose" (191). Leila was so identified with domesticity that, walking through a museum, her friend "pointed to a caryatid, a Greek woman holding up a building, a woman in the form of a structural column.

'That's you, Leila. Caught in stone'" (174).

Lives unfold along the fault lines of domesticity. In *A Thousand Acres*, when Ginny recalled how she had waited meekly to hear what horrible things her father had said about her, she said, "I dropped my eyes to the vinyl tablecloth, red and white plaid" (195). Earlier, she had described a strong flashback: Mrs. Ericson "wearing an apron with a red and white checked dish towel sewn to it...wiped her hands on the towel as she sat down" to tell Ginny, just after her mother's death, that she and her husband were moving away (135). Ginny had received her attitude toward domesticity largely from her mother, whose death sharpened her attention to domestic details as well as her undertaking of domestic responsibilities. That generational movement continued through the novel; we saw one of Ginny's young nieces carefully shaking the popcorn pot, anxious to please; another was busily crocheting a sweater. Similarly, in *Beloved*, Sethe wanted to get back home and "set these idle girls to some work that would fill their wandering heads," perpetuating her own dutiful use of domesticity to give her life anchor and purpose (99).

The downward movement of domesticity through the generations is clear and easy to trace. The horizontal movement to the other gender is far less sure, but my sense is that, despite the still-frequent ridiculing of househusbands and still bitter resentment of unevenly divided chores, we are slowly beginning to honor men's domestic qualities and engage them more generally in domestic pursuits. Indeed, the final strong impression I took from the novels was the well-developed, healing, nurturing domesticity of the most lovable male characters. In *Tracks*, when Edgar Pukwan dragged weak, ill Fleur in a sled, bouncing her over potholes and tipping her in the snow, Nanapush told us he "followed the sled, encouraged Fleur with songs, cried at Pukwan to watch for hidden branches and deceptive drops, and finally got her to my cabin, a small tightly tamped box overlooking the crossroad" (4). Through the novel, Nanapush tended, healed, fed, advised, watched over and cried over the people he loved.

In *The Other Side*, we saw Dan, who tenderly released the two thin braids imprisoned under Ellen's pillow (9). When his wife took a job in the medical library, Dan took care of their infant daughter, and in the midst of the associated bottle-warming and laundry he "felt for the first time that he took part in the life that other human beings always had been leading but from which he'd been cut off" (24). In *The Longings of Women*, sweet Zak worried about his hideous draperies and told Leila easily, "The least I can do is make you lunch," asking considerately, "What don't you eat?" (207). In *A Thousand Acres*, the man Ginny fell in love with, Jess, was a gentle vegetarian who thoughtfully poured her a cup of coffee; not once did we see her husband pour her anything (36).

If all these sensitive domesticated males sound too tender for realism, we have to remember how assiduously women have disdained any male version of domestic activity. In *A Thousand Acres*, Ginny and Rose were appalled by Harold, who was planning quite practically to put a concrete floor in his kitchen, "green tinted concrete that slopes to a drain so he can just hose it down when it gets dirty" (78). Harold's freezer, predictably enough, was "pulled away from the wall, stinking of that sour frozen smell, and, faintly, of meat and blood"; clearly testosteronal territory (158). And one of the first signs of the father's madness was the way he left kitchen cabinets outside rotting in the elements (80), not to mention his purchase of an absolutely inappropriate white brocade sofa (155).

The genders, as we have said, do not yet enjoy a common approach to domesticity—not in mainstream America, and not in most of its sub-cultures. The practical result of this disparity is that, when women juggle domesticity with a career, both suffer. Instead of fully sharing domestic rituals with domestic partners, most women make a halfhearted attempt to elicit their help, then resent it when the spoons wind up in a different drawer and the whites get washed on warm. Meanwhile, the women are doing a halfhearted job on the remaining chores—which, because the powers and meanings of domesticity remain hidden, carry only the humble status of drudgery.

We are confronting changed economic demands, evolving technologies, gender and relationship tensions, the chaos of deregulation, the clash of generations, conflicting expectations and mutually exclusive priorities. In the maelstrom, domestic tasks have kept their attachment to femaleness, but they have lost their connection to the core of life, and those who perform them have lost the dignity of fulfilling a role essential to sustain their loved ones. It's all drudgery now; there's no time for any of it, and what's done is often joyless, unskilled and unproductive, with little power to order even a room, let alone the soul.

When Charlotte Perkins Gilman envisioned community dining facilities, she wasn't thinking McDonald's. Her point was hot nutritious food cooked efficiently by a few people of either gender and served in better surroundings, freeing most women for tasks generally perceived as more intelligent and constructive. Gilman pointed out the multitude of professions involved in "our clumsy method of housekeeping," and suggested specialization to divide labor more efficiently (*Women & Economics* 245). She found it ironic that dainty woman, placed so delicately on a pedestal,

> has by common consent been expected to do the chamber-work and scullery work of the world. All that is basest and foulest she in the last instance must handle and remove. Grease, ashes, dust, foul linen, and sooty ironware,—among these her days must pass. As we socialize our

functions, this passes from her hands into those of man. (Women &
Economics 246–7)

Gilman's goal was to turn the home into a place of peace, rest, love and
privacy, so "the union of individuals in marriage would not compel the
jumbling together of all the external machinery of their lives" (*Women &
Economics* 299). Oakley would later remind readers that "the status of
housework is interwoven specifically with the status of married women,"
whose domestic responsibilities blocked their progress toward equality
(*Woman's Work* 5).

Throughout the twentieth century, feminist thinkers of various per-
suasions have followed in Gilman's footsteps, proposing a variety of
alternatives to traditional domesticity. Boiled down, they include keeping
but revaluing the traditional role of homemaker; opening it to males; inte-
grating it with the public sphere; redividing the tasks; changing standards and methods; or, as Aptheker suggests, dissolving the entire concept. "If the occupation continues to exist," she warns, "it will continue to
be part of the female domain and hence inherently disadvantaged" (184).
Once the role has lost its distastefulness as well as its gender link, society
can resurrect it in new form.

William Beer, one of those literary househusbands who write about
the experience, has the opposite opinion: he says housework should be
"held up and praised as a way of escaping the estrangement to which
many are subject in modern life." Rather than make a housewife or husband into a salaried worker, he advises preserving housework as the last
area of preindustrial craft that's still prevalent. With computers, faxes and
modems bringing us home in high-tech cottage industry, he adds, men
and women could resume an interwoven, mutual involvement in all
aspects of daily life (116).

Beer's sentiments are not unlike Gilman's 100 years before him, but
while he advocates going home again, this time in a more worldly fashion, she wanted us to move out into the world and make ourselves at
home there. On the last page of *The Home: Its Work and Influence,* she wrote
that home "should be the recognized base and background of our lives;
but those lives must be lived in their true arena, the world." Gilman firmly believed that the sweet ordering principles of domesticity could
expand. As soon as both men and women have full scope for exploration
and involvement, she promised, the whole world "will grow to have the
sense of intimacy, of permanent close attachment, of comfort and pleasure and rest, which now attaches only to the home" (347).

Instead of moving in that direction, we continue to criticize each
other for our relation to domesticity (or lack thereof). When human
beings feel they have been schooled and expected to behave in a certain

way or fill a certain role, they tend to indulge in smug, all-knowing, right-eous criticism of anyone else's faltering attempts. I hear myself using the possessive pronoun at the oddest times: it is "my dishtowel" that has gone astray, "my ironing" that awaits. Working an odd schedule, my hus-band once called me at work to ask how I mopped the floors; he was home and willing but didn't want to do it "wrong." It will be interesting to see what happens to our language, methods and expectations as more couples begin to care equally for their homes; if more of us are able to cre-ate more personal, satisfying relationships to the places we live in and the objects we use every day, we may recreate domestic rituals that look very different from the nineteenth century "cult of domesticity" we have been trying so hard to erase. As women's proprietary rights and internalized standards vanish, we may find ways together to bring back those vaunt-ed domestic rewards of stability, safety, peace, comfort, intimacy and har-mony.

Or, we may simply hire each other to perform tasks we persist in see-ing as drudgery, allowing them to scrub our lives clean for us. In which case, our souls will remain untouched.

BIBLIOGRAPHY

Primary Sources

Erdrich, Louise. *Tracks.* NY: Harper & Row, 1988.
———. "Nests." *Ladies Home Journal CX:5* (May 1993): 84-85.
Gordon, Mary. *The Other Side.* NY: Viking, 1989.
———. et al. *Spiritual Quests: The Art and Craft of Religious Writing.* Boston, MA: Houghton Mifflin, 1988.
Morrison, Toni. *Beloved.* NY: Alfred A. Knopf, 1987.
———. "Memory, Creation and Writing." *Thought* 59:235 (Dec. 1984): 388.
———. "Rootedness: The Ancestor as Foundation." *Madison* 492-497.
Piercy, Marge. *Stone, Paper, Knife.* NY: Knopf, 1983.
———. *The Longings of Women.* NY: Fawcett Colombine, 1994.
Smiley, Jane. *A Thousand Acres.* NY: Fawcett Columbine, 1991.
———. Interview with Jane Smiley in St. Louis, MO, April, 1995.
Tan, Amy. *The Kitchen God's Wife.* NY: G.P. Putnam's Sons, 1991.
———. Interview with Amy Tan in St. Louis, MO, November 28, 1995.

On the Writers

Allen, Paula Gunn, ed. *Voice of the Turtle: American Indian Literature 1900 -1970.* NY: Ballantine Books, 1994.
———. "Something Sacred Going on Out There." *Madison* 547-559.
Barnouw, Victor. *Wisconsin, WI Chippewa Myths & Tales and Their Relation to Chippewa Life.* Madison: University of Wisconsin Press, 1977.
Bjork, Patrick Bryce. *The Novels of Toni Morrison: The Search for Self and Place Within the Community.* NY: Peter Lang, 1992.
Bloom, Harold, ed. *Toni Morrison.* NY: Chelsea House Publishers, 1990.
Broker, Ignatia *Night Flying Woman: An Ojibway Narrative.* St. Paul: Minnesota Historical Society Press, 1983.
Butler-Evans, Elliott. *Race, Gender and Desire: Narrative Strategies in the Fiction of Toni Cade Bambara, Toni Morrison, and Alice Walker.* Philadelphia, PA: Temple University Press, 1989.
Carmean, Karen. *Toni Morrison's World of Fiction.* Troy, NY: Whitston Publishing Co., 1993.

Chang, K. C., ed. *Food in Chinese Culture: Anthropoloical and Historical Perspectives.* New Haven, CT: Yale University Press, 1977.

Christian, Barbara. "The Highs and the Lows of Black Feminist Criticism." Bloom 44–51.

Cook-Lynn, Elizabeth. "You May Consider Speaking About Your Art," Madison 440-444.

Cooper-Clark, Diana. "An Interview with Mary Gordon." *Commonweal* 197:9 (May 1980): 270-273.

Densmore, Frances. *Chippewa Customs.* Minnesota Historical Society, 1979.

Deo, Veena S. "The Creative Black Woman in Toni Morrison's Novels." Diss. University of Kentucky, 1989.

Dixon, Melvin. "Like an Eagle in the Air: Toni Morrison." Gates 115-142.

Dorris, Michael. *The Broken Cord.* NY: Harper & Row, 1989.

Dreifus, Claudia. "Chloe Wofford Talks About Toni Morrison." *The New York Times Magazine* 11 Sept. 1994: 72-75.

Duffy, Martha. "The Case for Goneril and Regan." *TIME* Magazine 11 Nov. 1991: 92.

Evers, Larry and Ofelia Zepeda, eds. *Home Places: Contemporary Native American Writing from Sun Tracks.* Tucson, AZ: University of Arizona Press, 1995.

Gates, Henry Louis, Jr., ed. *Reading Black, Reading Feminist: A Critical Anthology.* NY: Penguin, 1990.

Gates, Henry Louis Jr. and K. A. Appiah, eds. *Toni Morrison: Critical Perspectives Past and Present.* NY: Amistad, distributed by Penguin USA, 1993.

Giles, Paul. *American Catholic Arts and Fictions.* Cambridge, UK: Cambridge University Press, 1992.

Green, Michelle. "Of Serpents' Teeth in Iowa." *People* Magazine, 13 Jan. 1992: 59-60.

Hallowell, A. Irving. *Culture and Experience.* Philadelphia, PA: University of Pennsylvania Press, 1955.

Hicks, Walter J. "An Essay on Recent American Fiction" Diss. University of North Carolina, 1973.

Holloway, Karla F.C., and Demetrakopoulos, Stephanie. *New Dimensions of Spirituality: A Biracial and Bicultural Reading of the Novels of Toni Morrison.* NY: Greenwood Press, 1987.

hooks, bell. "Homeplace (A Site of Resistance)." Madison 448-454.

Hunnewell, Susannah. "What It's Like to Live in a Female Body." *The New York Times Book Review.* 8 Aug. 1993, sec. 7: 25.

Je, Jennie R. and Dorothy Lonewolf Miller. "Cultural Survival and Contemporary American Indian Women in the City." Zinn and Dill 185-202.

Jones, Bessie W. *The World of Toni Morrison: Explorations in Literary Criticism.* Dubuque, IA: Kendall/Hunt, 1985.

Jones, Jacqueline. *Labor of Love, Labor of Sorrow: Black Women, Work and the Family from Slavery to the Present.* NY: Basic, 1985.

Kegg, Maude. *Portage Lake: Memories of an Ojibwa Childhood.* Edmonton, Canada: University of Alberta Press, 1991.

Keyishian, M. Deiter. "Radical Damage: An Interview with Mary Gordon." *The Literary Review: An International Journal of Contemporary Writing* 32 (Fall 1988): 69-82.

Kim, Elaine. *Asian American Literature: An Introduction to the Writings and Their Social Context.* Philadelphia, PA: Temple University Press, 1982.

Klinkenborg, Verlyn. "Smiley's People." *Mirabella* (Nov. 1991): 90-91.

LaDuke, Winona. "From Resistance to Regeneration: The Next 500 Years." *The Nonviolent Activist* (Sept.-Oct. 1992): 3-6.

Landes, Ruth. *Ojibwa Religion and the Midewiwin.* Madison, WI: University of Wisconsin Press, 1968.

——. *Ojibwa Sociology.* NY: Columbia University Press, 1937.

——. *The Ojibwa Woman.* 2nd ed. NY: AMS Press, 1979.

Lerner, Gerda, ed. *Black Women in White America.* NY: Random House, 1972.

Levine, Paul. "Recent Women's Fiction and the Theme of Personality." *The Origins and Originality of American Culture.* Ed. Frank Tibor. Budapest: Akademiai Kiado, 1984.

Lim, Shirley Geok-Lin and Ling, Amy, eds. *Reading the Literatures of Asian America.* Philadelphia, PA: Temple University Press, 1992.

Ling, Amy. *Between Worlds: Women Writers of Chinese Ancestry.* NY: Pergamon Press, 1990.

Madison, D. Soyini, ed. *The Woman That I Am: The Literature and Culture of Contemporary Women of Color.* NY: St. Martin's Press, 1994.

McKay, Nellie Y. *Critical Essays on Toni Morrison.* Boston, MA: G.K. Hall, 1988.

——. "An Interview with Toni Morrison." *Contemporary Literature* 24 (1983): 413-429.

Metress, Seamus P. *The Irish-American Experience: A Guide to the Literature.* Washington, D.C.: University Press of America, 1981.

Mitchell, Louise. "Slave Markets Typify Exploitation of Domestics." *The Daily Worker* (5 May 1940). *Black Women in White America.* Gerda Lerner, ed. NY: Random House, 1972.

Neithammer, Carolyn J. *Daughters of the Earth.* NY: Collier, 1977.

Nelson, Ronald. "The Renewal of the Self By Returning to the Elements." Walker and Hamner 73-90.

Pearlman, Mickey, and Katherine Usher Henderson. *Inter/View: Talks with America's Writing Women*. Lexington, KY: The University Press of Kentucky, 1990.

Perry, Ruth. "Mary Gordon's Mothers." Daly and Reddy 209-221.

Peterson, Shawn. "Loving Mothers and Lost Daughters: Archetypal Images of Female Kinship Relations in Selected Novels of Toni Morrison." Diss. University of Oregon, 1993.

——. "Gender and Afro-Americanist Literary Theory and Criticism." *Speaking of Gender*. Ed. Eileen Showalter. NY: Routledge, 1989. 56-70.

Rigney, Barbara Hill. *The Voices of Toni Morrison*. Columbus, OH: Ohio State University Press, 1991.

Shands, Kerstin. *The Repair of the World: The Novels of Marge Piercy*. Westport, CT: Greenwood Press, 1994.

Shkilnyk, Anastasia M. *A Poison Stronger than Love: The Destruction of an Ojibwa Community*. New Haven, CT: Yale University Press, 1985.

Spicer, Edward H., ed. *Perspectives in Indian Culture*. Chicago, IL: University of Chicago Press, 1961.

Spillers, Hortense. "A Hateful Passion, a Lost Love." Bloom 27-54.

Stepto, Robert B. "Intimate Things in Place: A Conversation with Toni Morrison." *Chant of Saints: A Gathering of Afro-American Literature, Art, and Scholarship*. Ed. Michael S. Harper and Robert B. Stepto. Chicago, IL: University of Illinois Press, 1979. 213-229.

Tanner, Helen Hornbeck. *The Ojibwa*. NY: Chelsea House Publishers, 1992.

Tedlock, Dennis, comp. *Teachings from the American Earth: Indian Religion and Philosophy*. NY: Liveright, 1975.

Walker, Alice. "In Search of Our Mothers' Gardens." Madison 516-523.

Walker, Margaret. "On Being Female, Black, and Free." Sternburg 95-106.

Walker, Sue. "Marge Piercy: An Overview." Walker and Hamner 132-147.

Walker, Sue and Eugenie Hamner, eds. *Ways of Knowing: Essays on Marge Piercy*. Mobile, AL: Negative Capability Press, 1991.

Ward, Susan. "In Search of 'Ordinary Human Happiness': Rebellion and Affirmation in Mary Gordon's Novels." *Faith of a (Woman) Writer*. Eds. Alice Kessler-Harris and William McBrien. Westport, CT: Greenwood, 1988. 303-308.

Washington, Mary Helen. "The Darkened Eye Restored: Notes Toward a Literary History of Black Women." Bloom 30-43.

Wax, Murray L. *Indian Americans: Unity and Diversity*. Englewood Cliffs, NJ: Prentice-Hall, 1971.

Williams, Sherley Anne. "Some Implications of Womanist Theory." Bloom 68-75.

Wisker, Gina, ed. *Black Women's Writing*. NY: St. Martin's Press, 1993.

White, Ruth Trotter. "Autoethnography and the Sense of Self in the Novels of Toni Morrison." Diss. University of Iowa, 1992.

Wong, Hertha D. "Adoptive Mothers and Thrown-Away Children in the Novels of Louise Erdrich." Daly and Reddy 174-192.

Wong, Sau-ling Cynthia. *Reading Asian American Literature: From Necessity to Extravagance*. Princeton, NJ: Princeton University Press, 1993.

Zinn, Maxine Baca and Bonnie Thornton Dill, eds. *Women of Color in U.S. Society*. Philadelphia, PA: Temple University Press, 1993.

On Domesticity

Abraham, Laurie, et al. *Reinventing Home: Six Working Women Look at Their Home Lives*. NY: Plume, 1991.

Aburdene, Patricia and John Naisbitt. *Megatrends for Women: From Liberation to Leadership*. 1992. NY: Fawcett Columbine, 1993.

Adams, Charlotte. *Housekeeping after Office Hours: A Homemaking Guide for the Working Woman*. NY: Harper & Brothers, 1953.

Aldous, Joan, ed. *Two Paychecks: Life in Dual-Earner Families*. Beverly Hills, CA: Sage Publications, 1982.

Aptheker, Bettina. *Tapestries of Life: Women's Work, Women's Consciousness, and the Meaning of Daily Existence*. Amherst, MA: University of Massachusetts Press, 1989.

Arendt, Hannah. *The Human Condition*. Chicago, IL: University of Chicago Press, 1958.

Bailer, Dorice. "Orderly House, Orderly Mind." *The New York Times* 18 Dec. 1994, sec. CN: 6.

Banner, Lois W. *Women in America: A Brief History*. 2nd ed. NY: Harcourt Brace Jovanovich, 1984.

Barber, Elizabeth Wayland. *Women's Work: The First 20,000 Years: Women, Cloth, & Society in Early Times*. NY: Norton, 1994.

Barker, Diana Leonard and Sheila Allen. *Dependence and Exploitation in Work and Marriage*. NY: Longman Group Ltd., 1976.

Beecher, Catherine E. *A Treatise on Domestic Economy*. (1841) NY: Schocken Books, 1977.

Beer, William R. *Househusbands: Men and Housework in American Families*. NY: Praeger, 1983.

Bender, Sue. *Plain and Simple: A Woman's Journey to the Amish*. San Francisco, CA: HarperSanFrancisco, 1989.

Brown, James W. *Fictional Meals and Their Functions in the French Novel: 1789 - 1848*. Toronto, Canada: University of Toronto Press, 1984.

Cardozo, Arlene Rossen. *Woman at Home*. NY: Doubleday, 1976.

Chapman, Elizabeth and Maggie Kassner and Karen Kriberney. *The Modern Woman's Guide to Life*. NY: Harper & Row, 1988.

Cowan, Ruth Schwartz. *More Work for Mother: The Ironies of Household Technology from the Open Hearth to the Microwave*. NY: Basic Books, 1983.

Daniel, Robert L. *American Women in the 20th Century: The Festival of Life*. NY: Harcourt Brace Jovanovich, 1987.

Davison, Jane. *The Fall of a Doll's House: Three Generations of American Women and the Houses They Lived In*. NY: Holt, Rinehart and Winston, 1980.

Davison, Jane and Lesley. *To Make a House a Home*. NY: Random House, 1994.

Day, Christopher. *Places of the Soul: Architecture and Environmental Design as a Healing Art*. San Francisco, CA: The Aquarian Press-HarperCollins, 1990.

Douglas, Mary. "Deciphering a Meal." *Daedalus* 101:1 (1972): 61-81.

———. ed. *Food in the Social Order: Studies of Food and Festivities in Three American Communities*. NY: Russell Sage Foundation, 1984.

———. *Purity and Danger: An Analysis of the Concepts of Pollution and Taboo*. (1966) London: Ark Paperbacks, 1984.

Douglas, Susan J. *Where the Girls Are: Growing up Female with the Mass Media*. NY: Times Books, 1994.

DuVall, Nell. *Domestic Technology: A Chronology of Developments*. Boston, MA: G.K. Hall, 1988.

Ehrenreich, Barbara, and D. English. *For Her Own Good: 150 Years of the Experts' Advice to Women*. Garden City, NY: Doubleday, 1978.

Eisen, Carol G. *Nobody Said You Had to Eat off the Floor... The Psychiatrist's Wife's Guide to Housekeeping*. NY: David McKay Company, Inc., 1971.

Fraser, Nancy, and Linda Gordon. "A Genealogy of *Dependency* Tracing a Keyword of the U.S. Welfare State." *Signs: Journal of Women in Culture and Society* 19:2 (Winter 1994): 309-337.

Frederick, Christine. *The New Housekeeping: Efficiency Studies in Home Management*. NY: Doubleday, 1914.

———. *Household Engineering : Scientific Management in the Home*. Chicago: American School of Home Economics, 1919.

Foy, Jessica H. and Thomas J. Schlereth, eds. *American Home Life, 1880 - 1930: A Social History of Spaces and Services*. University of Tennessee, 1992.

Gerson, Kathleen. *Hard Choices: How Women Decide about Work, Career, and Motherhood*. Berkeley, CA: University of California Press, 1985.

Gilman, Charlotte Perkins. *Women and Economics.* (1898) NY: Harper & Row, 1966.

——. *The Home, Its Work and Influence.* NY: McClure, Phillips & Co., 1903.

——. *The Living of Charlotte Perkins Gilman.* NY: Harper Colophon, 1975.

Hayden, Dolores. *The Grand Domestic Revolution: A History of Feminist Designs for American Homes, Neighborhoods, and Cities.* Cambridge, MA: The MIT Press, 1981.

Hellmich, Nanci. "Superwomen Find Themselves Grounded by Housework," *USA Today.* 11 Aug. 1994: 05-D.

Heloise. *Heloise's Housekeeping Hints.* NY: Pocket Books, 1965.

Hess, John L. and Karen Hess. *The Taste of America.* NY: Grossman Publishers, 1977.

Laing, Dilys. *The Collected Poems of Dilys Laing.* Cleveland: The Press of Case Western Reserve U, 1967.

Larson, Kay. "Women's Work (or Is It Art?) Is Never Done," *The New York Times.* 7 January 1996: H-35.

Lawlor, Anthony, AIA. *The Temple in the House: Finding the Sacred in Everyday Architecture.* NY: G.P. Putnam's Sons, 1994.

Letter to the editor, *Harper's* 287:1721 (October 1993).

Lopata, Helena Znaniecki. *Occupation Housewife.* NY: Oxford University Press, 1971.

Lévi-Strauss, Claude. *The Origin of Table Manners.* John and Doreen Weightman, transl. NY: Harper & Row, 1978.

Malos, Ellen. *The Politics of Housework.* London: Allison & Busby, 1980.

Masnick, George and Mary Jo Bane. *The Nation's Families: 1960 - 1990.* Cambridge, MA: Joint Center for Urban Studies of MIT and Harvard University, 1980.

Matthews, Glenna. *"Just a Housewife": The Rise and Fall of Domesticity in America.* NY: Oxford University Press, 1987.

McCarthy, Mary. *Occasional Prose.* NY: Harcourt Brace Jovanovich, 1985.

McGrath, Earl J. and Jack T. Johnson. *The Changing Mission of Home Economics.* NY: Teachers College Press, Teachers College, Columbia University, 1968.

McHugh, Kathleen Anne. "Keeping House: Discourses of Domestic Economy." Diss. Indiana University, 1991.

Mead, Margaret. *Sex and Temperament in Three Primitive Societies.* (1935) NY: Morrow Quill, 1963.

Mennell, Stephen, and Anne Murcott and Anneke H. van Otterloo. *The Sociology of Food: Eating, Diet and Culture.* London, UK: SAGE Publications, 1992.

Myerson, Abraham. *The Nervous Housewife.* Boston, MA: Little Brown, 1920.

Norris, Kathleen. "It All Comes Out in the Wash." *The New York Times Magazine*. 22 Aug. 1993, sec. 6: 16.

Oakley, Ann. *The Sociology of Housework*. NY: Pantheon Books, 1975.

——. *Woman's Work: The Housewife, Past and Present*. NY: Pantheon, 1974.

Ogden, Annegret S. *The Great American Housewife: From helpmate to wage earner, 1776 - 1986*. Westport, CT: Greenwood Press, 1986.

Oxenhandler, Noelle. "Fall from Grace: How Modern Life Has Made Waiting a Desperate Act," *The New Yorker*, June 16, 1997.

Oxford English Dictionary. The Compact Edition, 2 vol. Oxford, UK: Oxford University Press, 1985. Vol. 1.

Palmer, Phyllis M. *Domesticity and Dirt: Housewives and Domestic Servants in the United States 1920 - 1945*. Philadelphia, PA: Temple University Press, 1989.

Parker, Gail. *The Oven Birds: American Women on Womanhood 1820-1920*. Garden City, NY: Anchor, 1972.

Peet, Louise Jenison and Lenore Sater Thye. *Household Equipment*. NY: Wiley, 1955.

Rabuzzi, Kathryn Allen. *The Sacred and the Feminine: Toward a Theology of Housework*. NY: Seabury, 1982.

Rand, Ayn. *Atlas Shrugged*. NY: Signet Press, 1992.

Ruddick, Sara, and Pamela Daniels, eds. *Working It Out*. NY: Pantheon, 1977.

Rybczynski, Witold. *Home: A Short History of an Idea*. NY: Viking, 1986.

Shelton, Beth Anne. *Women, Men and Time: Gender Differences in Paid Work, Housework and Leisure*. NY: Greenwood Press, 1992.

Sinnigen, William G. and Charles Alexander Robinson Jr. *Ancient History: From Prehistoric Times to the Death of Justinian*. 3rd ed. NY: Macmillan Publishing Co., Inc., 1981.

Smith, Daniel Scott. "Family Limitations, Sexual Control, and Domestic Feminism in Victorian America." *Clio's Consciousness Raised: New Perspectives on the History of Women*. Eds. Mary Hartman and Lois W. Banner. NY: Harper Colophon Books, 1974. 119-36.

Starr, Tama. *The "Natural Inferiority" of Women: Outrageous Pronouncements by Misguided Males*. NY: Poseidon Press, 1991.

Strasser, Susan. *Never Done: A History of American Housework*. NY: Pantheon, 1982.

Thom, Mary, ed. *Letters to MS., 1972 - 1987*. NY: Henry Holt and Company, 1987.

Tyler, Anne. "Still Just Writing." Sternburg 3-16.

USA Today. "Who Made Their Bed Today?" 10 Jan. 1995: 01-D.

U.S. Bureau of the Census. Current Population Reports, P-23-181. *Households, Families, and Children: A 30-Year Perspective*. U.S. Government Printing Office, Washington, D.C. 1992.

Usdanfky, Margaret L. "White Men Don't Jump Into Chores." *USA Today*. 8 Aug. 1994: 01-D."Working Women Polled—Family Top Priority." *San Francisco Chronicle* 10 Sept. 1984: 1.

Literary Criticism, Myth and Symbol, Feminism

Abel, Elizabeth, and Marianne Hirsch and Elizabeth Longland. *The Voyage In: Fictions of Female Development*. Hanover, NH: University Press of New England, 1983.
Aldridge, John W. *The American Novel and the Way We Live Now*. NY: Oxford University Press, 1983.
Anderson, Douglas R. *A House Undivided: Domesticity and Community in American Literature*. NY: Cambridge University Press, 1990.
Ascher, Carol, Louise DeSalvo, Sara Ruddick, eds. *Between Women: Biographers, Novelists, Critics, Teachers and Artists Write About Their Work on Women*. Boston, MA: Beacon Press, 1984.
Atwood, Margaret. "Paradoxes and Dilemmas: The Woman as Writer." Eagleton 74-76.
Baym, Nina. *Woman's Fiction*. Ithaca: Cornell University Press, 1978.
——. *Feminism & American Literary History*. New Brunswick, NJ: Rutgers University Press, 1992.
Bell, Catherine. *Ritual Theory, Ritual Practice*. NY: Oxford University Press, 1992.
Bergmann, Barbara. "The Job of Housewife." *Feminist Philosophies*. Eds. Janet A. Kournay, James P. Sterba and Rosemarie Tong. Englewood Cliffs, NJ: Prentice Hall, 1992: 171-184.
Bigwood, Carol. *Earth Muse: Feminism, Nature, and Art*. Philadelphia, PA: Temple University Press, 1993.
Bolen, Jean Shinoda. *Goddesses in Every woman.: A New Psychology of Women*. San Francisco, CA: Harper & Row, 1984.
Cirlot, J.E. *A Dictionary of Symbols*. 2nd ed. NY: Philosophical Library, 1971.
Clayton, Jay. *The Pleasures of Babel: Contemporary American Literature and Theory*. NY: Oxford University Press, 1993.
Cooper, Barbara Eck. "The Difficult Arts of Family Life: The Creative Force in the Domestic Fictions of Six Contemporary Women Novelists." Diss. University of Missouri-Columbia, 1986.
Daly, Brenda O. and Maureen T. Reddy, eds. *Narrating Mothers: Theorizing Maternal Subjectivities*. Knoxville, TN: The University of Tennessee Press, 1991.
Didion, Joan. "Why I Write." Sternburg 17-26.

Dillard, Annie. *Pilgrim at Tinker Creek*. NY: Harper's Magazine Press, 1974.

Dinnerstein, Myra. *Women Between Two Worlds: Midlife Reflections on Work and Family*. Philadelphia, PA: Temple University Press, 1992.

Donovan, Josephine. *After the Fall: The Demeter-Persephone Myth in Wharton, Cather and Glasgow*. University Park: Pennsylvania State University Press, 1989.

Douglas, Ann. *The Feminization of American Culture*. NY: Avon, 1978.

Driver, Tom F. *The Magic of Ritual: Our Need for Liberating Rites That Transform Our Lives and Our Communities*. San Francisco, CA: HarperSan Francisco, 1991.

DuPlessis, Rachel Blau. *Writing Beyond the Ending: Narrative Strategies of Twentieth-Century Women Writers*. Bloomington, IN: Indiana University Press, 1985.

Eagleton, Mary, ed. *Feminist Literary Theory: A Reader*. Oxford, UK: Basil Blackwell, 1986.

Elshtain, Jean Bethke, ed. *The Family in Political Thought*. Amherst, MA: University of Massachusetts Press, 1982.

Estés, Clarissa Pinkola. *Women Who Run with the Wolves: Myths and Stories of the Wild Woman Archetype*. NY: Ballantine Books, 1992.

Faludi, Susan. *Backlash: The Undeclared War Against American Women*. NY: Crown Publishers, Inc., 1991.

Ferguson, Mary Anne. "The Female Novel of Development and the Myth of Psyche." Abel, Hirsch and Longland 228-243.

Flanagan, Kieran. *Sociology and Liturgy: Re-presentations of the Holy*. NY: St. Martin's Press, 1991.

Foucault, Michel. *Power/Knowledge: Selected Interviews and Other Writings, 1972-1977*. NY: Random House, 1980.

Friedan, Betty. *The Feminine Mystique*. NY: Norton, 1963.

Gilbert, Sandra M. and Susan Gubar. *The Madwoman in the Attic: The Woman Writer and the Nineteenth-Century Literary Imagination*. New Haven, CT: Yale University Press, 1979.

Gimbutas, Marija. "Goddess-Oriented Old Europe." Spretnak 22-31.

Hedges, Elaine and Ingrid Wendt. *In Her Own Image: Women Working in the Arts*. NY: McGraw-Hill, 1980.

Heilbrun, Carolyn. *Toward a Recognition of Androgyny*. NY: Knopf, 1973.

———. *Writing a Woman's Life*. NY: W.W. Norton & Co., 1988.

Hill, Mary A. *Charlotte Perkins Gilman: The Making of a Radical Feminist 1860 - 1896*. Philadelphia, PA: Temple University Press, 1980.

Hulley, Kathleen. "Interview with Grace Paley." *Delta* 14 (1982): 27.

Hunter College Women's Studies Collective. *Women's Realities, Women's Choices* NY: Oxford University Press, 1983.

Jacobus, Mary. *Reading Woman: Essays in Feminist Criticism.* NY: Columbia University Press, 1986

Jones, Amelia. "Postfeminism, Feminist Pleasures, and Embodied Theories of Art." *New Feminist Criticism: Art, Identity, Action.* Eds. Joanna Frueh, Cassandra L. Langer and Arlene Raven. NY: HarperCollins, 1994.

Jong, Erica. "My Grandmother on My Shoulder." *Writers on Writing,* Eds. Robert Pack and Jay Parini. Hanover, NH: University Press of New England, 1991.

Kaplan, Cora. *Sea Changes: Culture and Feminism.* London: Verso, 1986.

Kelley, Mary. *Private Woman, Public Stage: Literary Domesticity in Nineteenth-Century America.* NY: Oxford University Press, 1984.

Kourany, Janet, James Sterba, Rosemarie Tong, eds. *Feminist Philosophies: Problems, Theories and Applications.* NJ: Prentice Hall, 1992.

Kraditor, Aileen. *Up from the Pedestal: Selected Writings in the History of American Feminism.* Chicago, IL: Quadrangle, 1968.

Kristeva, Julia. "Women's Time." Trans. Alice Jardine. *Signs* 7 (Autumn 1981) 5-25.

Labovitz, Esther Kleinbord. *The Myth of the Heroine: The Female Bildungsroman in the Twentieth Century.* NY: Peter Lang, 1986.

Lenz, Elinor and Barbara Myerhoff. *The Feminization of America: How Woman's Values Are Changing Our Public & Private Lives.* Los Angeles, CA: Jeremy P. Tarcher, Inc., 1985.

Lerner, Gerda. *The Majority Finds Its Past: Placing Women in History.* NY: Oxford University Press, 1979.

Lesniak, James G., ed. *Contemporary Authors.* New Revision Series: 30. Detroit, MI: Gale Research, 1990.

Luepnitz, Deborah Anna. *The Family Interpreted: Psychoanalysis, Feminism and Family Therapy.* NY: Basic Books, 1988.

Luke, Helen M. *Woman, Earth and Spirit.* NY: Crossroad, 1981.

Marcus, Jane. "Invisible Mending." *Between Women: Biographers, Novelists, Critics, Teachers and Artists Write About Their Work on Women.* Eds. Carol Ascher, Louise DeSalvo and Sara Ruddick. Boston, MA: Beacon Press, 1984. 381-395.

Metzger, Deena. "In Her Own Image." *Heresies* I (May 1977).

Miller, Nancy K. *The Poetics of Gender.* NY: Columbia University Press, 1986.

———. *Subject to Change: Reading Feminist Writing.* NY: Columbia University Press, 1988.

Mills, Sara and Lynne Pearce, Sue Spaull and Elaine Millard, eds. *Feminist Readings/ Feminists Reading.* Charlottesville, VA: University Press of Virginia, 1989.

Modleski, Tania. *Feminism Without Women: Culture and Criticism in a 'Postfeminist' Age.* NY: Routledge, 1991.

Moore, Thomas. *Care of the Soul: A Guide for Cultivating Depth and Sacredness in Everyday Life.* NY: HarperPerennial, 1992.

Payant, Katherine B. *Becoming and Bonding: Contemporary Feminism and Popular Fiction by American Women Writers.* NJ: Greenwood Press, 1993.

Paz, Octavio. *Convergences: Essays on Art and Literature.* Transl. Helen Lane. NY: Harcourt Brace Jovanovich, 1987.

Powers, Meredith A. *The Heroine in Western Literature.* Jefferson, NC: McFarland & Co., Inc., 1991.

Pratt, Annis. *Archetypal Patterns in Women's Fiction.* Bloomington, IN: Indiana University Press, 1981.

Rainwater, Catherine and Scheick, William J., eds. *Contemporary American Women Writers: Narrative Strategies.* Lexington, KY: University Press of Kentucky, 1985.

Renzetti, Claire and Daniel Curran. "Gender Socialization." Kourany, Sterba and Tong 31-42.

Rich, Adrienne. *On Lies, Secrets and Silence: Selected Prose 1966–1978.* NY: W.W. Norton, 1980.

——. "Prepatriarchal Female/Goddess Images." Spretnak 32-38.

Ries, Julien. *The Origins of Religions.* Grand Rapids, MI: William B. Eerdmans Publishing Co., 1994.

Roberts, Michele. *The Visitation.* NY: Interlink Publishing, 1984.

Romines, Ann. *The Home Plot: Women, Writing & Domestic Ritual.* Amherst, MA: University of Massachusetts Press, 1992.

Rose, Jane Ellen. "Gender Politics in American Literature of Domesticity, 1830-1860." Diss. Purdue University, 1992.

Roszak, Betty and Theodore, eds. *Masculine/Feminine: Readings in Sexual Mythology and the Liberation of Women.* NY: Harper Colophon Books, 1969.

Ruoff, A. LaVonne Brown and Jerry W. Ward Jr., eds. *Redefining American Literary History.* NY: Modern Language Association, 1990.

Ryan, Mary P. *The Empire of the Mother: American Writing about Domesticity, 1830 to 1860.* NY: Copublished by the Institute for Research in History and Haworth Press, 1982.

Sewell, Marilyn, ed. *Cries of the Spirit: A Celebration of Women's Spirituality.* Boston, MA: Beacon Press, 1991.

Sexson, Lynda. *Ordinarily Sacred.* NY: Crossroad, 1982.

Showalter, Elaine, ed. *The New Feminist Criticism: Women, Literature and Theory.* NY: Pantheon, 1985.

———. *Sister's Choice: Tradition and Change in American Women's Writing.* Oxford, UK: Clarendon Press, 1991.

———. *Speaking of Gender.* NY: Routledge, 1989.

Smith, Barbara. "Toward a Black Feminist Criticism." Eagleton 77-80.

Spacks, Patricia Meyer. *The Female Imagination.* 1975. NY: Avon, 1976.

Spender, Dale. *Women of Ideas: And What Men Have Done to Them.* 1982 UK: Routledge and Kegan Paul Ltd. Reprinted in 1990 by Pandora Press, London, UK.

———. *The Writing Or the Sex? Or Why You Don't Have to Read Women's Writing to Know It's No Good.* Columbia University Press, NY: 1989.

Spretnak, Charlene, ed. *The Politics of Women's Spirituality: Essays on the Rise of Spiritual Power Within the Feminist Movement.* NY: Anchor Books, 1982.

Sternburg, Janet, ed. *The Writer on Her Work.* NY: W.W. Norton & Co., 1980.

Trosky, Susan M., ed. *Contemporary Authors,* Vol. 136. Detroit, MI: Gale Research, 1992.

———. *Contemporary Authors.* New Revision Series, Vols. 41 and 44. Detroit, MI: Gale Research, 1994

Jeannette Batz Cooperman holds a Doctorate in American Studies and a Bachelor's in Philosophy and Communication from Saint Louis University. A senior editor and columnist at *The Riverfront Times* alternative newsweekly, she's won numerous awards for her reporting on health, education, women's issues, and social justice. Dr. Cooperman has written *Half Life: What We Give Up To Work* and the educational text for *A Child's Story: Recovering Through Creativity.*

W·R·I·T·I·N·G A·B·O·U·T W·O·M·E·N
Feminist Literary Studies

This is a literary series devoted to feminist studies on past and contemporary women authors, exploring social, psychological, political, economic, and historical insights directed toward an interdisciplinary approach.

The series is dedicated to the memory of Simone de Beauvoir, an early pioneer in feminist literary theory.

Persons wishing to have a manuscript considered for inclusion in the series should submit a letter of inquiry, including the title and a one-page abstract of the manuscript to the general editor:

Professor Esther K. Labovitz
Department of English
Pace University
Pace Plaza
New York, NY 10038
(212) 488-1416